'This is a really exciting book about the visions and prophecies of the tribal peoples in North and South America. Patricia Mercier has done impeccable research and is also a shaman-seer in her own right. She sifts out the doom and gloom interpretations and reveals a prophetic worldview that is profoundly realistic, insightful and practical. These visions are immediately relevant to our contemporary social and environmental crises, and, if acknowledged and acted on, provide solutions.'

William Bloom, author of *The Endorphin Effect* and founder of the Foundation for Holistic Spirituality http://www.williambloom.com

'A powerful journey of the heart and a tale for our times. Patricia journeys as deeply into her self as she does the rainforests and the mysteries of the Mayan people.'

**Nicholas Breeze Wood, *Sacred Hoop Magazine*
Sacred Hoop Magazine: www.sacredhoop.org
Nicholas Breeze Wood: www.nicholaswood.net**

'The ancient prophecies of the Maya, Hopi, Kogi, Lakota and Inca speak directly to these days and this time!

Weave a new way of life through the hidden depths of this intriguing and enjoyable journey into the sacred teaching of many indigenous cultures. Deepen your perspective and grasp the "Threads of Time" that build a path through the morass of conflicts and dilemmas of your modern life, into a brilliant, light-filled future, guided by compassion and balance. Many layers of teachings are revealed by the multiple facets of the author's crystal skull.

Timely, powerful and important, the journey of *The Maya End Times* offers an intriguing vision of Maya teachings, myths and legends, clarifying and illuminating our future.'

LionFire, Master Shaman, and author of *Secrets of the Maya Chakra Temples* http://thelighthows.com/lionfire/bio_david.htm

D0112879

'From now through 2012 we are walking what the Maya call "The Road of Awe" – *Xi Balba bih*. The unique feminine perspective on the wisdom of the many indigenous sources Patricia has touched in her spiritual journey is very illuminating to our own journeys and can help prepare us to walk the Maya's Road of Awe with more grace! Reading this book makes one grateful to be alive during this astoundingly transformative time on Earth!

This book is uplifting and inspiring as to how we can participate in the creation of the higher octave of reality that we are both receiving as a new template and synergistically creating during this next few years on Earth. I wholeheartedly recommend this book!'

**Ariel Spilsbury, co-author of *The Mayan Oracle: Return Path to the Stars* and *The 13 Moon Oracle: A Journey Through the Archetypal Faces of the Divine Feminine*
www.holographicgoddess.com**

'An exciting literary gem that embraces the looming and inevitable rapid evolution of human presence on the earth. The great cycle is closing, another is being birthed. Where will you be in 2012? What will be your offerings to the Power that returns to evolve us?'

**Chief Sonne Reyna, Yaqui-Carrizo-Coahuilteka Nations, North America – Turtle Island
http://www.lightstreamers.com/Chief_Sonne_Reyna.htm**

Patricia Mercier (Alloa), author and artist, is co-director of The Sun & Serpent Maya Mysteries School, a focal point for healing and shamanic training in the UK and Spain. She has studied and travelled widely throughout Central America. In 1995 and 2000 she was initiated at the great pyramid of Ku-kuul-kaan in Chichén Itzá at the invitation of Maya elders, shamans and wisdom teachers.

You can contact Patricia at www.mayasunserpent.com or www.myspace.com/alloapatriciamaya, or email her at mayasunserpent@hotmail.com.

By the same author

Maya Shamans – Travellers in Time
Secretos de los Chamanes Mayas (to be published 2008)
Chakras
The Chakra Bible

THE
MAYA
END TIMES
A SPIRITUAL ADVENTURE

MAYA PROPHECIES FOR
2012

PATRICIA MERCIER

WATKINS PUBLISHING
LONDON

Distributed in the United States and Canada by
Sterling Publishing Co., Inc.
387 Park Avenue South, New York, NY 10016-8810

This edition first published in the UK 2008 by
Watkins Publishing, Sixth Floor, Castle House,
75–76 Wells Street, London W1T 3QH

1 3 5 7 9 10 8 6 4 2

Designed and typeset by Jerry Goldie

Printed and bound in Great Britain

Library of Congress Cataloging-in-Publication data available

ISBN 10: 1-905857-57-8

ISBN 13: 978-1-905857-57-9

For information about custom editions, special sales, premium and
corporate purchases, please contact Sterling Special Sales
Department at 800-805-5489 or specialsales@sterlingpub.com

www.watkinspublishing.co.uk

DEDICATED to all courageous indigenous peoples of the Americas. They are our modern warriors and prophets who, despite 500 years of repression, endeavour to walk traditional ways and regain their indigenous nations' individual and collective rights at governmental and United Nations levels.

ACKNOWLEDGEMENTS

I particularly wish to thank Maya day-keeper Hunbatz Men, Itzá Maya Tradition, Mexico; Don Alejandro Cirilo Perez Oxlaj, Guatemala; and Chief Sonne Reyna, USA, for their insights and contributions, as well as Maya researcher/author John Major Jenkins, USA; Maya visionary, artist/author José Argüelles, USA; and crystal skull keeper Elmera, UK. In addition, thanks to Palden Jenkins, editor, and of course Michael Mann, publisher. Lastly to my husband Mikhail for his inspiration and research into continued injustices perpetrated against indigenous peoples.

CONTENTS

List of Plates   xi
Foreword: Chief Sonne Reyna   xiii
Preface: Hunbatz Men   xv
Introduction   xvii
Map: The Mayalands of Central America   xxiv

Part One: The Earth's Lament

1 Day of the Solstice   2
2 Predictions in the Ring of Fire   15
3 The Serpent Turns   36
4 Madre Tierra – Mother Earth   54
5 The Children of Time   70

Part Two: The Song of the Skulls

6 Harvest of the Gourd of Ashes   90
7 Evolution and our Return to the Stars   116
8 The Cloud People   132
9 The Singing Skulls   151
10 The Call of the Cosmic Maya   168

Part Three: Time – After Time

11 Jaguar Paw Stone   185
12 The Blessing of the Crystal Skulls   199
13 Song to *Homo Spiritus*   217

Appendices

1 Prophecies: Hunbatz Men   233
2 The Seven Fires Prophecy of the Anishnabe People
   and the Process of Reconciliation   239
3 Prophecies of the Americas   243
4 Maya Timekeeping and Archaeological Periods   246
5 Known Crystal Skulls   249
6 Life-Sustaining Systems of exchange and Reciprocity   252

   Bibliography   254
   Index   258

LIST OF PLATES

1 Temple of the Seven Dolls, Dzibalchaltún, Mexico – M Baker

2 Temple of the Sun, Nah Chan (Palenque), Mexico – M Baker

3 Carved serpent head, Chichén Itzá, Mexico – M Baker

4 Don Alejandro, Mayapan, Mexico – M Baker

5 Sunset at Frontera de Corazal, Mexico – M Baker

6 Small amethyst crystal skull – M Baker

7 Ebmnagine, a life-size quartz crystal skull – M Baker

8 Group of small figures with elongated heads – M Baker

9 Hunbatz Men, Itzá Maya Tradition day-keeper – M Baker

10 Part of frieze at Ek' Balam, Mexico – M Baker

11 The Maya Sun God 'Kinich Ahau', Mexico – M Baker

12 Colossal Olmec head – M Baker

13 Cave at Tulum, Mexico – M Baker

14 Great pyramid of Ku-kuul-kaan, Chichén Itzá, Mexico – M Baker

15 Huayna Picchu, Peru – M Baker

16 Temple of the Sun God, Apu Inti, Machu Picchu, Peru – C Friar

17 Lost city of the Incas, Machu Picchu, Peru – C Friar

18 Inca ruins at Machu Picchu, Peru – C Friar

19 Xamuk'u, a life-size crystal skull – M Baker

Foreword

We now live in extraordinary end times. Prophetic signs and portents are everywhere. In the swirl of confusion and denial, ancient native wisdom shares precious values and insights. Native wisdom is natural wisdom relevant toward divining our present challenges upon the heart of the earth. We now behold modern science and native science converging on undeniable natural truths.

Upon the heart of the earth, the four seasons of nature teach us about our humble, sacred and conscious presence here now. In the heart of heaven, the vast and profound galactic seasons of nature periodically teach us absolute humility and undeniable reverence. We then remember that a greater power of love and compassion rules all of divine creation.

This unique book is Patricia Mercier's emotional personal sojourn with enchanted native peoples and native wisdom. It recounts her personal journey, seeking and finding some of the wisdom from the heart of the earth and the heart of heaven, that eternal wisdom that claims all humans as native.

We are now inside an emerging galactic season of obvious change. Like the divine snake, the living earth and the living sun are changing their skins. We the humans are their living skin. We are also changing. A wealth of natural wisdom and resources is out there now to help guide us. This exciting book shares some of these insights.

Climatic natural cycles are the beacons of profound reconciliation for the human race. My people, the Yaqui, say there are only two personalities in the human race: Yoeme (our tribal name), those with enchantment and love in their heart; Yori, those with confusion and fear in their heart. Together we hold hands and reclaim enchantment and love in the heart of humankind. And liberate the fear in the heart of humankind. We do so for the children, for they will inherit a better life from us.

So, thoroughly enjoy Patricia (Alloa) Mercier's global spiritual adventure. And celebrate the cosmic birthing of *Homo Spiritus*.

Yahete, with enchanted love from my heart,
Chief Sonne Reyna, Yaqui-Carrizo-Coahuilteka Nations,
North America – Turtle Island

Chief Sonne Reyna: hereditary eagle nawal, traditional sun dancer, sun dance society peace chief, ambassador for natural-supernatural worlds, global advisor: reconciliation and healing with nature, Vietnam war veteran, ceremonial singer, artist, film-maker, writer. Books in progress: *The Great Awakening* and *Healing and Blessing the Storms*, to be published in 2008.

Chief Reyna can be contacted at tayekonake@hotmail.com.

Preface

The Maya civilization was born in the memory of time. It was born when the Maya people started worshipping our Great Father Sun as part of the universe.

Many prophecies have been told in the Maya culture – as for instance, those of the Brother Tree, the Arrival of White Men in America and the Return of the Maya gods. These days, all human beings have an obligation to understand the Maya prophecies. As humans, we hope all the good prophecies get fulfilled, but at the same time we hope the harmful ones that might hurt our Mother Earth and humankind never get fulfilled.

Humankind is being led toward self-destruction by modern society. Wars in the name of democracy are held to benefit the personal interests of a few people who want to exploit natural resources. The Maya prophecy about our Brother Tree says: 'When the last tree dies, then the animals that live on and in it will die, too. This will cause an ecological imbalance and, consequently, human beings will also die.'

This is because our Brother Tree provides food to all the animals and plants and to human beings, too. Once we have killed all the trees, there will be no food or other benefits for the animals and human beings. Therefore, our breathless hearts will expire.

The crystal skulls are very important, but modern human beings do not care about them. This modern Western culture has spoiled humankind and led it to a world of ignorance. So the need for people to understand the importance of the crystal skulls has become urgent.

We can get many benefits from the crystal skulls. They can awaken our ancestral memory and our mental and corporeal powers. Many ancient peoples around the world used to worship these crystal skulls, which let them have a more advanced knowledge than any modern society now.

The ancient Mayas were one of these wise peoples. The most perfect crystal skull in the world was found in the Maya temples of Lubaantún, Belize, in Central America by Anna, the daughter of F A Mitchell-Hedges, in 1924. When someone makes a meditation with this skull, it gives off a halo around itself.

How much mystery surrounds the crystal skulls? When all the crystal skulls around the world work together, it will be the right time for the beginning of a new age, which will be an era of wisdom.

This book by Patricia Mercier unveils some of the secrets and responds to some of the questions many initiates and ordinary people usually have. The most important thing in these modern times is to be open-minded in order to understand. This is the only way to acquire cosmic wisdom.

Hunbatz Men
Itzá Maya Tradition

Hunbatz Men: day-keeper, Itzá Maya Tradition. Ceremonial and initiatic journey leader. Author of several books, founder of the world-wide Maya Mysteries Schools and Mayan Ceremonial Centre Lol Be.

Hunbatz Men can be contacted on mayan20@prodigy.net.mx and website www.themayas.com.

Introduction

Amaruka is a very old name given to the western hemisphere by some of its indigenous inhabitants long before Amerigo Vespucci sailed across the Atlantic to its shores. Amaru in Inca means snake or serpent and Ka signifies location or place.

This book is an adventure into dimensions of time – the messages and wisdom of Central American indigenous peoples, who still live close to nature. It poses choices that fundamentally affect you and me. It mentions crystal singing skulls, prophecies, cosmic beings, time and hidden, mysterious cities.

Prophecy has long been associated with the peoples of the Americas, and the crystal skulls are fundamental to the prophecies of the Maya. Mystics and visionaries who have held the crystal skulls have accessed information that can only be explained as coming from other dimensions – the skulls have something to sing about!

Alive and well today are some six million people of pure Maya descent. Add to this the millions of other indigenous peoples living across the Americas – Turtle Island – and we have a rich cultural 'choir' of voices, including those of the Cherokee, Seneca, Anishnabe, Inca, Hopi, Kogi, Zuni and Sioux.

As you read this book you will be introduced to knowledge and wisdom from these indigenous peoples. You will hear about their ancient cultures that produced outstanding achievements well before Columbus or indeed even the Chinese ever set foot in the Americas. But the point of this knowledge and wisdom is of no value unless we *use* it in our lives today. It is a living knowledge coloured with wisdom of the ages and the tears of Mother Earth, recounted for us in the prophecies of the indigenous peoples.

As we listen around their fires of knowledge we shall begin to understand a particular Maya prophecy concerning the date of 21 December 2012. This is the completion point of a 5,125-year calendar count of time called the Long Count. It marks a change from one age or Maya Creation to another. Maya wisdom teachers, along with other indigenous peoples of the Americas, give urgent warnings to humanity concerning the critical times in which we now live, and the possible demise of the human race.

In a search for the truth behind these prophecies and predictions I undertook a quest across the Americas over a period of years. I am fortunate to have studied with Hunbatz Men from the Yucatán, Mexico, a day-keeper of the Itzá Maya Tradition. Hunbatz Men has studied Maya teachings and been instrumental in inviting outsiders to take part in numerous ceremonies. In 1995 he brought many hundreds of people to the Yucatán to ceremonially reopen a number of sacred places in ancient Maya cities.

Subsequently scores of people were initiated as Solar Initiates, remembering their starry origins. In 1996 Hunbatz Men founded the worldwide Maya Mysteries Schools, autonomous groups studying the mysteries of the cosmos, universal truths, Maya teachings and mysteries from their own lands. Thus my husband Mikhail and I started the Sun and Serpent Maya Mysteries School in UK, and now we carry out holistic shamanic training and spiritual healing where we live in Spain.

Hunbatz Men was influential in organizing the fifth annual Gathering of Indigenous Elders and Priests of the Americas in 2003. I attended as an observer and met some of the participants. From these colourful and inspiring people I was inspired to collect prophecies from indigenous Americans and present them as a story from the mouths of the singing crystal skulls.

On my path I gained insights and guidance from invisible beings from whom I believe the prophecies originate. These beings are not attached to any one nation, race, time, place or dimension. Some elders and shamans access subtle dimensions through ceremony, visions and sacred shamanic tools such as the 'singing skulls'. They have preserved powerful esoteric knowledge throughout the ages by passing it down through family lineages. A Maya saying goes, 'We are the Lords, the Travellers in Time'.

The Maya peoples carry with them a long history reaching through aeons of time. The present-day Maya are widespread throughout parts of Mexico, (principally the states of Yucatán, Quintana Roo, Campeche, Tabasco and Chiapas) and Guatemala, Honduras, El Salvador and Belize. They speak 30 different languages. Archaeologists say they have an identifiable history spanning 3,000 years. Others say they are adept at tuning in to nature, to the starry cosmos and to the pulse of life – the beat of the indigenous heart, the Web of Life.

The ancient Maya are best known for their achievements between the years 300 and 843 CE, the Classic Period, when they built large and impressive cities containing temples, flat-topped stepped pyramids, observatories, palaces and living quarters. But they long pre-existed that time. Their cities included architecture that enhanced and amplified sound and light, using scientific, mathematical and astronomical knowledge. These cities, today mostly located deep in semi-tropical rainforests or on dry scrubland, defy present-day logic. How were they able to organize complex building works when they lived in such apparently harsh climatic situations?

Theirs is a living, evolving tradition and many of today's Maya still live deep in the rainforests or in remote locations, continuing to enact ceremonies to keep them in close contact with nature. Others live in villages or towns, but they nevertheless carry a serene dignity linking with their ancestral heritage, with the *halach uinic*, Mayan for 'true people'.

The Maya have a tradition of prophecy, memories of extraterrestrial contact and an unrivalled understanding of time cycles. The 'true people' foresaw the Spanish conquest and the horrors that would come with it. Even today the rights of the indigenous of the Americas are still overshadowed by the doctrine of discovery and a papal bull dating back to 1452 in which Pope Nicholas directed King Alfonso of Portugal to 'capture, vanquish, and subdue the Saracens, pagans, and other enemies of Christ', 'to put them into perpetual slavery' and 'to take all their possessions and property'. This papal bull and another dated 1493, directly subjugating the Maya, have never been rescinded despite repeated requests to the Vatican.

Maya calendrical prophets named an important date called One Reed, when an ancestor god was prophesied to return, 'coming like a butterfly from the east'. In our Western Gregorian calendar, One Reed was Easter Sunday, 21 April 1519. It happened to be the day that Hernándo Cortés and his fleet of 11 Spanish galleons arrived off the coast of what is now Vera Cruz, Mexico. When these ships came towards the shore the Maya people were waiting. The billowing sails of the ships reminded them of butterflies skimming above the ocean – they didn't use sailing ships themselves.

Their prophecy was fulfilled and Cortés, after fighting his first battle at Tabasco, founded the town of Vera Cruz, marched to Tlaxcala, and made allies of some of the indigenous people. During subsequent incursions into Mexico he was generally not resisted. His small force of soldiers, many on horses, overcame thousands of indigenous inhabitants – not least with fatal diseases. He marched on the Aztec capital, Tenochtitlán, in central Mexico, capturing and tricking the king, Montezuma. But the Aztecs rose against him, and Cortés was forced to flee. Later he launched a bloody and successful siege of the capital, defeating the Aztecs. He was formally appointed governor and captain-general of New Spain in 1522 by the Spanish king. In this way the enormous change and ensuing carnage equivalent to an indigenous holocaust, in what Europeans called the New World, was anticipated by a single prophecy.

Often priests or simple individuals received prophecies. Some of them have been recorded, such as in the books of Chilam Balaam and the prophecies of a woman called *Xnuc K'in* of Mani. There are many prophecies from diverse parts of Turtle Island that confirm we are now living in the 'end times'. When taken together these indigenous predictions and prophecies have crucial messages of the risk of impending destruction and yet, conversely, many of them contain hopeful, illuminating messages. Destruction is not inevitable.

We may well question the validity of such predictions. However, indigenous peoples who have received such prophecies, predictions and revelations have found themselves in a particular time and place coordinate that enables them to connect into a greater whole. An intuitive part of their mind, a higher consciousness, can 'read' signs which come as feelings, visions, voices, words or pictures. These signs are part of a record of all that is, has been and is to come, called the Web of Life – in Western traditions, the Akashic Record. I prefer to call it the WorldWideWeb of Light.

Clearly there is not just one possibility for the future. Maya time-keepers say that lines of time are bundled together into strands that become part of a woven 'Mat of Time'. It is the task of skilled shamans and recipients of prophecy to pull out a time strand from the mat and interpret it.

There is a formula available to resist what appears to be an awesomely bleak future. Through environmental actions and self-empowerment we may connect into the WorldWideWeb of Light, which continuously streams around, bathing our planet from the centre of the cosmos. The Maya describe this centre as the House of *Hunab K'u*, the One Giver of Movement and Measure – in our terms, the one God. When we feel our connection into the WorldWideWeb of Light there is the possibility that we can avert even the direst of predictions. For example, the Hopi Prophecies talk of a critical mass of 144,000 people being needed to 'awaken' before the nexus point of 21 December 2012.

I contrast the potentially fearful statements implied in some prophecies with positive steps that may be taken to prepare us for coming times, drawn from mythic stories and signs such as those of White Calf Woman, The Returning White Brother and other predictive messages from the Hopi, Sioux and Kogi peoples.

Throughout this book I place the prophecies before you as powerful statements that have influenced generations of indigenous peoples. I ask you to listen to the positive elements in them, deep within yourself. You then become the one to make the necessary life choices. In the deepest part of your soul and spirit, develop a burning desire to understand how you could spin yourself a different thread of life in the years leading up to, and beyond, the critical date of 21 December 2012.

The reason for taking control of your choices becomes apparent as you begin an exploration into the worlds of elders and shamans. As you read the prophecies, be aware that they represent our *possible* futures. They are not yet written in stone.

The recipients of prophecy have, in the main, opened themselves up through ritual or ceremony to other dimensions that normally are closed. For example, a group of Guatemalan elders received a particular prophecy. They were meditating in a room with raindrops playing musically on the roof when apparently they drew a particular time thread towards themselves. The elders, all at the same time, saw and 'read' the prophecy as if they were pictures projected one after another onto a wall. They did not doubt the validity of what they saw, for they came from an ancient culture where such prophetic tidings were commonplace for wise ones and shamans.

This is an important lesson – we too must believe that, even in our modern culture, we can affect the threads of future time. The outcome depends on every one of us making choices from moment to moment, moving gracefully in and out of different states of awareness.

Our minds risk being lulled into a state of inertia by a type of 'cultural hypnosis' induced by our Western materialistic worldview. But by exercising our full human potential, its strangling grip will be loosened. The more we release ourselves from this cultural hypnosis, awakening to our soul purpose and taking guardianship of our planet, the more we will come into a harmonic resonance with the true inner spirit of life. When every decision we take enhances life, then our own little lives will become one with the greater life of Spirit.

Patricia Mercier (Alloa)
Andalucia, Spain, 2007

Notes

I have used the modern Western dating system. Thus BCE (before the Common Era) and CE (Common Era) replace the more familiar BC and AD.

As with all prophecies there are confusions and some differences of opinion as to the veracity of future dates. I have chosen to use the 2012 date because its popularity has the advantage of focusing our minds upon the great need for positive change – then our hearts will follow.

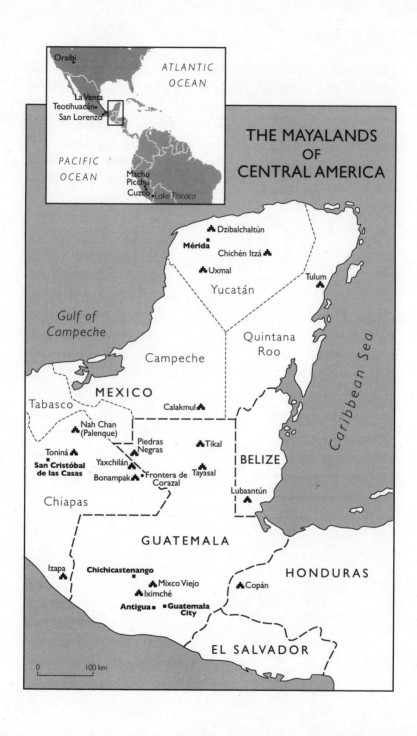

THE MAYALANDS
OF
CENTRAL AMERICA

Oraibi

ATLANTIC
OCEAN

La Venta
Teotihuacán
San Lorenzo

PACIFIC
OCEAN

Machu
Picchu
Cuzco Lake Titicaca

Dzibalchaltún

Mérida
Chichén Itzá

Uxmal

Tulum

Yucatán

Gulf of
Campeche

Quintana
Roo

Campeche

MEXICO

Tabasco

Calakmul

Nah Chan
(Palenque)
Piedras
Negras

Tikal

Toniná
San Cristóbal
de las Casas

Yaxchilán

BELIZE

Bonampak Frontera de
Corazal

Tayasal

Caribbean Sea

Chiapas

Lubaantún

GUATEMALA

Izapa

Chichicastenango

Mixco Viejo
Iximché

HONDURAS

Copán

Antigua Guatemala
City

EL SALVADOR

0   100 km

Part One

The Earth's Lament

CHAPTER 1

Day of the Solstice

Spirituality is a state of connectedness to life,
it is an experience of being, belonging and caring.

It is sensitivity and compassion, joy and hope.

It is the harmony between the innermost life
and the outer life, or the life of the world and
the life universal.

It is the supreme comprehension of life in time and
space, the tuning of the inner person with the great
mysteries and secrets that are around us.

It is the belief in the goodness of life and the
possibility for each person to contribute goodness
to it.

It is the belief in life as part of the eternal stream
of time, that each of us came from somewhere
and is destined somewhere, that without such belief
there could be no prayer, no meditation, no peace
and no happiness.

U Thant, Secretary General of the United Nations, 1961–71

The Twin Pyramids

I walk slowly up the hill to Mixco Viejo, ancient capital of the Guatemalan Pokoman Maya, high on the sun-scorched plains, with a panoramic all-encompassing view. The city has deep rocky ravines all around it and I pass across them by way of a causeway. The ochre-coloured earth shimmers with a heat haze; the temperature rising as midday approaches.

Beneath the purple shade of a welcoming flowering jacaranda tree, its blossoms hanging heavy with pollen, are a group of immaculately dressed schoolchildren. They chatter and play, unaccustomed to the countryside, for they have come by bus from the capital Guatemala City. Like so many colourful parakeets they flit from one thing to another, jumping up and down excitedly. I note their electronic game toys in hand, their walkmans and earplugs, insulating them from the beauty of nature that surrounds them.

A teacher, seemingly only a little older than the kids, slowly ascends the path from the ravine and they dutifully gather around her. A moment of silence sweeps across the group as she begins to tell them, in Spanish, about the Maya Indians and this ruined city that is part of their Maya heritage. Some faces look puzzled. Just one or two seem inquisitive. Few really seem to be interested as she starts to talk of the Maya peoples, whose nations now inhabit the present-day countries of Guatemala, parts of Mexico, Belize, Honduras and El Salvador.

Having finished, she points towards two smallish stepped pyramids, seemingly identical, each with a flat top. The particular placing of these pyramids by their builders was in a special alignment to catch the energy of each spring equinox sunrise. This was just one of many such alignments in the Mayalands of Central America, that the ancient Maya arranged perfectly to align with the rising and setting points of specific solar phenomena.

At that same moment an elder who is a 13th-generation Maya high priest called Wandering Wolf appears. He is dressed in his traditional colourful clothes, standing between the two pyramids in exactly the position that the sun's rays strike at the spring equinox. Sunlight catches the red woven cloth tied around his head, ready for the special

3

ceremony that is to follow. He holds his hands in the air, honouring Father Sun. The children turn, a magic moment captured in their collective awareness. Their eyes, at first dulled by a seemingly boring and irrelevant lesson, suddenly light up. They leave the schoolteacher and rush towards Wandering Wolf, eager to see his next move.

Almost imperceptibly he nods approval at them and begins to talk in Kiché Mayan to the children, who follow him and then quietly gather in a circle as he prepares for a time-honoured ceremony. It is to be a traditional fire ceremony where a small fire is specially laid out on the bare dusty earth and very ancient prayers are made as it burns.

Accompanying Wandering Wolf are Elizabeth and Rosemarie, fire priestesses, who each carry a heavy sacred bundle of offerings for the fire, wrapped in a large hand-woven red cloth. Mikhail, my husband, and I are laden with bunches of white lily flowers freshly purchased from the market in a nearby village. Wandering Wolf selects an auspicious spot and begins to make the layout of the fire. First, a cross is made from sugar (or sometimes honey), with arrows to the four compass directions of east, west, north and south. Then a circle about a metre wide is drawn around it on the ground.

Copious amounts of copal incense (a type of tree resin), fragrant kindling wood and what I consider to be unusual offerings of cigars, sweets and chocolate are placed at the centre of the as yet unlit fire. Each of the four directions is coloured with powdered sugar in red, white, blue and yellow, and small coloured offering candles are laid down around the centre. Wandering Wolf signals to me and I gently put down the lilies, taking care that they face inwards, to give themselves willingly to the flames that will soon start to consume the little piles of kindling wood. El Maestro Wandering Wolf, respected elder, begins a lengthy incantation of prayers and lights the ceremonial fire.

The ceremony here at Mixco Viejo attracts the children like a fiery magnet. It is open to everyone, since in such fire ceremonies no one is excluded. Every day, in traditional Maya villages, people make sacred fires and pray for the health of their families and the world. Typically the words are said: 'May we end this day as we started – in health, strength and peace.'

As I stand in the circle of children around the fragrantly smoking fire

I wonder what this humble, peaceful man, who is so rich in wisdom, thinks of greedy bankers, industrialists, businesspeople and all those who plunder the Earth, using it for personal gain. I dare not ask Wandering Wolf what blackmail and corruption he has witnessed in his own 'Land of Guatemaya', for it would break the energy building up for the ceremony.

Not so long ago Guatemala's élite controlled the country and argued whilst army and militias fought a civil war, surrounding the villages and shooting dissenters alongside innocent children. Now Maya children, descendants of such atrocities, just one generation on, form into a tight eager circle around the fire. I wonder, can this ancient ceremony awaken them to their destiny? Can it invoke in them an awareness of the part they each could play in the future, during this critical time for the world?

Young eyes, rich in dark liquid beauty, turn towards Wandering Wolf as he begins reciting the ancient Maya calendrical count of days. The old calendar counts, very different to our Western Gregorian calendar, are vital in order for the Maya shamans to weave intricate life-patterns on what, in their cosmology, they call the Threads of Time.

What are these Threads of Time? The shamans explain this by alluding to a hand-woven mat. Such mats are commonly made and used in the Mayalands. From a traditional Maya perspective everything and everyone on the planet sits upon a 'mat', a kind of grid reference point, that holds us in a time-space position. We carry personal time-threads that are the sum of all our past experiences in this life and others.

Then there are the Threads of Time Future. These are bundles of possibility and potential destiny, or 'callings', each with its own particular 'colour', vibration or frequency, that we may activate during the course of our lives. We can choose the threads we will follow – to what extent we will honour the Earth and to what extent we will degrade her. Every thread gives us a choice to make from moment to moment. Visionaries and prophets access these threads when receiving prophecies.

Shamans can help us weave these threads into a meaningful whole. They can take us on journeys into other worlds of perception, just as the smoke, heavy with aromatic incenses, drifting up from sacred fires, invites us to dream with it and move into an altered state of consciousness. The ceremonial fire can open a glimpse into other dimensions: it is a doorway or portal through which to leave our physical limitations behind, to travel in other realities and then to return to awareness of our bodies.

A Quantum Leap into the WorldWideWeb of Light

Here is an example of this 'dimensional travel'. It occurred that day at Mixco Viejo. Suddenly I was propelled into a recollection. I experienced a strange sensation, as if I had regrown my umbilical cord. Something was pulling me, dragging me. Startled, looking down at my solar plexus, I see what appear to be threads of light streaming from it. Then there came a reverberating sound of drumming, and instantaneously I saw a circle of serious brown faces eerily lit up by the occasional sparking of a wood fire in the centre of a tipi.

Chanting and women's soft sobbing came to my ears. My first thought was that I was back in my mother's womb and, baby-like, I moved my hands to cover my ears. But nothing stopped this vision coming through my eyes – an intense scene swirling within smoke and flames. Chanting and crying were all around me. I jumped, my feet moving of their own accord in some kind of earth-stomping dance. Across the circle of faces I could see another dancer, a medicine man, who had an intense glow around him and an even stronger golden glow from the centre of his bare-skinned chest.

I was drawn towards the medicine man. I could see now that he was dancing around the body of a man lying on the ground, dying. The body had very little auric glow and I saw that the usual light in the centre of his chest was all but extinguished. He was shaking and going into spasms as I held him down and the medicine man sucked at the top of his head, vigorously spitting a stream of dark-looking liquid to one side. I somehow knew this sick man had been bitten by a snake on his ankle.

I applied herbs as the medicine man worked. We moved together, knowing exactly what to do. Then another part of me –

me in my present life – pushed into my mind, saying, 'Hey, wait, let's get a real doctor'. But then I 'jumped' back into the tipi and the sobbing of the women had subsided. Within moments the sick man was sitting up, and there appeared an ever-increasing golden glow around his chest.

I began to rationalize what was happening: somehow I had been pulled by one of those Threads of Time back into the past. How had it happened? I am normally very clear-headed. I felt that either Great Spirit or Wandering Wolf had something to do with it. As I rationalized my experience, it began to fade. But by being drawn into this fractal picture, the medicine man had shown me the weakness of the sick man's 'assemblage point' and how his shamanic power had restored life to the man. I remembered the teachings of an old Mexican who lived way out in the Sonora Desert – Don Pedro Bravo had told me that the assemblage point is where we personally 'sit' on the Mat of Time. It is where our own 'grid reference' coordinates of light meet, keeping us alive.

I thought of my days as a yoga teacher and reflected that this intense energy point, rather like a chakra, an energy centre in our body's subtle energy system, is held within our auric field. When we are born it is situated over our abdomen and, gradually, in our first seven years of life, it moves to its optimum position over the right side of our chest. While we are alive it maintains this position, but at the point of death it drops lower until it disappears. Then, when we leave our body, it reunites with the Source, called 'Great Spirit' by Native Americans.

Sometimes our assemblage point is knocked out of position by trauma, illness or the abuse of drugs or alcohol. An experienced shaman can rectify this in a healing ceremony. They may also undertake soul retrieval, in which the soul may be trapped in and released from other dimensions. Shamans and medicine men and women say that moving the soul back to its correct place in a patient's body is a risky business. Clearly the shaman's ceremony that I saw in my vision had managed to save the man with the snakebite.

As I continued to re-establish myself in 'ordinary' reality and the vision dimmed, I realized that these shamanic ways are as old as the history of Earth herself, and as relevant today as they have ever been. I mused how we Westerners rush to our doctors when we are sick or plagued by psychological issues, seeking solace in some costly drug to suppress rather than release the dark poisonous liquid in which we are rotting. Our ailments are like rotting fruit hanging lifeless upon a mythic World Tree. A shaman sucks this dark poison out of us to bring healing.

Maya villagers in Guatemala, living a life rich in tradition and imagery, talk of owing their lives to the existence of the 'Earth Fruit' that grows upon the World Tree. Don Pedro's explanation of life was multi-dimensional, just like the fractal picture I had been shown in the tipi. This is a reality well travelled by the shamans, seers and prophets of many ancient cultures.

After my deep experience I was still trying to come to grips with the everyday world, and recalled a time some years before when I had visited a card reader for a consultation. This woman had explained her skills to me: 'I can prophesy the future by reading signs on the Threads of Time.' I remembered her soft contralto, almost monotone voice lowering as she leaned forward to me, saying, 'These threads enable us to predict personal events as well as things like weather patterns and other natural cyclical occurrences.' She had reminded me that 'prophecy', originating from Greek and Latin, means divinely inspired future prediction.

I remember asking her why Nostradamus researchers say that, after the year 2000, his prophecies seemed to end. She said, 'He knew that, after that date, the evolution of humanity would cause humans to be raised to new realizations and a higher plane.' This would make it difficult for Nostradamus to see what would happen next. Her reply set me off on a long quest to understand the workings of time. It led eventually to my travels throughout the Americas, to uncover the indigenous peoples' rich store of prophecies.

At that consultation I thought how useful it would be to be able to select our future from a bundle of threads – a bundle of possibilities! Now, some years on, I had recalled something from the past in the 'vision' I had at Mixco Viejo. I began to wonder how I could tap into the future too. I had heard rumours that something cataclysmic could happen around the year 2012, and that this date had been anticipated by the Maya of Central America thousands of years ago. That's why I had come to Mexico and Guatemala. I was on a quest to find out what secrets the Maya held.

The Basis of the 2012 CE Prophecy

When we look beyond our immediate world situations at what Maya wisdom teachers call 'sacred science', an evolutionary soul-awakening process becomes apparent. An example is in the Maya sacred book, the *Popul Vuh*, a mythic story which describes in poetic terms how the lesser gods 'blinded humanity' back in prehistory, limiting our potential. Accordingly we have been held, fixed, unable to realize our full human potential, for the past 5,000 years – we have been 'sleeping'. Yet the global situation of today – climate change and current world events – demands that we wake up out of our destructive habits and cultural hypnosis to *choose* our futures, if we are to survive.

The Maya Long Count calendar divided history into a series of ages, and this reckoning is still followed by people living in the Guatemala highlands. If we place the origin of the story of the blinding of humanity at the beginning of this current Maya age, precisely dated at 11 August 3114 BCE, and count from this date to the end of the age in an unbroken chain of days, as the Maya did, we come to the prophetic date of 21 December 2012 CE. Appendix 4 explains more about how they did this.

Some writers on this subject have predicted dire circumstances will occur in 2012 – leading to a disaster of enormous, global proportions. But none of the Maya, or others whose prophecies are mentioned later, have actually predicted disaster as an inevitability – though they do say that it is a possibility. Gloom-and-doom predictions are mostly the work of Westerners, adding their own interpretations. Present-day Maya people who follow traditional counts of time do know, without any doubt, that a date in their calendars equivalent to our year 2012 marks the end of a Great Age and the beginning of a new one. They repeatedly say that the rest is up to us, and the future is not set in stone.

As this book progresses, more details about the Maya prophecies will emerge and, with them, the variety of viewpoints of other native peoples of the Americas. They are not like the 'People of the Book', Christians, Jews and Muslims, who adhere to a written doctrine. Instead, they follow truths indigenous to their own tribes and lineages, passed down verbally from generation to generation and therefore quite varied in their details.

In view of the uncertainties that the prophecies appear to present us, one may well ask, 'What can I do in the face of potential disaster?' Keeping an open mind is the first step towards unlocking ourselves from a debilitating matrix of fear that has been built up in Western nations boasting a material economy based on 'liberal democracy' and 'negative freedom'. The second step is to begin a path of reunification with Source, with Great Spirit or the God Within. The third step is to 'travel' the Threads of Time consciously, to make informed choices for our individual futures and for the future of all humanity.

This is a kind of *remembering* which also informs the future and asks each and all of us to travel into Time Future, to 2013 CE and beyond. This is the year when the next Age will unfold, based upon our actions in the moment that is Now. In this remembering we lose the 'blindness' that the lesser gods inflicted upon us. We wake up. Once we each know about the Threads of Time we are able to make a transformed choice through our *hearts*, not so much our heads. With this we can truly affect the future. In this process we remember our soul mission, carried into our present life from wisdom set in the deep distant past.

Choices are presented to us every day. One way to empowerment is to make ourselves fully alive to possibilities that are *con*structive and non-harmful to other life forms, to Mother Earth and to other humans. Doing this on a day-to-day level is not easy, but once we have learned the art we become more adept at it. A positive outcome for the future depends on every one of us making choices from moment to moment, moving gracefully in and out of different states of consciousness, surfing the Web of Life.

Not so long ago I met a grandmother, a wise elder of the Plains Indians in the United States, who clearly understood the Web of Life. Dressed in her traditional clothes, colourfully decorated with beadwork patterns, with her long greying hair tied back into two plaits, she looked deeply into me with her dark, sad eyes and said, 'If our Earth is to survive as a viable home for our grandchildren's children, through the next seven generations, we must wake up *now* to our soul purpose, walk our talk and take responsible guardianship of our inheritance of planet Earth, and for generations yet to be born.'

At that time I was too shy to quiz her about what exactly she meant. So I decided to set up a little shamanic experiment I had heard about. Waiting until dark I put a candle beside me and sat before a large mirror. It is said that guidance always comes to you when you do this. Gazing at my reflected face, I began to question myself. What did 'walk our talk' mean? What did the peoples of Turtle Island (the Americas) know that others did not? Does it mean that I should never say one thing while doing another? Does it mean always living from a higher centre of consciousness, with grace, compassion and nonviolence? Like the Native Americans, should I show loving awareness of nature, only taking what I *need* and not what I *want*?

In the dim light of the flickering candle, my face in the mirror receded in and out of my field of vision. I heard the words, 'Be true to yourself. Do not eat more than you can grow, or live with more than you can carry on your back.' Looking intensely at the mirror I glimpsed the image of a young Indian brave standing behind me, the candlelight catching his handsome features, a feather headdress and bone beads around his neck. As a kind of spirit guide, he transmitted these words to me: 'Live the Beauty Way. Walk your talk and never *ever* speak with forked tongue.'

As his image faded, I began to think about those words. If we all truly mean what we say and if every decision we take is life-enhancing, our collective experiences will become one with the Source and we will know that we are not separate from one another. We will be empowered to change the course of world events and avert disaster. By adopting a simple code of living we can take full responsibility for our thoughts and actions. We will base them on life-enhancing principles. It's a tall order, but not impossible. What is at stake is our futures.

Making these new connections in order to walk our talk also works in terms of the WorldWideWeb of Light, the all-encompassing subtle earth energies and light grids in and around our planet. In order to walk our talk, as part of an interconnected human race, our position on this web of light is determined by every person's own assemblage point and by an overlay of the Threads of Time from past and future, all intersecting in the Now. This gives us a kind of personal 'grid reference point'.

Back in the heat of the midday sun at Mixco Viejo, the fragrant blue smoke of the sacred fire caressed my senses, spiralling into the air like the frequently depicted Maya Vision Serpents of old. My gaze turned to the other participants in the circle. Beaming smiles linked our hearts with an inner recognition. The children had stood quietly for a long time and, as the fire ceremony came to a close, they held hands in pairs and jumped nimbly across the dying embers. I caught a glimpse of tears in the corner of Wandering Wolf's bright, piercing eyes.

Duality

The fire ceremony over, I wandered towards the twin pyramids a little way from the site chosen by El Maestro, Wandering Wolf, for the fire. These pyramids are about 30ft (10m) high, with a small flat platform on top. Their smooth stones seemed to have grown organically out of the hard sun-baked earth, of similar ochre colour. There is much spiritual science to be learnt from ancient sacred places.

Demonstrating an advanced knowledge and culture, every old Maya city had at its centre many profusely decorated ceremonial buildings, temples, pyramids, astronomical observatories and centres for teaching. Their outward appearance often hides a whole history that has been steeped in the stones, hidden from the sight of tourists, encoded there for those who can access such things. They are a repository of time past, time future, star maps and sound-vibration encodements. Sometimes the tall single standing stones, called *stelae*, are carved with images or Maya hieroglyphs. The two twin pyramids at Mixco Viejo do not have any carvings on them.

I decided to explore the hidden energies of the two pyramids, first by climbing them, then by standing at the foot of each, resting my back against the wall so that my spine became a sensing 'barometer' of the energies held in each stone. The left pyramid held strong feminine qualities. The right-hand one seemed to exude a masculine quality. Finally I positioned myself in the power spot between them, where Wandering Wolf had first stood upon his arrival at Mixco Viejo. The pyramid builders made astronomical observations and cleverly positioned the twin pyramids so that the rising orb of the sun on 21 March , the Maya New Year in many of the calendar counts, would rise between them.

As I stood there a realization came to me: *clearly these pyramids have a lesson to teach us about duality*. Wandering Wolf had been showing us something. To me it seemed that he stood between them, experiencing the tension caused by duality, but then he chose to walk away to a new position outside the tension. I wondered about the tensions that duality holds, keeping this world captive. What can we learn as individuals if we explore the duality within us?

For each of us a burden of fearful, negative knowledge highlights our fragility and that of life on this planet, and it can cause huge tension and despair. There is fear of losing material comforts, of doing without, of becoming underprivileged or subjected to control and manipulation. Over much of the world we see a 'live now, pay later' society. Even people of integrity are lured into acting as reluctant accomplices, either by choice, out of negligence or perhaps arising from a feeling of helplessness derived from living in an unsustainable society where, before long, the world will not have a quality of life suitable for the majority of human beings.

Metaphorically speaking, we are eating our great-grandchildren by stealing from them the possibility of a sustainable life in the future. An example was given by the New Economics Foundation in spring 2006: for everyone in the world to live at the level of consumption experienced by people in Britain, we would require 3.1 Planet Earths. Yet, looking at the positive side of duality, we are being shown the possibility of a new time, a new Creation, as predicted by the Maya, the Inca and others, so long ago.

Gradually we are becoming aware that we are not as separate from each other or from our environment as we previously believed. This is something the world's indigenous people have long known. The twin Maya pyramids at Mixco Viejo illustrate that, while they represent duality, standing between them when the sun rises at the equinox, the contradictions of duality are resolved. We discover the unifying dynamic behind the image of the sun, as so often demonstrated in sacred science. That is, if we free ourselves of the dualities built into our cultural conditioning, we experience unity.

Mystics might refer to this dynamic as the 'third vector', a resolution of dualism and an aspect of arcane knowledge known to many ancient peoples. The ancient Maya, builders of the sun pyramids, who honoured the mystery behind the sun, revered this knowledge, calling it *Ahau*, or Lord. The solar priests who instructed the population in this arcane knowledge were called *Ahau Kines* and everyone was called *Kin*, or 'a little piece of the sun'. Even in the English language 'kin' refers to our wider families. *Ahau* was a gateway to higher consciousness or superconsciousness. The ultimate creative deity, *Hunab K'u*, was named 'the One Giver of Movement and Measure', for it was this that was all-powerful and 'set the worlds in motion'.

Under the Teaching Tree

My companions were nowhere in sight. The day was getting hotter and I decided to seek some shade. The sound of a great mass of buzzing bees caused me to investigate the nearby trees. The drone of the creatures almost hypnotized me as I watched their movements in and out of the flowers.

Then I walked across and sat beneath the same flowering jacaranda tree where the children had received their teachings. I was reminded of a story that originated in a land far away from the Maya. One day, according to an Eastern story, the gods decided to create the universe. They created the stars, the sun and the moon. They created the seas, the mountains, the crystals, the flowers and the clouds. Then they created human beings. Finally at the end, they created truth. At this point a problem arose: where should they hide truth so that human beings would not find it right away? They wanted to prolong the adventure of the search.

'Let's put it on top of the highest mountain,' said one of the gods. 'Let's put it on the farthest star,' said another. 'Let's hide it in the darkest and deepest of abysses.' 'Let's conceal it on the secret side of the moon.'

At the end, the wisest and most ancient god said, 'No, we will hide truth inside the very hearts of human beings. In this way they will look for it all over the universe, without being aware that they have it within themselves all of the time.'

CHAPTER 2

Predictions in the Ring of Fire

The time is out of joint; O cursed spite,
That ever I was born to set it right!

***Hamlet**, William Shakespeare*

I want to tell you about the Maya 'cosmovision', the basis of the Maya prophecies, accessed by developing 'superconsciousness'. The prophecies are not best explained by logical means – instead I want to give you a taste of the awareness with which the people of Central America developed their calendrical and prophetic thinking. So I shall take you to visit the ancient Olmecs, one of the first city-dwelling peoples of the Americas, then I shall recount an experience I had with a Maya shaman and 'day-keeper', followed by more about the Maya prophecies, and finally a story about a trip to the top of a Guatemalan volcano. But first, a little about superconsciousness.

Superconsciousness

Years of meditation practice had left their calming signature upon me. But, try as I might, a higher consciousness eluded me until something happened to time itself. At first it appeared to be speeding up. My daily routine at home was normal. To begin with I thought I was tired, and I didn't want to engage in everyday conversations. Our pine *cabaña* on the Andalucian mountainside in Spain was also my art studio. It was there that I realized it wasn't time that was speeding up – something else was changing. I began to see something new in the sketches and paintings I had done of the sacred sites and mythology of the Mayalands. They became like windows, giving me, their creator, quite different perceptions.

This propelled me into periods of enhanced understanding, a higher state of being or superconsciousness. I have since talked with shamans about how to understand superconsciousness in the ways that many indigenous peoples do. With minds uncluttered by possessions, materialism and greed, generally they have a much greater acceptance and contentment with life. They know somehow that their awareness interacts with the environment in which they live, in a way we seem to have lost in the Western world. We, in our objective detachment, have become separated, preoccupied with our own affairs and interpretations of life, failing to read the messages we receive from the world around us, and within us.

By staying in close touch with the mystery of the Earth, indigenous peoples have an unspoken communication with their surroundings. In every cell of their bodies they honour Great Spirit. They know that the environment includes the body and brain matter of all other living things, and therefore that at some level we are all interconnected. Nowadays, modern thinking appears to confirm ancient wisdom by observing that, when we enter into another quality of consciousness – superconsciousness – all is One. Sometimes the Maya call this solar consciousness, or *cosmovision*, or attaining the qualities of the *Ahau*, the Sun Lord. In superconsciousness, truths of the greater mystery hidden within life, the truths of the Unknown, become instantaneously available – but the Unknowable remains unknowable, yet a sense of reverence compensates for that.

It is up to each of us to decide to take up the challenge of remembering our inherent superconsciousness. It is our choice to become the *Ahau*, connecting ourselves into the WorldWideWeb of understanding, through Light as a carrier of information. We can choose a traditional way of accessing Light through meditation. Another way is to study the inner nature of Earth's mysteries that so many 'simple' native people understand.

Jaguar Priests – the Olmecs

Maya elders, who are connected to the Threads of Time Past and Time Future, recount many tales of ancestral beings, as if these beings are still living and real. To understand this, we need to step back in time to one of the former peoples who lived in the lands of Central America, known as the Olmec.

Although their original name and much of their history remains as yet undiscovered, they were given the name Olmec, or 'rubber people' because, as well as growing improved varieties of corn and other crops, they made good use of rubber trees, collecting the latex sap and trading it. Some speculate that these dark-skinned, thick-lipped, rather negroid-looking people expanded in Mexico from 2000 BCE, having crossed the ocean from Africa in far-off days.

Others say that perhaps the Olmec established themselves in Central America after the destruction of Atlantis. A repeating theme in most stories about Atlantis portrays a great civilization going through a period of massive destruction in its end times. Whether you believe this to be myth or history doesn't really matter. Wherever these stories come from, they are embedded deep within the human psyche. They also suggest a portent of cataclysm symbolic of our situation today.

By 1500 BCE the Olmecs lived in farming villages such as San Lorenzo, on a branch of the Coatzalcoalcos River in southern Mexico. This later developed into Central America's earliest known religious and political centre. With great effort and social organization they con-structed a plateau on which to build San Lorenzo. According to Maya historian and archaeologist M D Coe, this was some kind of effigy mound, looking like a gigantic bird flying eastwards toward Africa. The largest structures uncovered by archaeologists in San Lorenzo were for ceremonial use. It has the earliest known ball court, together with evidence of the unique bouncing rubber balls the Olmecs used for playing a ballgame which had cosmic undercurrents.

The Olmec are best known today for the colossal stone heads they carved, as enigmatic as the Easter Island statues. At least eight of them once stood in prime positions at San Lorenzo, making a strong statement about the power held within the head and the skull. They were possibly connected with ancestor worship. The skilful artisans who carved the stone heads worked with flint tools, making objects of serpentine and mica, iron ore beads and decorative ear spools, incorporating obsidian mirrors derived from the highlands of Mexico and Guatemala.

The Olmec traded textiles, exotic plumes, sacred books and wooden religious items with people far and wide, who regarded the Olmec as cultural and religious models to emulate. Their stone objects have been discovered all over Mesoamerica. But, like the later Maya, their civilization was not to last. Around 900 BCE chaos suddenly engulfed San Lorenzo. Someone – who, we do not know – apparently ordered the end of the city. The massive stone monuments, thrones and sculptures were dragged into lines, smashed and then buried. Over the subsequent years their temples and elaborate basalt-columned tombs succumbed to the searing tropical sun, and their memory and colourful traditions faded into the twilight of time.

La Venta, another Olmec town, was first occupied about 1100 BCE and maybe became the political and ceremonial successor to San Lorenzo. The remains of this town continue to stand on a fluted mound that took an estimated 800,000 man-days to complete. Even after erosion, it is still about 100ft (30m) high. Nearby there are also sacred landscape configurations that represent a massive jaguar mask positioned eight degrees west of north, aligned astronomically with the heavens of 3,000 years ago. Clearly guided by shamanic visions, the La Venta jaguar priests went to the trouble of constructing three intricate mosaic pavements of jaguar masks from serpentine stone slabs. Then they ceremonially covered them on completion. But, like San Lorenzo, La Venta was totally destroyed around the year 400 BCE.

I sat in a park in modern La Venta, where some of the massive Olmec remains have been placed, looking at one of the giant stone heads. I mused upon its meaning. Why did the Olmec go to such trouble to portray just a head – why not the whole body? Was it a warning to us not to let our power 'go to our heads'? Or, more likely, was it to say that consciousness is held there, ready to be activated and ennobled into superconsciousness?

Other Olmec sculptures and items of pottery display strong links with the jaguar, as if this creature also has something to convey to us.

Indeed, some of these images show jaguar priests or similar personages shape-shifting into their animal *nagual* (a shamanic term for a power animal, spiritual guide or one's magical inner self). Olmec peoples, like the Maya, revered this fierce stalker of the night that moves stealthily on softly padded feet between the duality of darkness and light, able to stalk with a sense of sight and smell far superior to that of the human. The creature became an emblem of the Underworld, where people go after death. The Underworld was not seen as a 'hell' in the Christian sense. Rather it was a place where another existence, an afterlife, another timeline or dimensional reality, was possible for humans.

Gene and George Stuart, in *Lost Kingdoms of the Maya* (Am. Soc. of Civil Engineers, 1993) said: 'The jaguar was considered to be the intermediary between the world of the living and the dead, and a protector of the Classic Maya royal houses.' In 1988, excavations next to Altar Q at Copán, Honduras, revealed 16 jaguars sacrificed by ruler Yax Pac in a masonry crypt – a jaguar for each of his royal ancestors.

In its savage beauty the jaguar connected the Olmec and, later, the Maya, to the raw energy of nature, for they feared and, more importantly, honoured this beautiful beast. They felt the raw energy move through their own bodies and, in refining it within themselves, they used their superconsciousness as a tool that connected them into the world of prophecy. With their inscrutable, colossal head sculptures the Olmec also left us a question for the future, on a Thread of Time from the past. Why were the heads lined up and systematically destroyed so long ago? Being wary not to allow our own cultural matrix to permeate our thinking, we might ask whether this was the fulfilment of some long-forgotten prophecy.

On my journeys through Mexico I found that the Olmec people were well recorded, although they are little spoken of today. What interests me is what happened on the Threads of Time. How can we explain the enigma of their demise and the apparent disappearance of whole societies in the past, including the Anasazi people of Chaco Canyon, Arizona, and the Maya at the end of the Classic Period? Modern theories of drought, pestilence or warfare fail to explain it. I believe there is a parallel between these occurrences, which has some sort of prophetic message for us to interpret and heed at this crucial point in our history.

The past, while it has much to teach us, is insignificant compared to the present moment, the *Now*. It is only in the Now that we can put into practice anything that we experience while travelling on the prophetic Threads of Time, past or future. It is up to each of us in this present moment – in the Now, as you read this page – to learn from the past, whether from the Olmec, the Maya, other ancient civilizations or from our own ancestors, in order to be able to interpret the Threads of Time and move forward into a secure future for planet Earth. *This is the inner essence and teaching of prophecy and prediction.*

The Prophetic Serpent of Time

The shaman beckoned me over. 'Follow me. Great Spirit has told me that I must show you something.' I was with a small group of people who had just completed a sunrise ceremony at the Temple of the Turtles in Uxmal, Mexico. I followed as he purposefully strode off in the direction of a long grey wall. Behind it, a huge quadrangle, with steps on three sides leading up to numerous small rooms and temples, cast lengthy shadows in the early morning light. A flock of white doves swept past as we entered through a graceful pointed Maya arch, stepped into a silence and the unexpected searing heat within the quadrangle. He pulled on my arm to bring me to an abrupt stop.

'Look along there. Look at the carved serpent with a human head in its mouth.' The angle of the sun perfectly cast its light and shadow upon an enormous serpent, twisting along the whole façade of one side of the quadrangle, sinuously making its way through the intricate carved stone decoration. The shaman looked at me with piercing eyes and began to speak, partly in English and partly in Spanish.

'Time is like this great serpent that periodically rises up and speaks to humanity of the future. This is one of the meanings of the carved images of serpents with human heads in their mouths, which you can see in sacred Maya city sites. For our ancestors in Mexico – Olmec, Maya, Aztec, Teotihuacáno – there was a deep fascination with time. Even the archaeologists have noticed it!'

'Can you tell me more?' I asked, already knowing that archaeological research confirmed this in nearly every investigative dig and study of temple alignments and astronomical recordings done so far.

He sucked in his breath through his flashing golden teeth and paused. 'The ancient astrologers and day-keepers, who kept the count of the days, comprehended both the circular and cyclical nature of time. Our history of the Earth tells us that events occurring once are likely to occur again in another cycle, providing a continuous linking of past, present and future. You are interested in divination, señora?'

'Yes,' I replied, perhaps too eagerly, realizing that he had picked my next question right out of my mind! I knew that the Mayalands were fertile ground for divination.

Then, drawing me into one of the small temples and sitting upon a moss-covered stone bench, he sank into deep thought while we both breathed in the slightly acrid and distinctive smell of bats, hanging above us. He tightened the red woven sash he wore around his waist, a sign of his authority as a day-keeper in his community.

'At one time prediction and divination were a normal part of life in every village community in rural parts of Mexico and Guatemala. They gave continuity to the hard and difficult lives that people endured after the Conquistadors ravaged our lands. They enhanced life with meaning, purpose and connectedness to nature and the elements. If you wish, señora, I can give you a divination.'

This was exciting. I had heard that, if you are lucky, you might still find a special shaman or calendar priest who would give a personal divinatory reading.

'First I must pray to our Creator God, the One Giver of Movement and Measure, whom we call *Hunab K'u*, and who lives in the stars of Orion.'

Switching suddenly into some kind of Maya language that I did not understand, he began to sway backwards and forwards while he drew a red cloth, crystals and red oval seeds from a small pouch. It seemed he was praying to a litany of gods and goddesses, for I was able to pick out a few of their names.

In a hypnotic way the intense heat and his words worked their magic on me. I closed my eyes and let myself travel to the stars of Orion. The

21

shaman was still swaying back and forth in a trancelike way as I opened them again. He said, 'Heart of Heaven, Heart of Earth, Serpent, Sun, *Ahau*, bless this woman, let her hear the words she needs to hear.'

He motioned for me to choose a handful of the red seeds and began his divination, placing them in sets of four and reciting more prayers and names of the days in Mayan. '*Ik, Akbal, Kan, Chicchan, Cimi...*' The last was the day associated with death. Here he paused and looked questioningly across at me. '*Manik, lamat, muluc, oc...*' And so he went on, counting the 20 day-names and repeating them many times over, but each time stopping ominously at *Cimi*. The day *Cimi* was represented by the picture of a skull.

Finally he looked up. 'Ah, señora, you will have an interesting life. A life of excitement and danger as you follow the road of prophecy. Be aware of the skull. All is not what it seems. Take care. Watch the serpent. You should ask the Virgin of Guadaloupe for protection, for if you peek under her mantle into the worlds of the ancestors you must take the consequences!' Then he went on with some personal comments and guidance. I wondered about this enigmatic Virgin whom many of the Maya had substituted for their old Classic Period corn and Earth goddess, called Tonantzin, after the Catholic religion was imposed upon them.

'Can you tell me more about the prophecies?' I asked respectfully, knowing that it was not done to ask too much of a genuine shaman. He turned, emerging from his trance and smiled at me.

'You have all the information you could ever need in your own skull – you just have to find where it has been hidden. Study all the prophecies.'

He seemed to look past me, into the starry depths of Orion. 'I see you holding a crystal, a huge, rounded crystal – yes, it is a head, or a skull. Beware the portal of death, before your mission is done.' The shaman closed his eyes and would say no more. I was left wondering what this mission was, and how dangerous it might be. Why did he keep mentioning a skull? It sounded a bit scary to me.

The reading over, I thanked the shaman and left, leaving him sitting in the small temple. As I went to leave the quadrangle, the pointed Maya arch was nowhere to be seen. To one side a carved image of a man sitting in a meditation pose looked down on me, as I found my way out through a small gap between the buildings. Looking back, I saw the graceful Maya arch, but it had been filled in with stones centuries ago! I was left wondering how I had got into the quadrangle and just where on Earth I had been for the last hour or so.

Later, when I shared this experience with Mikhail, he replied, rather strangely, 'I think you slipped into another time, and perhaps your mission isn't in this world!'

When we decide to venture into indigenous prophecies, it becomes apparent that much of what they reveal is already happening to us at this present time. Events described in prophecies are either real, or they have happened already, or they are future possibilities on the Threads of Time. Prophecy may also be a 'working out' in unseen and subtle levels other than in everyday life on Earth. This is particularly true of passages within prophecies that are somewhat enigmatic or at first difficult to understand. Mikhail's comment could well be right.

I had already collected a number of prophecies from the Americas. They fall into two distinct categories: those promising empowering situations and those of the doom-and-gloom type. Events like tsunamis, the melting of the polar icecaps and the destruction of the rainforests imply that we are perhaps in the midst of prophecies relating to End Times. But I knew it was important not to be fearful or despairing. I needed to take heed of the warnings in the shaman's reading. It was imperative to keep myself clearly informed, to watch and learn from the signs, in order to change despair to empowerment.

The Prophecy of the Nine Hells – and False Prophecy

My belief is that the ancient Maya, some 5,000 years ago, began an unprecedented experiment to refine human consciousness through study and ceremony, leading to what we might now call superconsciousness. One of the results of this was their cosmovision perception of very long and very short periods of time. The shamans of the age became adept at keeping calendars that are considerably different to our

understanding of time, dates, seasons and cycles. They became special-
ized calendar 'day-keepers' and understood at least 17 distinct calendars.
Such day-keepers, even now, can read the signs for each day, in a unique
blend of intuition, shamanic journeying and astrological prophecy.

Maya calendars, so complicated that they are a lifetime's study in
themselves, count time in days or 'little pieces of the Sun', called *k'in*,
running from sunset to sunset, with clearly different qualities and traditional guiding principles for every day. The best-known Maya calendar
is the sacred *Tzolk'in*, (or *Cholq'ij*) comprising 260 days in each cyclical
round. At first encounter this number of days seems rather strange to
us, accustomed as we are to a solar 365-day calendar. The 260 days are
linked to a cycle of the Pleiades stars and were also once the period of
human gestation. The Maya used these complex calendars to track
Times Past and Present, and to predict important future events on the
Threads of Time.

One of the best-known prophecies relates to the years leading up to
the 16th century, when a large council meeting of calendar day-
keepers identified a critical time to come in the future. They did not
know exactly what would happen but they identified a day in their
calendar called One Reed (or *Ce Acatal*). They foretold that, on this day,
an important ancestor would return. The returning one was said to be
'coming like a butterfly' and would be white-skinned. There was also
an ancient story about the bringer of wisdom to the Maya, named *Ku-
kuul-kaan* or Quetzalcoatl. He was a tall bearded white man who had left
the shores of the Mayalands on a raft made, according to the tradition,
of serpents, promising to return from the east in future times. These two
stories became confused with each other.

Subsequently the two prophecies were told throughout the lands.
But no one really knew what to expect and, by chance or by fate, the
prophesied person arrived in the year 1519, in the form of a Spanish
explorer. It was Hérnando Cortés who stepped ashore, commander of
his sailing fleet of 11 Spanish galleons with tall, white, billowing sails.
Of course, the Maya living along the coast had not seen galleons
before, and those sails presumably looked something like huge white
butterflies in the distance. Thus the arrival prophecy was fulfilled and
the invader Cortés, unwittingly also resembling a returning ancestor,

met little opposition as his small army rode a trail of destruction across the lands of the Maya and the Aztecs.

The fulfilment of such an important prophecy came at the start of a new calendar cycle. There were great upheavals, barbarous acts against the Maya and Aztecs, leading to feelings of doom amongst the people. They had never before known such cruelty and were especially shocked by the abuse of one of their sacred symbols, the World Tree, which took the form of a wooden cross. The invaders carried this symbol before them, on which there was an image of a man being crucified, when normally the World Tree would be decorated with flowers.

For them this perverse new symbol spoke of the violent nature of the coming time and the brutality of the Conquistadors. It was not long before traditional Maya priests were calling the new cycle Nine *Bolontikus*, or Nine Hells. Each cycle ran for 52 years, and there were to be 9 of them, adding up to 468 years. As these nine cycles unfolded, land and freedom were taken away from the Maya. European diseases transmitted by the invaders decimated the native people and many thousands succumbed to the cruelty of the Conquistadors.

Those Nine Hells ran, one after another, through the succeeding centuries, until a prophesied date that equates in our calendar with 16 August 1987. In the West, this was given the name 'Harmonic Convergence', which many people worldwide gathered together to celebrate. On that day many Maya welcomed the global focus on Maya ideas that the Harmonic Convergence brought. The presence in Mesoamerica of thousands of American and European participants and observers gave the quiet, unassuming Maya a certain degree of protection while they went about their ancient ceremonies to celebrate the ending of the Nine Hells, in accordance with the prophecy. At last the memories of the 'false prophet' Cortés were being laid to rest.

As people focused on peaceful ceremonies at ancient Maya sacred sites, they prayed for a smooth transition into the new Fifth Age of the Maya. This was to occur in the year 2012. Times were still harsh for the Maya, however, in 1987. For all those indigenous people present, undertaking such ceremony was risky. Successive dictatorial governments had consistently denied the Maya people, descendants of the pyramid builders and inheritors of very old ceremonial traditions, the basic right to conduct their shamanic ceremonies. They kept them jobless and in poverty, stealing their land. As I was to learn on my quest to understand time and prophecy, following shamanic traditions and the calling of one's heart can be hazardous.

The Prophecy for 2012

With the prophecy of the Nine Hells completed, present-day Maya day-keepers, wisdom teachers and indigenous elders tell us that we are now living in a time of transition leading to the end of the present age. They have explained to me: 'The Time of Preparation is here. There are just a few years left – up to 2012.'

I could see that, alongside environmental changes, wars and atrocities, the whole of humanity is being given an unprecedented challenge. So the question is, *how do we change things*? How do we move from a state of war and violence to a state of peace, within ourselves and at an international level? How do we move away from 'I want' to 'What are our real needs?'

Again the voices of the indigenous people ring in my ears: 'Time is short. Act now.'

Maya elders continue to emphasize: 'We are in crucial transitional times. The fate of the world is precariously balanced. We give you dire warnings of what could happen if the people of the world acquiesce, if we are complacent. All must rise up and become guardians of our planet. As our shamans say, we must become Warriors of the Light.'

As I gathered together the predictions relating to these critical times, one in particular stood out from the others. It concerns a time period of 5,125 years in a most important Maya calendar count of time, the Long Count, that is due to end on or around 21 December 2012. Something unprecedented is set to happen to human consciousness around that day. It has been named the end of the Maya Fourth Creation.

But even their leaders say: 'This may or may not be the exact date when a great change will happen, because our count of the ages was severely disrupted during the period when the Conquistadors tried to erase our civilization. Our teachings and mythology, that you see in a few surviving books and carved upon temple walls, show all the three previous time periods or ages recorded by us, the Maya, to have ended in cataclysm.'

This is the most crucial and relevant prediction coming to us on the Threads of Time Past. It is to be seen in a special ancient sacred book of the Maya, known to academics as the *Dresden Codex*. This folded, illustrated book predicts that massive global floods will accompany the end of this Fourth Creation. So, remembering that the Fourth Creation is set to end around 2012, from now on we must be prepared for anything to happen!

It is for this very reason that today's indigenous leaders are releasing their prophecies to the world. All those who hear them have a responsibility to sound the alarm bells. This time around, the human race is in a better position to avoid catastrophe simply because, individually, we can choose to prepare ourselves, using our developing superconsciousness to access the WorldWideWeb of Light.

What can we expect to happen? It is prophesied that on 21 December 2012, at the winter solstice in northern countries, and over a period of days and years around that date, there could be the potential for either destruction or renewal. Simultaneously the whole world will be moving gradually from the fourth to the fifth great age of the Maya.

The elders emphasize: 'The transition period in any Maya time count is always critical and hazardous. In particular, the last 13 years up to 2012 will set the tone as the 'seating' years for the post-2012 period, or the Fifth Age. Coming up to that date, the Threads of Time will slowly but surely be rewoven together into a new pattern of energy for the next age.'

Upon reflection, I considered that the elders were giving us a partially cloaked clue about 2012. It is not in their nature to reveal all their wisdom at once – especially to a *gringo*! (their name for a white person). Clearly the changes on Earth could be understood as 'energetic' changes, which would also affect the physical world. Energetic movement can be either quite subtle or massive, depending upon one's own state of spiritual development. It slowly began to dawn upon me that 2012 might not mean an apocalyptical resolution to our lives, but a watershed and a critical marker point upon the Threads of Time, as if a preset cosmic alarm clock had just rung to wake us up from complacency and cultural hypnosis.

My intuition then told me that the Web of Life and the WorldWideWeb of Light would be incorporated as a pattern or essential 'grid' upon which the potential renewal of the human race could be laid. Just *how*, I was not sure. I steeped myself in mythology, astrology and astronomy like the sages of old. I participated in Guatemalan fire ceremonies in the time-honoured way. I sought the wisdom of the elders, the unfathomable depths of the shamans and the smiles of the village children. Then there were to be many days wandering around humid, mosquito-ridden, ancient cities, before the sacred voices of the ancestors whispered to me and gave me more clues to follow. The Threads of Time do not give up their secrets easily!

But the elders were always very clear. 'A new Maya count of time will occur from around 22 December 2012. Transitions at the turning of the ages are so momentous that we Maya prefer to call them "Creations". In your calendar's terms we can say that the whole world will be entering the period of the Fifth Creation around the year 2012 – to us it will be Year Zero.'

The first time I met Wandering Wolf was in St James's Church, Piccadilly, in London, where he came to give a talk to a packed audience. He made a mysterious reference to 'the Year Zero' and to prophecies that say 'Volcanoes will wake up in an uproar, as if they are in concert with one another'.

He said, 'The erupting volcanoes and the contamination from them, darkening our skies, will slowly rupture the planet's "veil".' This is the Earth's outer atmosphere, that present-day Maya wisdom teachers call the Crystal Veil or Shield. Almost as a postscript, he warned that 'Nuclear explosions have already damaged the veil'.

Over the years I got to know Wandering Wolf better. This quiet, unassuming man's name is Don Alejandro Cirilo Perez Oxlaj, and he is the most senior elder of the Maya National Council of Elders, *Xincas* and *Garifunas* of Guatemala. He has represented the Maya people at the United Nations, he had an audience with the Pope and he now travels the world 'trying to make it conscious'. He was the receiver of a powerful End Times prophecy that he shared with me. Despite his not admitting that he is a shaman, I have seen him use shamanic powers, especially when 'reading' the omens in the smoke of the sacred ceremonial fires and giving very accurate divinations.

Again and again I asked myself, can it really be that the Earth is being prepared for the fulfilment of ancient prophecies? Heeding Wandering Wolf's messages, I was certain that his words had more than an echo of ancient truth about them. Events such as the massive Asian tsunami on 26 December 2004 confirmed this to me.

Repeated journeys to the lands of the Maya for study, ceremonies and initiations with the shamans and elders left me convinced that a number of temple buildings in the Mayalands were deliberately left as 'time markers' for the End Times. Today's multidisciplinary archaeologists have discovered that Maya architects were skilled at planning the layout of sacred cities to reflect specific star groups or cosmological concepts; they call this archaeoastronomy. Buildings were laid out with geometrical precision displaying a highly developed knowledge of the movements of the sun and moon and the behaviour of light and sound effects – the twin pyramids at Mixco Viejo are an example. Some places were designed so that, at particular times of the year, 'Great Father Sun' or 'Sister Moon' caused light and shadow effects through apertures, onto steps or onto carved pictorial stones at these ancient places.

I went to Dzibalchaltún, Mexico, for the 2006 spring equinox. I waited at dawn to observe how the sun rises dramatically through a temple door, illuminating a long ceremonial path leading up to the temple. That year, it seemed to the waiting crowd, and also to me, that it was inexplicably off the 'normal' mark by around 5 degrees. I was told that, in another famous sun-and-shadow phenomenon at that time, the usual 'serpent' light effects were dimmed.

This evidence from these solar markers, seen with my own eyes, left me wondering if something dramatic really had happened to time, when atomic clocks had to be reset after the Asian tsunami (owing to a slight change in Earth's rotation at the time). Is the Earth herself rotating slightly differently? Whatever the answer is, it certainly seemed to be an omen.

I set out to learn more from the elders of the Americas about what we could expect in the years to come. My first initiation task was with the element of fire – to find an active volcano!

Volcán de Pacaya

Leaving La Venta, I stayed a few days in Antigua, the old capital near Guatemala City, and then decided to journey to the part of Guatemala that its people, who are natural poets, call 'the heart of the world'.

Indigenous Guatemalans have a deep appreciation of natural phenomena. They live daily with life-threatening situations generated by the Earth, such as hurricanes, earthquakes and volcanic eruptions. Much of the Maya world lies in a volcanic region, with more than a dozen volcanoes stretching in an east-west line from the Pacific across their land.

Guatemala is located on the edge of the Cocos Plate, one of the Earth's tectonic plates, and the country's volcanoes are part of the 'ring of fire' surrounding the Pacific Ocean, encompassing 75 per cent of the world's active and dormant volcanoes. One of the most active volcanoes is Volcán de Pacaya, 18 miles (30km) southwest of Guatemala City, part of a range including the caldera of Lake Amatitlán. It has consistently erupted with spectacular nightly displays since 1965.

I have long had a fascination with volcanoes. Whilst in Guatemala I wanted to visit Volcán de Pacaya – something important seemed to be calling me there. So I set off to make contact with my friend Rafael, who lives in the village of Amatitlán, next to the lake and near the road to the volcano. Getting out of the crowded bus I walked to his house, which nestled amongst flowering trees, with the inevitable scraggy turkey ceaselessly scratching in the dusty yard. The old roof of his veranda was now hanging a little crazily. Its sunburnt paint, a poor imitation of the famous 'Maya blue' with which the chambers of pyramids and royal tombs were decorated, was flaking off in large irregular pieces. It created a dappled effect as a magical kind of late afternoon light played upon the orange rusted tin of the roof.

I called out, asking, '¿Rafael? ¿Rafael? ¿Dónde está Rafael?' (Where is Rafael?) and a little girl with a beaming smile came running to the door. She pointed towards the trees where, deep in their shadow, I could see a figure. It was Rafael, resting from woodcutting. I walked over to greet him. Rafael's face split into a wide grin as he saw me, for it had been many years since we had last met. We shook hands enthusiastically. My Spanish had improved, so I asked him, 'Are you married now? Is that your daughter?'

'Yes,' he replied. 'She called Ixchel, after the Maya goddess of healing and childbirth.'

Later, over a cool drink, I told him of my desire to visit the volcanic cone of Pacaya. 'It is a dangerous place now,' he said, and I assumed he was referring to the continuous eruptions. But no, there was a danger of being attacked and robbed, even raped and murdered. I asked what we could do to ensure our safety if we went there. He explained that most people just wanted to see the view and take photos, rather than to honour Pacaya, as his ancestors had done. This rather callous, touristic approach was the cause of the danger.

With his words ringing in my ears we went together the next day down a small track to the village of San Vincente Pacaya, from which trails lead up the volcano's lower green slopes. On the way we passed coffee and tobacco plantations, until vigorous native trees eventually took over in wild abandon, as they do in such climates. I gathered a small bunch of white forest flowers as I pushed my way through the thick vegetation, for I knew it would be important to do a ceremony using the flowers to placate the volcano and any other dangers, before making the final climb.

Rafael, a wise man who had followed the old shamanic ways all his life, suddenly stopped and pointed to a clearing ahead. This was to be the place for a traditional fire ceremony to honour the spirit of Pacaya. In preparation he scratched a cross on the ground and then a circle. This was the pointer to the four directions and, just like Wandering Wolf, he was making a medicine wheel for 'good medicine' to accompany us on our experience with Pacaya. He untied a cloth bundle he was carrying, retrieved handfuls of copal incense, shiny golden nuggets of fragrant tree resin, then proceeded to pile them in the centre of the circle on some kindling wood.

This was the signal for me to lay down the flower blossoms, with their beautiful faces turned in toward what would become the centre of the fire. Usually coloured offering candles are laid around the fire, red in the east, blue in the west, white in the north and yellow in the south, but Rafael had not been able to go to such expense. Instead he handed me some pieces of flat black incense and, rather strangely I thought, a handful of sticky, coloured sweets for me to use as my fire offerings.

He started his prayers, mumbling in what, to me, was an unintelligible Maya tongue, lighting the fire as he did so and calling the names of ancient gods. He watched intently to see how it would burn, paying attention to how the smoke 'spoke' to him. Understanding the sacred fire is one of the main ways of prophecy that has survived from times past. Not only shamans but also ordinary people would observe the fire, in much the same way as your granny may have read tea leaves.

I knew from other fire ceremonies that the outcome of his deliberations would determine the course of the rest of the day for us on the summit of Pacaya, and our eventual safety. He began the ritual count of days and I gave my offerings to the fire and the volcano. I asked for the wellbeing of all peoples upon Mother Earth, that they would live in peace and respect the world of nature.

The fragrant smell of burning sweets and copal started to weave their spell and, as had happened before, I slipped into the dreamtime of the Maya, seeing all manner of images passing before my closed eyes. In my trancelike state I could just about hear Rafael, now whispering in Spanish, asking for Pacaya to keep talking gently to people. By this he meant that, if the volcano erupted only a little, the people felt safe and knew that a big explosion was not about to happen.

He whispered that we loved the rocky slopes of her skin and her fiery belly and that our fire ceremony was just for her. He implored her to keep us safe as we climbed to her summit – keep us safe from crazy people who could harm us. I opened my eyes a little, and the red of the fire, the black of the earth and the white of the rapidly wilting flowers etched an indelible archetypal image in my mind, giving me a sense of connection to goddess worship the world over, and especially to my own Celtic roots. Rafael took a stick and stirred the fire into fresh life for a moment before it finally settled into a smoking pyre. How appropriate, I felt, to honour this volcanic fire goddess of the Earth with our own little fire.

Once again, as I had experienced many times before, the teachings of the Maya came to me in a gentle way. There was no formal study, just a growing understanding of the part we all have to play in the dance of life and the balancing of elemental forces. Indigenous people have always known about this, but so many of us have forgotten. Why would we want to harm the Earth, our mother?

It must be a forgetting, a kind of blindness that has descended like a vulture upon us, from our dominant world culture of materialism and greed. Indeed, in the sacred book of the Kiché Maya, *Popul Vuh*, they say that the gods deliberately inflicted a blindness and a limit to what, and how far, humans could see. They did this at the beginning of our present time-cycle, the Fourth Creation. Their teachers say that our challenge, as we move into the Fifth Creation, is to see clearly again, to restore our vision of paradise on Earth.

The ceremony over, and the fire safely extinguished, we continued on our way, climbing over rocks and lava-strewn paths, finally reaching the summit of Pacaya as dusk fell. We were prepared with warm blankets to stay all night to see the spectacular fire show just metres away. With a large boulder sheltering us from the worst of the deadly sulphur in the air, we looked up towards the ash cone of the volcano, knowing that we could go no further unless we wanted to risk sliding into the fiery interior itself.

Occasionally the heart of the Pacaya volcano goddess pulsed out red-hot ash, high into the air, as a sparkling firework display, whilst her belly rumbled beneath us. Just a little way to our right was a fissure with a constant outpouring of lava running downwards in black rivulets as its red heat cooled in the sulphurous night atmosphere. Beneath the black crust forming on the surface of these rivulets, cracks appeared, and we could see super-hot, orange-red veins of molten lava – the veins of the Earth Mother herself.

For a moment I felt the need to look away from this splendour. Upon gazing upwards I was drawn towards the three main stars (comprising the left one in the 'belt' and the two 'feet'), in the constellation Orion, which the Maya name the Turtle. The Maya know these stars as the Hearthstones of Creation. They were shining brightly, pulsing out a variety of colours through the clear, unpolluted sky beyond the low clouds of sulphur fumes around the summit.

I had never before felt so *present*, so in the Now, as I was on Pacaya. The combination of the potential immediacy of death from the belching fire and fumes and the sheer primal magic of the volcano held me spellbound, with no thought for the past or future. I was totally in the Now, the only true state of being.

A Teaching of Being in the Now

We stayed overnight on the slope of Pacaya, wrapped in our blankets, meditating, trying to stay awake. My thoughts in the half-darkness, lit by glowing volcanic light, ranged over the words of people who had taught me, including famous people I had never met. I used their words to focus my mind when I started to drift into sleep...

Nelson Mandela had once said, 'It is not the kings and generals who make history. It is the masses of the people.' And here's a really appropriate ancient Chinese proverb: 'The miracle is neither to fly in the air nor to walk on the water, but to walk on the Earth.'

Such words are not just rhetoric. They affect the way that this current Maya Creation is completed around the critical end date of 21 December, 2012. Such inspirational and creative words take us into magical realms while we are still in the midst of the mundane. By giving us positives, with rhyme and beauty, they overcome negative mind-effects of the daily news and daily-life stress. They can counter even dire prophetic texts, which may otherwise shock us into a helpless state of inertia. They light us up, give us courage to be Warriors of Light, bonding us more strongly with the vibrant life-stream of the WorldWideWeb of Light. I felt close to the sentiment of a former American astronaut, Edgar Mitchell, who said: 'The consciousness of man has an extended nature which enables him to surpass the ordinary bounds of space and time – suggesting that there is another dimension beyond the material world.'

Our walk back down Pacaya next morning was inspirational too. As I traversed the path below the lava slopes I could see every tree's energy field surrounding it in a halo-like, coloured brilliance. The birds' morning chorus took on the quality of a great natural symphony.

A small cloud in the azure sky blushed with pink, taking on the shape of a serpent.

All this gave me a feeling I had just ingested some hallucinogenic substance. But no, I was totally in the Now. Superconsciousness was heightened by the night-time experience of Pacaya. My feet seemed to dance across the rocky, downward trail. We quickly reached the scattered houses of St Vincente Pacaya down below.

On my way down I had thought about Leonard Peltier, whose indigenous name is 'Wind Chases the Sun'. He is an indigenous rights activist and political prisoner in USA, mentioned by Amnesty International. He was jailed for 24 years, allegedly for killing two FBI agents. This is what he has to say:

> American Indians share a history rich in diversity,
> integrity, culture and tradition. It is also rich in tragedy,
> deceit and genocide. As the world learns of these
> atrocities and cries out for justice for all people
> everywhere, no human being should ever have to fear
> for his or her life because of their political or religious
> beliefs. We are in this together, my friends, the rich, the
> poor, the red, white, black, brown and yellow. We share
> responsibility for Mother Earth and those who live and
> breathe upon her. Never forget that.

From the official newsletter of the Leonard Peltier Defense Committee, *Spirit of Crazy Horse*, July/August 2002

CHAPTER 3

The Serpent Turns

T his chapter looks at destruction and the momentous endings of ages of time. We start at Tayasal, where the last remnant of a Maya city outlasted the fateful coming of the Spanish Conquistadors for nearly 200 years. Then we visit North America to hear the perspective of native people there, to return later to today's Tayasal, now called Flores, and a meeting I had with an old gentleman. But first we shall travel back to a time just before the final destruction of the culture of the ancient Maya, who were on a par, in the scale of their achievements, with the ancient Greeks and Egyptians.

Tayasal and the End of the Ancient Maya

It is the year 1526 in our calendar. The zenith of the Maya period and the ruling dynasties of kings and queens is long gone; archaeologists refer to it as the Classic Period, which lasted from the 300s to the 800s CE. By the beginning of the 16th century the vast, archaic, sacred Maya cities and pyramids were already hidden beneath a tangled carpet of jungle vegetation. A few scattered groups of people remained, living the old ways of the wise ones. Among them were the proud and resourceful Itzá Maya, who had retreated from the cruel onslaught of the Spanish Conquistadors.

These remaining Maya were settled around the shores of the beautiful Lake Petén Itzá, with a stronghold in the town of Tayasal (now Flores, in Guatemala) on an island joined to the shore by a kilometre-long causeway. They were among the last people still carrying the knowledge of the old temple architects, the astronomers, artists and craftsmen who, nearly a thousand years before, had begun their colossal construction programme of magnificent cities, built for gods and kings, from the tip of peninsular Yucatán in Mexico to the south of El Salvador, and to the border areas of Honduras and Nicaragua.

Tayasal, one of the last independent Maya cities, was holding off the rabble of European soldiers and pious monks who, like a cancerous growth, had been spreading from the coast of the Gulf of Mexico into the seemingly inhospitable, mosquito-infested interior of the Petén. By the 1500s this was an area of rainforest trees and lakes, hiding the mounds of fallen stones which recorded the history of the earlier Maya.

In 1526 the Itzá Maya of Tayasal were calmly going about their lives. Using hollowed-out tree canoes they criss-crossed the still, glassy surface of Lake Petén Itzá to collect crops of forest fruits and nuts. Some days were particularly propitious to plant maize, a staple food that they grew in little clearings around the lake and waterways, later to be called *milpas*. This crop needs human intervention to separate the seeds from the cob in order to grow. Prayers were said to the maize god as three seeds were planted in each hole – one seed for the god, one seed for the birds and creatures, one seed to grow into a flourishing plant for people to grind into flour. At harvest time their canoes were piled high with ears of maize, which they regarded as the gods' golden sunshine. Itzá Maya villagers also began to cultivate *ahaucatl*, 'the food of the gods', known to us as avocado and in Spanish as *aguacate*.

Akin to other indigenous peoples at this period of history, they took only what they needed for their immediate sustenance, maintaining strong interdependence with numerous gods and goddesses whom they believed to provide the right spiritual conditions for successful cultivation. They had an awareness of the 'spirit' of the sun as Father, our planet as Mother and the moon as Sister. Their calendar priests consulted unique agricultural calendars, to find auspicious times to plant and to harvest – in itself a type of prediction that would optimize the results of the crop. These principles have long since been forgotten, except perhaps by biodynamic growers in today's Western world. They even had a bee and bat calendar to connect them to other strands on the Web of Life.

At this time in Tayasal, the grand, exotic and elaborate ceremonies from the days of the splendid Maya kings and queens were past, and a type of council ruled the region. It was a typical sleepy afternoon, with the heat causing a haze of vapour to rise above the mirror-glazed surface of the lake. Here and there children perched on rocks near the bank, throwing crude fishing hooks and line into the lake, causing a swirl of water and a splash as they landed an occasional slippery catch.

The townspeople were aware from predictions made by priests, who kept the holy predictive calendars and thus the count of days, that their lives would soon change. In order to protect their families many dozens of spearmen were positioned, always ready and alert, on the stone causeway separating the island from the mainland. Watchers in elevated positions suddenly saw a dust cloud approach the nearest part of the mainland – a sight they did not wish to see, for it signalled a small band of Conquistadors.

Urging the women and children to safety in the temple on the highest point of the island, they quickly organized more men with spears. Wearing dignified battle regalia, thick leather protection, golden discs with the face of the sun god over their chests and shields with a frightening image of the god of war, the Itzá Maya awaited the onslaught. But strangely, the approaching troops, a sickly looking rabble of soldiers and mercenaries, of whom they had heard such wild tales of terror from passing traders, marched slowly and forlornly across their narrow causeway.

Also emerging from the cloud of dust were strange creatures. The watching Maya were astonished by the horses that some of the soldiers were riding, for they had never seen such animals before. At first they even believed man and horse were one creature, a kind of frightening chimera. Although overawed, the Maya soldiers lined up, weapons at the ready, to fight off the invaders on their odd steeds. But the Spanish soldiers, exhausted from travel and sickness, merely needed a place to rest.

The leader of the group was no less than Hérnando Cortés who, four years before, had written to King Carlos I of Spain describing the bloodthirsty cruelty of the Aztecs of central Mexico. Travelling extensively across the inhospitable Maya lands, he was now trying to reach the coast of present-day Belize with his sickly crew and a horse that had become ill and unable to move on. The soldiers did not attack but merely requested provisions.

The ailing animal was tethered in the shade and cared for. It was still too ill to continue on the arduous march when the soldiers left a few days later, to cross wild marshland and mountainous rainforest, so it was left behind. The Tayasal inhabitants, unused to seeing horses, and having got over their fears, marvelled at the beautiful creature and carefully nursed it back to health. Eventually the horse died, but over the subsequent years, out of respect for the majestic animal, a cult of the horse developed and offerings were made to a new god – the horse god!

In the ensuing period Tayasal resisted all further efforts to take it. The town was eventually destroyed by a small army of 235 men led by Martín de Ursua, almost two centuries later in 1697, thus marking the end of the last independent Maya region. As had happened in other conquered towns, de Ursua ordered the small temples of Tayasal to be torn down and the stones rebuilt into churches. Then people were forced to accept the new Christian religion, which amazed them with its apparent cruelty.

Unlike some other peoples of Central America such as the Aztecs (Aztekas), whose originally pure religion had degenerated by this period of history, the Maya did not involve themselves in human sacrifice. So they, like the coastal Maya who had first encountered the Spanish were also astounded when the military conquerors, together with pious friars in black robes, urged them to worship a bleeding, sacrificed god, Jesus, hanging on what they regarded as a most sacred symbol – the World Tree.

I went to Tayasal, now Flores, to ponder upon the way that the Conquistadors had been able to conquer proud warriors with such a small number of soldiers, over vast areas of hostile unwelcoming land.

The town is nowadays a cool haven in the seemingly endless hectares of rainforest, a Biosphere Reserve stretching across an area larger than England. Situated on what is almost an island on the lake of Petén Itzá, it is still reached by the same causeway described above, or by boat. It is an excellent place for contemplation and relaxation.

I wondered why Maya people with their unique culture and their strong feeling for the land appeared to have surrendered to foreign ways in just a few centuries, from the time of the Conquistadors onwards – no length of time at all in the great time-span of civilizations on Earth. Why had the images of a bleeding Christian god, nailed to a cross, managed to oust the long-held sentiments of the Maya, their earthy religious practices and what we would now call shamanism? But I also knew that, like many other conquered civilizations, the Maya had taken on only a thin veneer of the new Christian religion. In secret caves and on quiet lakesides hidden from view, the old customs were still ardently practised.

These customs, steeped in colourful history and wrapped up within the Threads of Time, enabled adepts to travel shamanically into the future as well as into the past, as had their forebears, the shaman-priest-kings and queens of yesteryear. Stemming from the archetypal mythic start of their Long Count calendar, spanning over 5,000 years, to its end in 2012 CE, awareness remained of the possibilities and choices to be made upon the Threads of Time.

The shamans continually took guidance from what had happened in past cycles, as well as from astrological and astronomical happenings in the solar system. Family and tribal ancestors were contacted through shamanic ceremony, in order to receive guidance from them for future actions. Many images still exist, carved in stone or wood, of rulers who undertook such ceremonies and met magically transformed guiding ancestors in order to contact the 'Vision Serpent' who 'spoke' to them.

Yet this was more than a fascination with time and ancestor worship. Using complex astronomical calendar calculations, they knew that sun, Earth, planets and cosmos were inextricably entwined in cycles of growth and destruction. Their calendars were intrinsic to the art of prophecy. There is some archaeological and much modern anecdotal evidence of at least 20 different calendars, recording short periods of earthly time and long cycles of cosmic time. The shamans and shaman-priest-monarchs guided by the calendar day-keepers knew how to travel the Threads of Time, both past and future.

Just after their civilization peaked, many Maya 'left' around 890 CE (I shall explain soon). Those that remained were carriers of ageless wisdom from beyond this world. They, like those of previous eras, were guided by mystical keepers of Time Future, known as Lords of Time. They were given a mission to tell those who would be alive in the End Times how to prepare for and evolve into the Fifth Creation.

In their uncluttered lives, close to the land and without our level of materialism, the people of this great civilization understood and 'read' signs that environmental damage was often a precursor to unrest, bringing stress to the population and resulting in battles for land and water. They also respected all aspects of tradition and learned from their living elders as well as from their starry ancestors – the star people, inter-galactic travellers, whom they believed founded and still guided their culture. We, who are alive today, are experiencing the dilemma of global disasters that they foresaw so long ago. Those Lords of Time are messengers in our present time, warning us about damaging the precious fragility of Mother Earth.

Early one morning I left the oasis of green-hued shade in my small lodging house, overhung with hanging ferns. I walked along the stone causeway, past the dusty hustle and bustle of the neighbouring town of Santa Elena on the mainland. Sitting contentedly at the lakeside, I watched while brightly-dressed women waded out to favourite stones at knee depth with their laundry and proceeded to wash it.

In a nearby *palapa* (thatched building) the men and boys of one family were carving beautiful animal totems in wood. Skilfully made turtles, red-plumed macaws and fearsome jaguars were lined up in rows, offered for a few pesos, awaiting new homes far from the rainforest. Such trinkets are a sure sign that tourists regularly visit the region in their metallic diesel monsters.

In contrast, peering through the wisps of mist caressing the surface of the lake, I saw a hewn-out tree canoe being punted along in the shallow water with a wooden pole, a reflection on the glassy surface from times long past. However, it was loaded up not with maize but with six young schoolchildren in immaculate blue uniforms, and a motherly figure who poled the craft speedily towards the shore. Thereafter, every weekday, I watched the children boating in these 'water taxis' from their homes in lakeside villages to their school lessons in Flores.

Mission Completed!

I would like to explain more about a happening that has baffled many people. It concerns how, in the 9th and 10th centuries, most of the Maya citizens, in a widespread area, just 'left' and apparently merged into the rainforest to live very simple lives. Or, alternatively, they died off in large numbers. This has long been an enigma because dozens of Maya cities, seemingly at the peak of their culture, declined into oblivion within a period of just over 100 years from 790 CE to the last Long Count date recorded at Toniná, Chiapas, in 909.

Historians and archaeologists believe that increasing population and reduced harvests brought about this demise. There are many other theories as to why this civilization suddenly declined, ranging from war, family in-breeding, an unjust, inward-turning ruling élite who paid no respect to the farmers who supported their vast cities, or disruptive sunspot cycles affecting climate changes, starvation and drought.

I offer another view. The rulers, deeply in touch with the Spirit of the Land, knew from the ancestral and cosmic guidance they received whilst in shamanic trance, listening to the Vision Serpent, that it was simply time to withdraw from the Earth. All the indications are that the rulers in the region communicated their intention to one another. The task of the great ruling lineages of the Maya kings and queens of the Classic Period was over. Whole ruling families living in the sacred cities over a wide area inexplicably disappeared. All records on stones ceased. The common people were left to their own devices and, I believe, wandered off to subsist in the forests. I have heard people who are able to travel the Threads of Time say that the mission of the great rulers was successfully accomplished.

And what of this mission?

In their cities the Maya left markers and messages concerning Time Past and Time Future. Their knowledge of different calendars was vast, many calendars being synchronized with cosmic cycles. The élite shaman-priest-kings who had formulated accurate prophetic calendars knew the beginning date of the Fourth Creation, and their mission was to leave vital information for us to decipher at its end in 2012. Their messages were carved upon stones, to survive the ravages of time and the searing sun. Within a few hidden books of folded bark paper, they wrote important and intricately convoluted, but accurate, astrological/astronomical tables.

Present-day epigraphers and archaeologists continue to find more fascinating evidence in the form of inscriptions, names, dates and calendars and, in the case of San Bartolo, Guatemala, an amazing painted mural, surpassing that of Bonampak. The precision and timing of their calendars was part of the ancient Maya mission. The astounding accuracy of one of them was confirmed by NASA, who stated that the Maya Long Count is correct to a mere 0.00000001 seconds on the atomic calendar clock and that, when these seconds are added together, it is just one day out of synchronization in over 180,000 years!

Following the Classic Period, in the northern part of the Yucatán, centred around Chíchén Itzá, aspects of Maya culture were taken up again by the Itzá Maya, who were under a distinctly Toltec influence. The royal Classic Maya culture was replaced by ruling military-religious councils, comprised of war-driven leaders belonging to the Orders of Eagles, Coyotes and Jaguars. As these leaders engaged in vast building projects, the lineages of royal families became just a memory of the old citizens, lost in the jungle as inexorably as their stone lineage monoliths were split apart by strangler fig vines. Then, by 1250, even Chíchén Itzá itself was abandoned, becoming jungle-covered ruins by the time the Spanish Conquistadors arrived.

All these tales of the past may well interest us, but the Western mind must take a quantum leap before it can become steeped in the rich history, mythology and cosmovision carried by the indigenous peoples – otherwise Western understanding cannot enter into the hidden prophetic messages. Best decoded by Spirit in meditation or shamanic trance, we need to understand these prophetic messages as we slide relentlessly upon the Serpent of Time toward the end-year of this Fourth Maya Creation, in 2012.

The Spirit of the Land

My teacher Hunbatz Men told me 'We need to understand the past in order to be able to walk into the future'. I set upon a quest to inform myself about the thoughts and feelings of the givers of prophecy and some of the issues facing modern Maya.

It was unsettling to discover that from northernmost Canada to Chile in the extreme south, indigenous peoples to this very day are fighting to regain or retain their rights to ancestral land. They call their continent *Abya Yala*, which means 'Continent of Life' in the language of the Kuna people of Panama and Colombia, or *Itzachilatlan*. In the Declaration of La Paz, made at the Continental Encounter of Indigenous Pueblos and Nations of *Abya Yala* on 12 October 2006 in Peru, they stated:

> Our struggle cannot be held back. We no longer resist only to resist: our time has come. Our path calls for coordination, articulation and to be in communication on a permanent basis, taking into account all of our problems, needs and proposals.
>
> We condemn the acts of terrorism and intervention which the government of the United States is conducting in many countries of the world and in the Americas in order to protect their interests. At the same time we stand in solidarity with the struggles of all peoples and governments that defend their right of self-determination, such as Cuba and Venezuela.

History always has something to teach us, and the Itzá Maya of Tayasal were exemplary. They lived in harmony with their surroundings, in a sustainable culture and ecosystem, right up to the time when an invading force imposed foreign controls upon them. Through their close interdependence with the Earth, water, winds and the power of the sun, they led lives of day-to-day tranquillity and simplicity.

As agriculturalists, perhaps the first permaculturists or biodynamic farmers, the Maya respected the Earth as a mother, as someone who supplied all their needs. They understood and treasured the inner Spirit of the Land that their ancestors had personified into numerous gods and goddesses – with special reverence being given to their main god *Ku-kuul-kaan*, in areas of present-day Mexico and Guatemala, and to Quetzalcoatl in central and northern Mexico.

Maya people have told me how they still pray to *Chaak*, god of rain, *Hurrukaan*, god of storms (from whom we take the word 'hurricane') and his consort *Ixchel*, the goddess of rainbows. Sometimes elders have reminded me that the land receives its spirit in many ways. For example, it receives it from the quality of light that bathes it from unpolluted skies – after all, few people fail to be transfixed by the colours of a rainbow or a stunning sunset. Indeed, nature herself arranges that lightning bolts and electrical storms produce nitrogen, an important fertilizer for plants in soils which might otherwise be deficient!

Earlier, at Mixco Viejo, we saw how the builders of the past knew how to align their pyramids and temples to capture the energies of sun or moon at specific times of the year, such as at solstices, equinoxes or the full moon, in order to give a boost of energy to the Spirit of the Land. At Chíchén Itzá in the Yucatán, they designed and built a stepped flat-topped pyramid with such a precise orientation that Earth Mother would be 'impregnated' by a uniquely merged symbolic serpent of solar energy flowing down the side of the pyramid into her at strategic times of the year.

Warriors of the Rainbow

Here I wish to recount a story of hope and rebirth from North America.

We drew close to one another around the stove as the wind howled through the pine trees like a pack of angry wolves. This year the snows had begun early and we were pleased to have stocked our cabin with provisions. Darkness covered the land. It was at times like this that Grandmother could be persuaded to tell her stories. Eager faces of the children looked up to her as she began.

'I am going to teach you about harmony, for people in all four corners of the Earth. Today we need to learn again how to live the "Way of the Great Spirit". You have seen the white man's greed, and I have told you already that there will come a time when the fish will die in the streams, the birds will fall from the air, the waters will be blackened and the trees would no longer live. The Earth herself will be sick. She will be poisoned and man will have completely plundered her body for minerals.

'Deadly ash will fall from the sky. There will be times when the Earth will seem to be crying and torrential rains for months on end will wash the ash away, along with all the cities. Even politicians and huge armies will not be able to keep control of the hungry people. Then humankind as we know it will all but cease to exist.

'But there is a time coming when the keepers of the legends, the wise ones and the callers of ancient tribal customs, will be needed to restore us to health. These people are both the red man's and white man's key to survival. They are the Warriors of the Rainbow.'

Grandmother paused, adjusting the knitted quilt over her bony old knees and drawing a long inhalation on her tobacco pipe.

'The Warriors of the Rainbow will show the people that Great Spirit is full of love and understanding. They will teach them how to make the Earth beautiful again. These warriors will give people principles to follow, to make their path straight. The warriors will teach people the ancient ways of unity, love and understanding.

'They will show everyone how to pray to Great Spirit with love that flows like a beautiful mountain stream. They will show us how to paddle along the river to the ocean of life. They will show us how to radiate from our hearts warmth, understanding and respect for all of nature, to listen to the birds singing in the willows and to respect the salmon in the streams.'

Again she paused. Her eyes glazed a little as she remembered her carefree youth and sifted back through the Threads of Time. Her voice became stronger.

'Like great eagles these Warriors of the Rainbow are many and powerful. There will be terrifying mountains of ignorance to conquer and they shall find prejudice and hatred. They must be dedicated, unwavering in their strength and strong of heart. They will find willing hearts and minds amongst you little ones, who will follow them on this road of returning Mother Earth to the Beauty Way.'

The cluster of children around her spontaneously clapped their hands in excitement and then settled down again, fully attentive to Grandmother's words.

'The day will come: it is not far away. That day we shall see how we owe our very existence to the people of all tribes that have loved their culture and the ways of the ancestors. They have kept their stories alive. With the knowledge that they have preserved, we shall once again live in harmony with Mother Earth and humankind.'

Grandmother looked fiercely at all present around her. 'This knowledge is our key to survival. You children will again be able to run in the meadows and enjoy the treasures of nature. The world will be free from poisons and destruction and the rivers will again be clear.

'The Rainbow Chiefs will be chosen by the men and women warriors because of their quality of spirit. They will show everyone that miracles can be accomplished to heal this world of its ills and restore it to health and beauty.'

Grandmother closed her eyes, leaned back in her chair and rocked gently back and forth.

This story is from a time just a few decades ago, when there still was hope. As we commence the 21st century, elders are now telling us that we are at the 'eleventh hour', with the clock getting ready to strike midnight. By listening to wise words, and by weaving backwards and forwards upon the Threads of Time, I want to remind you of today's really critical world situation.

It begins with you and I.

Globally, we are all locked into repetitive patterns within cyclical time, and we are also locked into personal patterns within ourselves. It is in our nature to be complacent or fearful of change but, at this point of human history, this attitude is potentially disastrous. We can change ourselves beneficially, but it is often a question of how we deal with our lives. Let me explain.

I learned from the shamans that crises and the pressures of life can put us in danger of collapsing into helpless inertia. They steal our energy and clarity, which otherwise would be dedicated to positive action in the world. So a powerful way to contest this 'disaster inertia' is to strengthen our inner light and positivity at every turn in our lives – by every means, whenever possible. We can choose to focus on things that are good, bringing joy and happiness.

Whenever we focus on what is harmful or risky, on the misery, the hurt and the pain, we add to it and reinforce it. We do no good for our inner self or for what lies beyond and outside our own little selves.

These universal truths once lay at the core of all the world's religious teachings, before the original intentions within religions became distorted and corrupted. Once they held an intrinsically wholesome goodness, for the benefit of humanity and all other life-forms.

Today it is vital to understand our codependence and interconnectedness with our larger 'Earth Family', including the creatures of the natural world. We can create genuine sustainable opportunities if we choose life-enhancing personal and planetary alternatives. If enough people do this there is real hope for humanity. We must follow our hearts, not our heads.

Many people, whether or not they are religious, believe that we are not alone. Great Spirit gifts us with 'beings of light' who reveal glimpses of Time Future to us, and prompt us to rise to our possibilities and full stature. These are the 'voices' we hear when waking, or the images we see with our mind's eye during quiet times, or 'knowings' and intuitions that come to us when we are receptive. Guidance can come in diverse ways.

For example, since my divination with the shaman at Uxmal I was fascinated with his statements about skulls made out of crystal. I have talked to a number of 'sensitives' who have worked with some of these 'singing' crystal skulls – objects of quartz, carved in the likeness of human skulls. They tell me that quartz is an ideal material to relay messages 'spoken' from the 'beings of light' who guide humanity. How I wished I could really hold one of those powerful crystal skulls.

Many messages from other realms have now become dire warnings of impending disaster if the wake-up alarm clock calls are ignored. We are even being primed to expect the worst by disaster films like *The Day after Tomorrow* (20th Century Fox, 2004). Yet there is still hope. I have found that a careful reading of the ancient portents prophesies a coming golden age. Within these signals there lies an optimism for a better future, like that which the grandmother predicted in her story of the Rainbow Warriors. The choice is still ours!

The Web and the Matrix

Mikhail and I were once invited to be observers at a great Gathering of Indigenous Priests and Elders of the Americas, held in Mexico. Each participant brought a strong message with them about the spirit of their own lands. There were Hopi, Inca, Aztec, Maya, Cherokee, Navajo, Penobscot, Sioux, Inuit, Yaqui and others, from the frozen north to the southern tip of the Americas. Each shared their concerns and love for their lands. Imagine our surprise when Mikhail was invited to take the 'talking feather' in the circle and to speak on behalf of the Rainbow Warriors!

One participant from northern Canada later told us: 'I come from the land of snow, but the Spirit of the Land, in any natural place, in whatever country, is a merging of its inner spiritual essence with the human inhabitants' quality of life, with wild and domesticated animals and with natural ecosystems that exist there. The Spirit of the Land pours forth its essence and enables a kind of magic to seep into the animals and into humans who work close to the land, promoting vibrancy and health for all that grows and lives there. Water, in the form of springs, lakes and rivers, carries the spirit, imbuing places with a specialness that can be sensed by humans, with a little practice.'

A woman elder from North America reminded me of the well-known speech by Chief Seattle, originally delivered in Salish language to over 1,000 of his people in 1854. Sadly, only one year after he spoke his famous words, a treaty was signed giving away most of their lands, upon which the invading white people built the city of Seattle, shamefully banning the Indians from living there. His speech has become one of the most poignant statements of present day eco-spirituality.

The elder reiterated Chief Seattle's famous words to me. 'How can we buy or sell the Earth? We do not weave the Web of Life. We are but a strand in the Web of Life. What we do to the Web we do to ourselves. All things are connected. Every part of this Earth is sacred to my people...' The elder lifted her shoulders in a shrug and a deep sigh racked her body. 'People never learn,' she said, and walked away.

I thought about how the energies of different lands differ widely and why the gentle indigenous teachers I have talked to understand that land has an intrinsic spirit, an energy of its own. That spirit is maintained at high level by those who work and care for the land. But when it is trashed and polluted, it is weakened till its life force declines or dies. In these days of fast transport, cocooned within the security bubble of a car or airplane, or living in cities, we are losing the ability to access the Spirit of the Land. But if we care to be still and listen, anywhere we choose to place our feet upon the bare earth holds within it an unequalled calmness, a feeling that all is well with Spirit and the subtle energy-web of Light and Life.

But on this planet, duality presently reigns and is growing stronger. The dark opposite of the WorldWideWeb of Light and Life is constantly around us and has come to be called 'the Matrix'. The Matrix is not life-enhancing or natural – it is an energy field of human beliefs and fears, based upon materialistic value systems in modern society which cause a kind of cultural hypnosis. Within the Matrix, hierarchies of government and multinational business lock humans into an unnatural materialistic grid, rendering us into items capable of control or manipulation. We live in a world in which 7 per cent of the people own 60 per cent of the land, while using 80 per cent of the available energy. Because many people are not really *awake*, the human race faces a number of threats that derive from our acquiescence in the Matrix.

The sinister machinations of the Matrix were to stalk me during my quest into the Maya prophecies. In my darkest hours I imagined hard-set masks of faces seeking to take control of people, and careless, destructive disregard for all that the indigenous elders hold sacred. Like a black flesh-eating *Zotz*, the Maya Bat of Death, hovering over my nights, I was deeply disturbed by the implications of the Matrix.

But fortunately some people are breaking away from their situations within this cultural hypnosis. They are listening to the deep old mellow drum of the indigenous heartbeat that beats in symphony with the heart of Mother Earth. And finally, within the resonance of the beat, they recognize that our very survival as a species is threatened.

Subcomandante Insurgente Marcos of the Zapatista movement said, in Mazatlán, Sinaloa: 'Where before we only grew up and died, now we grow up learning. Now we grow up with pride of being an Indian. We are not embarrassed by our colour, or our culture or our language.' (*The Other Mexico*, 13 October 2006.)

Prophecy – Doom and Gloom!

Back in the marketplace of Santa Elena, near Flores, I nearly bumped into an old man who, despite his apparent age and long white hair, was tall and strong. Looking at him in his old colonial-style white suit, now somewhat ragged around the collar, I realized he was European. I apologized in case I had hurt him and bade him 'good day'.

'Señora,' he said, in a guttural but perfect kind of English, 'I have a message to give you.'

Pulling me to the side of a stall, piled high with a choice of colourful tropical fruits, he said, 'Be discriminating when seeking wisdom – it is like choosing one of these fruits. There are many juicy fruits, many traps for the unwary. The monks who taught me prefer to say that one's spiritual path is strewn with rocks.

'You know, we swing like pendulums between our life experiences – the "good" ones and the "bad" ones. We may try to walk a good path but the rocks always seem to get in the way. We live in a world of duality that, at its basest, is positive and negative. Those people who swing between these two expressions experience pain or tension in their lives that will not go away.'

He looked me straight in the eye. 'Señora, do you feel this uneasiness, a feeling of all not being well? You know, for many people, they oscillate between their happy emotions and sad ones. Their lives are held in the grip of duality from which it is difficult to see the third option, the third vector, that is immensely greater than either the positive or the negative. They are blinded by their pain, and this is compounded by their distance from seeing a way out of their situations.'

And quietly, 'But you, señora, are not one of these.'

He seemed to look past me, as if sensing some energy connection around me. The market vendors went about their business but, for a moment, time stood still. The man took off his battered straw hat and wiped his forehead with a grimy handkerchief.

He went on rather breathlessly, 'How can prophecy about End Times help those people whose minds take complete control of their lives and give no space, even during their relaxing times, to really know themselves, or to "be in the Now"? They say that the material world is all there is.'

I wondered how he knew about my interest in prophecy.

His voice softened. 'For these sad people, their minds push them on and their superconsciousness potential within them is imprisoned. But what I have to tell you is most important, señora. Prophecies about End Times are ways to face our fears. They are a way to avoid just hanging on to life and screaming in the silence for release.'

The man almost shouted at me: 'We need to look deeply at our fears!' Rather taken aback, I started to speak. He cut me short.

'Look,' he said. 'You have much to learn. I have been living here for 25 years and I still don't know how *they* think.' He waved his arm across to the fruit-and-vegetable seller standing patiently, smiling at the world around him.

'Can we discuss this more?' I asked.

'No, I have no time anymore.' He turned quickly and walked away. I thought of rushing to catch up with him but, within seconds, he was gone from my sight. And anyway, I considered, he's told me enough to think about already!

At that moment I realized that we are all compulsive thinkers, over-working the analytical left side of our brain. Our constant identification with mind processes creates a blockage, rather like water pipes becoming calcified. The positive response to this is to utilize subtle energetic pathways within our minds and bodies, nurturing them with a constant impetus of 'light messages'. These travel from cell to cell, faster than the known speed of light, keeping the body healthy. In meditation and still-ness, an enhanced flow of visible light energy and spiritual Light allows deeper levels of intuition to develop within a calmed mind. This in turn leads to superconsciousness, to see beyond the apparent doom and gloom, the negativity of any prophecy or situation.

I decided to keep my eyes open for the man when I next went to the market. Two days later I found him again. Alone at one of the little market cafés, he looked rather out of place sitting on a red, plastic Coca Cola seat. He seemed a little lost in time. I asked if I could join him and, after brief pleasantries, he shifted his position, removed his sunglasses and took a large swig of water. My eyes became fixed upon his frayed shirt collar and crumpled old dingy white tropical jacket and he startled me as he began to talk, straight to the point.

'I have something important to say. Ask yourself: can you as an individual take responsibility for your mind, and find truth, your own truth, to realize your full potential? Because, eventually, if you learn ways to overcome negative thoughts – even those that are caused in your mind as you read alarming prophecies for the first time – you break the constantly debilitating stream of negativity. Then you experience a moment of "no-time". A tiny gap opens into the vast potential that is superconsciousness. Once within superconsciousness, an understanding of the unified field of "no-time" opens.'

Without interrupting his flow, I moved my chair a little more into the shade and continued to listen.

'Have you asked yourself how much of the doom and gloom of prophecy has already occurred? Why is it that some prophecies don't appear to happen? People are waiting on the mountaintop for the end of the world. "It didn't happen, so let's go down again and carry on our lives as before!" So we might say, "Oh dear, I feel foolish! Why hasn't it happened?" Maybe instead we should have given a thought for all those who, through suffering, positive action, heroic deeds, spiritual practice or devotion, have been able to alter fate, reselect the strands of time from the future, and change the course of events for humanity. But people have forgotten how to *pray*, how to meditate, how to go within themselves. Perhaps we should try doing that, instead of helplessly allowing all the world's troubles to get us down?'

I knew that at the core of this question is our human ability to move beyond duality, to know that everyone can do this, and to enter into the spiritual heart of the world.

I replied, 'When we move beyond duality we know that we can never be separate from each other, from nature and the cosmos. We are connected to the Web of Life, as Native Americans say. It is then that we become spiritually awake, the mist clears from our eyes and we move into superconsciousness.'

'Yes,' he replied, mopping sweat from his brow. 'Superconsciousness has nothing to do with thoughts. It has everything to do with our connections as part of the living web of light-encoded filaments that permeate the universe, and of which prophecy is but one small but very important thread.'

CHAPTER 4

Madre Tierra –
Mother Earth

*Native science uses the sacredness of nature as its
guidepost to what should or should not be done by
humans. To be sacred is to be inviolable, to be
treated with utmost respect. To have a sacred
contract with nature is to care for it, protect it, give
back to it as much as is taken. When the White
Brother's inventive genius comes together with the
Red Brother's deep wisdom, we will develop an
appropriate technology that does not violate the
Earth, but restores it and permits all creatures to live
in health.*

**Elisabet Sahtouris PhD, a planet biologist,
speaking at the UN Policy Meeting on Indigenous Peoples,
Santiago, Chile, May 1992**

My quest for answers about the Maya prophecies has not been
just an intellectual or a spiritual pursuit. It has been an
emotional journey too. This is where many of the issues start becoming
more gut-wrenching, not just a matter of principles or a dualistic battle
of light with darkness, but a feelingful matter of caring, of expressing our
love of life rather than withholding it or hoping our personal and
planetary problems will go away, somehow resolve themselves or be
fixed by someone else.

Earth Mother Crying

It was Nine *Ix* in the Maya *Tzolk'in* calendar. Each day on my journey I consulted the calendar so that I could better understand the day's omens. I walked along the white sandy beach on a remote part of the Mexican coast, north of Campeche, aware that the energy of the day had begun to weave its magic on the Threads of Time: I had read from my notebook, '*Ix*, The Jaguar. Day of the Earth, woman and Mother Earth. A day of fertility. A day to respect animals'.

The wading birds along the waterline suddenly took flight as an unexpected gust of wind brushed along the shore, blowing tiny grains of sand against my feet and causing the miniature crabs to scuttle into holes for shelter. In the shallows a black shape glided by – a huge winged manta ray searching for food. In the distance the wind began to moan. A low deep note sounded out to sea, followed by a whoosh as it hit the shore. *Why, it's Mother Earth crying out to us.* I realized I was hearing her voice. In the sound of the wind I recognized that her heart was hurting. She was calling to the sea to soothe her pain.

The mournful sound of the wind sped across the creamy, foam-topped waves and stirred the dry grasses on the beach in a long lament. I sat down for shelter behind a white, sun-bleached tree trunk, pushing aside the washed-up human detritus of tin cans and plastic.

I mused that the technology that spawned the problems of pollution on Earth could equally give birth to the answers. Scientists have all the facts and figures but increasingly despair that governments do not heed them or, at least, that they do not act resolutely on their pronouncements. At their fingertips are the possibilities for appropriate technologies to replace energy-hungry factories, vehicles and pollution, but lack of awareness and greed still get in the way.

So it is left to the indigenous soul, shouting from the shores of the ocean of life, pushing their flimsy fishing boats out to sea, living a life of simplicity and resonance with Mother Earth, to remind us of our responsibilities. Only now are we waking up, falling in love again with life, listening to her heartbeat and seeing her beauty.

The wind on the beach began to abate as I slipped into a reverie, held in the arms of two of the remaining branches of the hurricane-battered old tree trunk. I felt warm and comfortable thinking of the very special relationships we have with our physical mothers. For the indigenous native people of the world, Earth is their Mother as well, so this creates a mother-and-offspring relationship with her. For this reason they find a kind of madness in today's world – a world that takes all it can from her, like a spoilt child.

Reasoning that the surface of the Earth is her 'body' and the rivers and seas her 'blood' is indeed a mysterious sacramental kind of notion to a city dweller. I slipped in and out of my reverie as I realized that our task is to return to honouring the divine feminine – the same principle that the Maya embody as the jaguar in the calendar reading for the day. Today, in this imbalanced world, the worst qualities of masculine dominance, the Matrix, seek power to abuse and destroy the fragile balance of all life.

I looked far out to sea, where the horizon curved sensuously around the planet. I thought about women's wisdom, with its seed-teaching of nurturing and growth that is fundamental to the worldview of indigenous peoples. They were birthed by the waters of the Earth, sustained by her and to her they return upon death. So were we, but we have forgotten it.

As the voice of Mother Earth the indigenous peoples of the Americas are well placed to point out the principal theme running through their prophecies – that greed and unbridled devastation will finally cause destruction and the end of the Mother as we know her. How vital it is now for all of us to become global guardians, joining with messengers from the lands of the Eagle (North America), the Condor (South America) and the Quetzal bird (Mesoamerica), to act on the words of those ancestral souls who cry out prophetically from the Times before Time. There is a dire need for people to bring about change, not from the top down, but from the bottom up. Or both!

The gentle lament of the Earth Mother is becoming a shout from many directions. We are at last hearing the prophecies that the Maya, the Hopi, the Kogi and others understood so long ago. This is mainly due to the voices of a few courageous indigenous peoples who have kept their prophecies carefully, passing them from one to another through the ages, hardly daring to commit them to paper. Better to hide them in stories and songs, in secret litanies to Mother Earth. Safer to hold them in their hearts where the White Brother could not go. Reverently to keep a vision of beauty in their eyes that the White Brother could not see. But now, sensing the urgency, they are daring to speak out.

I didn't realize how much time had passed. Far out to sea a storm had been gathering, with great swirls of cloud building up, twisting in upon themselves, sucking up the water and then throwing it into Hurrukaan's up-turned gourd pot. The wrathful god poured down tropical rain, flashes of lightning and reverberations of thunder. The elements could not be held back – they were building up, gathering speed and now ready to soak the shoreline. The waves grew angry with white-topped, churning foam.

I thought it prudent to get back along the beach to my car. The wind was rising, with the heads of the palm trees almost ready to snap under the force. As I started running, a thought hit me: according to most prophecies, the powers of destruction lie all around us and we need only to open our eyes to see them. But sometimes they come to get us, whether we see them or not.

Uxmal

The divine feminine and masculine are still to be encountered in the sacred places of the Maya to this day. My search for truth within the prophecies carried me once again to the ancient Maya temples of the city of Uxmal, in the Yucatán peninsula, Mexico.

In common with other places used over the centuries to honour and worship the Earth and the stars, these temples still transmit a continuing resonance of spiritual energies. Walking around Uxmal's grassy plazas in the heat of the afternoon when all the tourist buses have departed, it is easy to imagine priests and priestesses giving their teachings here, as they did for centuries. It is as if it would take only a small shift of consciousness to see them going about their daily rituals, for the air seems heavy with their presence. Rather than reveal themselves, they have, I suspect, magically transformed themselves into the numerous large colourful iguanas who, motionless, watch my every step. Some are a whole metre long from their noses to the tips of their tails!

It was early in 1995, an important year for the fulfilment of a prophecy which said that many people would come to the ancient Maya temples to reactivate them in order to learn more of their mysteries. On a warm spring day I stood upon the steps of the Temple of the Sun at Uxmal. Spanish colonialists wrongfully named this building the Governor's Palace. Its 23 grey stone steps represent solar energy and sunspots, of which the Maya astronomers had great knowledge.

I imagined the far-off days when the *Hau K'in* solar priest would be standing at the top of the colourfully painted temple. *Hau K'in* translates as 'a person who knows about the sun' and the sun was called 'Great Father'. He would be wearing vibrant clothes of office – a short white tunic hung about with sacred objects, perhaps a jaguar skin across his shoulders and bright red macaw feathers set into the tiers of the headdress perched upon his sleek black hair. These headdresses bore the fierce animal heads of shamanic guardians. With a golden disc showing the face of the sun god upon his chest and carrying his staff of office, the priest would stand resplendent on the steps, a living embodiment of the divine masculine, before entering the central temple.

Visible to him on either side were seven doors through which solar energy activated the seven subtle energy centres or chakras of his body – this knowledge was part of the cosmovision, the sacred science of the Maya. Hunbatz Men once said that, in this temple, 'The Mayas worshipped with the technology of the Spirit'.

Archaeologists tell us that the building was completed sometime before 900 CE. At that time the solar priest, standing in the central doorway, could have looked southeast across to a distant pyramid 3 miles (5km) away. It marked the place on the horizon where Venus rose as the Morning Star when it was at its southernmost declination.

The façade of the Sun Temple also brings our attention to the symbol for Venus. More than 200 stone masks of *Chac*, the Yucatec Maya rain god, are carved there; their lower eyelids all bear the symbol for Venus. In front of him the solar priest would be able to see the double-headed jaguar throne on a small stone podium, just as it is today. This was, and still is, a most powerful initiatory place, serving in potent ceremonies to balance into unity the duality present within the human mind.

In the eyes of Maya elders, Uxmal stands apart from other ancient cities in the area because it is a 'cosmic university' intentionally dedicated to the divine feminine. An equally important centre of cosmic understanding is that of Nah Chan, or Palenque. However, Uxmal holds a special resonance, being dedicated to the sun, Venus and the moon. It was here that women would come to be initiated into the lunar mysteries appropriate to priestesses. Hunbatz Men showed me that the Mayan word *Ux*, pronounced '*oosh*', is a mantric incantation for preparing one's body to receive the power of the moon, and of water and liquids. Understanding the sacred liquids of the body is still taught to initiates today. It was, and still is, part of a progressive spiritual process to open to the eternal Light.

Another feminine initiatory temple is at Tulum, a city on the old coastal route for Maya trading canoes passing around the Yucatán peninsula. Women about to give birth were carried onto the adjacent white sandy beach. They were received in tiny birthing temples under the watchful gaze of *Ixchel*, goddess of childbirth and rainbows. The birth of a child would be joyful and an honour to the ancestors because, even before a girl child is born, she holds within her womb the eggs that will produce her own children. She will never naturally get more eggs. From the moment of her birth her every breath nourishes her growing body and, throughout her life, whatever she eats, drinks, sees, hears, smells and feels will become nourishment for her own unborn children.

Every woman is a manifestation of the feminine principle, sym-bolized by the moon. Her body flows with tides of blood just as the moon causes the oceanic tides to flow. First Mother, the Great Mother, was revered in all early groups of people worldwide. In shamanistic communities the cult of the Great Bear Mother stretched from the cold northern arc stretching from Finland to Siberia and on to North America. The Lion Mother was worshipped in Neolithic times from Turkey to Egypt, and with the coming of the domestication of crops and animals the Grain Mother, greatest of all the Ancient Ones, was worshipped. She was known by different names in different places: as Koré and her mother Demeter in Greece, or as Ceres in Rome, the goddess Ker in ancient Britain and as the Corn Maiden in the Americas, the goddess who created the first human beings.

Throughout the world the feminine impulse has always been a fertile womb for prophecy. Female prophets, tellers of fortune, those that could read the signs in the sky and earth, were equally respected alongside men. Travel the length and breadth of *Abya Yala* today and you will meet many Native American women who affirm that they wish to assert spiritual and political leadership in their societies, as they have done through the ages. Both the Haudenosaunee clan mothers and the Cherokee nation were traditionally led by what were called 'Beloved Women'.

Within most of these nations there was a parity in decision making, ownership of property, economic equality and, in some – for example, in the Lakota and Navajo societies – women held a preponderance of power in one or more of these spheres. In spiritual matters too, women were equals, an integral part of the intrinsic mystery of the Sacred Hoop of everyday life. It was quite usual for them to be the receivers of prophecy, often through quietness and rest during their 'moon times', but their words would have been shared with all the elders and it is likely that the chief relayed the prophetic messages to the whole tribe.

In most tribes, on day-to-day matters of living there was a certain division of work. When it came to large council meetings the male elders or chiefs would often be the ones to 'hold the feather' – meaning that they exerted their right to talk. Typically they made 'legal' judgements and rules, while the wise women or grandmothers would exercise more of a moral, tone-setting and ultimate sway over the principles by which this should happen. In other words, the women would often stay out of the day-to-day arguments, intervening only when there was a matter of principle at stake or when they deemed the chiefs to be in error or missing something. Their focus was to maintain traditions and represent *intuitive* truth or 'the final word'.

For me, it was time to leave the Temple of the Sun, under the watching gaze of at least three iguanas expertly camouflaged on the rocks. I walked down the steps and terraces from this temple, with its divine masculine energies still resonating in me, to connect with the strong feminine energies held in the Moon Temple of Uxmal. Again, this is a building that has been misnamed, since the invaders and tourist guides to this day call it the 'Nunnery Quadrangle'. Yes, there *were* women there – but nuns they were not!

Along with over a hundred other people, all of us white Westerners seeking a path of indigenous wisdom, we gathered at the request of Hunbatz Men to hear him share profound teachings, the depth of which became very apparent to us. While we stood waiting for the ceremonies to begin, we looked at the enormous snake carved in stone. We saw it stretching all along one side of the building that is built around a court-yard. In common with other snake effigies throughout the region, the mouth of this snake is inexplicably 'birthing' a human head.

Suddenly a great flight of butterflies, shimmering blue and yellow, descended towards the grass as Hunbatz Men, in full ceremonial regalia, stood in front of the typical Maya stone arch forming the original temple entrance, nowadays blocked with stone. He said, 'I am very pleased to bring you to the cosmic university of this place. Humanity has bad problems, for its education is not good. Personal education has been created to service "the Machine". If we want to work in the way of the Light we need another education – we need a cosmic education. We need eternal laws, because it is the truth, and we come from the eternal law of *Hunab K'u* (Great Spirit). In this sacred place the women were educated and understood the Eternal Light. I am happy because you are coming back to this school of education.'

Pointing to the arch he said, 'Archaeologists do not understand why the Maya built this kind of arch. They do not understand this because they have a Western culture. To enter into the Maya wisdom you have to go with your Spirit. The Maya arch is in the shape of the hands. Where is the gate where we say that the Spirit goes in and out of the body? It is this point (pointing to the centre of the chest), and when the Maya make this form (putting his hands in a prayer shape) the Spirit is going inside. We are going to go with our *Spirit* through the door to learn.

'This simple form of arch the anthropologists do not understand – they too were educated with a Western education. If you truly want to learn about Maya culture you have to go in through the arch with your Spirit. You have to move this force with the Spirit. The cosmic law of this cycle of time will do it.

'You are not here by accident or by chance. The Great Spirit sent you, for you to seek your destiny, and then you *had* to be here. You have the responsibility to be the future teachers of this new education. Humanity needs a new education. It is necessary to have cosmic education. This should make you feel happy because you are here, because Great Spirit sent you here, because of these sacred places.'

Turning to look up at Father Sun he said, 'Remember *Hunab K'u*. Three times we will say the name of *Hunab K'u*. We have an obligation to commune with "the above and the below". It is the only way we can keep balance. We need to know up and down, and this is the only way we can be close to *Hunab K'u*.'

All eyes turned skyward as we spoke the Yucatec name of the One God, Great Spirit, with great reverence. Then Hunbatz Men continued, 'You were born to be Maya because, in the same way *Hunab K'u* made the Maya, he made you. The only difference between us and you is the colour of the skin.'

Slowly we walked in silent procession to the inner courtyard of the Temple of the Moon, quietly anticipating the new cosmic education that we would receive there. It seemed like a dream that I had once passed through this Maya arch and met the shaman who told me about time. I was constantly seeking answers to the strange words he had spoken after the divination... 'I see you holding a crystal, a huge, rounded crystal – yes, it is a head, or a skull. Beware the portal of death, before your mission is done.' Once again I saw his kind and proud Maya face and remembered how I had gazed into his piercing dark eyes. This time, with the group of initiates, I entered the Temple of the Moon by passing through the normal entrance.

In the Times Before Time

On another occasion, during the Gathering of the Indigenous Priests and Elders of the Americas in Mérida, Mexico, in 2003, the Guatemalan teacher Wandering Wolf told us that three native birds symbolize the indigenous peoples of the Americas: the Eagle of the North, the Quetzal of Central America and the Condor of the South. He went on to explain; the Maya prophecies proclaim that it is from the centre, meaning Central America, that we will understand how to forgive the Eagle of the North and the Condor of the South. We listened spellbound to this symbolic description.

He continued, his sincerity obvious and his hands held together in prayer, 'We will come together with all our brothers and sisters like the fingers of our hands, for we are One. We are children of the Sun, we are children of the Earth. Our culture is rooted in the heart of Mother Earth. The prophecies of our ancestors said that in the time of the Thirteenth Baktun we would see the return of the ancestors. This is the time in which we are now.'

To explain the calendrical cycles he mentioned here, each Baktun is made up of 144,000 days or approximately 394 years in the Gregorian calendar. A Great Cycle is 13 Baktuns or approximately 5,128 years. The current Great Cycle, the Fourth Sun, ends in 2012.

It would be comforting to think that the ancestors are returning to guide us, but many people still question whether are we poised on the brink of a new golden age or riding headlong into an apocalypse. I mused over the ways and means by which we could possibly evolve more rapidly in order to heed the cosmic education that Hunbatz Men told us about, and the ancestral prophecies spoken by Wandering Wolf.

At the end of the day I finally had time to consult the *Tzolk'in* calendar. It read: 'Four *Oc* – it represents the dog. It is a day of authority, of destruction and disequilibrium, corruption and uncertainty, but also of reconciliation. The number four means that the energies will come in from all four directions of the Earth. The dog symbolizes an unfailing devotion and is often used as imagery in lands where wolves do not live.'

So it seemed a fitting day for Wandering Wolf's words.

The Kogi – the Elder Brothers

My search to understand the prophecies took me in many directions. I had heard of the Kogi of Colombia, who call themselves 'the Elder Brothers', but it always seemed too difficult to travel to their lands and they permitted very few visitors. The Kogi were virtually unknown to the world until just a few years ago. Choosing to live deep within the richly forested mountain slopes, they came out of isolation in 1990 to give a message to the world, in a BBC documentary film by Alan Ereira called *From the Heart of the World – the Elder Brothers' Warning*. This film contained a strong and shocking message about the changes the Kogi were observing.

By good fortune, while in Mexico I came across a young anthropologist, Carmen, who had spent time with them. We were on adjoining tables at breakfast and struck up a conversation. My opening comment was, 'I am so pleased. At last, just recognition is about to be laid down on the UN statute books, with the Rights of Indigenous Peoples becoming recognized in the General Council meeting that is to be held in Autumn 2006.' [*Regrettably various countries, USA and UK amongst them, blocked the final ratification of these rights, an event which went unreported in the Western press.*] On 13 September 2007 the UN General Assembly finally adopted the, non-binding, text of the Declaration on Rights of Indigenous Peoples.

In response she began to tell me the history of the Kogi. 'We Europeans and Americans are called by them the Younger Brothers. None of us have respected the Elder Brothers' sacred Earth wisdom in the past, and even today we still violate their lands. It is 500 years since the tribal lands of the Kogi, the Hopi and many other indigenous cultures around the world were invaded and seized, on grounds dating back to a Papal Bull of 1493 announcing that infidels had no land rights, while Christians, the invaders, did!

'Indigenous peoples were identified as part of the "brute nature" that Christians were out to conquer and subdue for pope, king and country. In repeated genocidal waves, the Euro-American culture became dominant, perpetuating the dogma that indigenous people are backward, ignorant and impoverished without white man's intervention, and in any case they need converting to be saved!'

I replied, 'Yes, it is difficult to imagine the horrors of those times. By contrast, in the times-before-time-was-recorded, tribes lived peaceably together, usually cooperating as an extended family unit that was matrilineal – with power descending through the female line.'

I recalled reading about the founding of the United States, and explained, 'It was among the Native Americans of the Haudenosaunee League, whom they called Iroquois, that the founding fathers –

especially Benjamin Franklin – realized that democratic principles and practices were already in operation amongst them. The Haudenosaunee League was a peaceful and self-governing federation of tribes. The American settlers adopted these ways, especially since there were no democratic precedents in Europe at the time, but unfortunately they left out the equal position of women, as well as the role of children and the people's sacred contract with nature.'

She smiled, took a deep breath and continued, 'As we now know, the sacredness of the feminine impulse probably guided most early peoples of the Americas. Among the Haudenosaunee that you mention, chiefs were selected by the grandmothers, who had watched them grow up and knew who would serve their people well. It was also within the power of the grandmothers to remove chiefs from their positions if they did not govern as they should and keep traditional ceremonies. Generally, the women participated equally in all decisions. But this was another integral part of indigenous democracy that was rejected by the founding fathers.

'To this day women take a pivotal role in Maya and Hopi society. In the past, in those lands, held in the protective memory of the ancestors, indigenous peoples revered nature. They acknowledged that all beings were related and interdependent. The creatures roaming the land, mountains, trees, rocks, water, wind, the air, the fire, the stars and the guiding spirits within all things were held sacred. In this way everything was balanced by people's desire to give back to Great Spirit as much as was taken from nature.' She paused to continue her breakfast. Then in response to my questioning, she began to recount the story of the time she had spent with the Kogi.

'The Sierra Nevada de Santa Marta, in Colombia, is the highest coastal mountain range in the world. The indigenous groups that live on it – Kogi, Arhuaco and Assario – are descendants of the Tairona civilization that flourished there before the Spanish invasion. Unlike most South and Central American civilizations, the Taironas lived in relative peace with the Spanish for the first 70 years following the conquest, until Spanish demands finally caused a rebellion, which was then ruthlessly crushed. Tairona survivors fled up into the high parts of the mountain to regroup and restore their society.

'Now the three remaining tribes refer to themselves as the Elder Brothers, and white people they refer to as Younger Brothers – the name implying that we have much still to learn.'

Wanting to understand the culture from the beginning, I asked, 'Like the Hopi and other Native Americans, the Kogi have a creation story, don't they?'

'Yes, theirs tells of *Aluna*, Great Mother of the primeval waters, the source of all Creation. In her dreaming of the world she envisioned all the possibilities for all worlds and all times, and even before creating this world she went through great mental torment. To the Kogi she is known as Memory and Possibility. She created eight worlds before this one.

'But it wasn't until her ninth creation that she made humans, including the Elder and Younger Brothers. Younger Brothers were given a special kind of knowledge, that of science and technology, but in giving them this they were sent far, far away across the oceans. The Kogi told me that, 500 years ago, these Younger Brothers sailed back and began causing troubles in the peaceful lands of the Elder Brothers. Despite warnings from the Elder Brothers, to this day they continue to destroy the rainforests and dig out the heart of their Mother with mining.'

This reminded me of an old Maya proverb: *Whoever cuts the trees as he pleases cuts short his own life.*

Carmen continued, 'Do you know, it amazed me that every part of the Kogis' way of life reflects religious beliefs. They build traditional temples that are some 7 or 8 metres (23–26ft) high and 8 metres (26ft) in diameter, tied together with liana vines and rings of cane. The temples have two doors, exactly opposite each other, and each has four fires and four shelves on the walls. All of these elements are important symbols that guide their lives. An imaginary line joins the two doors and this separates light and darkness, good from bad, right from left, male and female. In what seems a very sophisticated and developed understanding, Kogis must try to balance all of these forces of duality during their daily lives.'

I asked, 'Do the Kogi respect their women?'

'Very definitely,' replied Carmen, 'since the temple is a mother's womb. The top of the temple is her vagina, and the Mamas (priests) place pots and vessels there like seeds, which symbolically fertilize her. Inside the temple, men lie in hammocks that symbolize their mother's placenta. They spin threads to hang from the top of the temple. These threads represent umbilical cords, helping them to be nourished with the Mother's wisdom. When they begin to talk together, it is rather like a confession instigated by the Mama who uses the occasion to give advice. In this fertile womb they tell their mythic stories, talk of the day's happenings and sing ceremonial songs to the ancestors.'

By now we had finished our breakfast of delicious juicy tropical fruits, rolls and coffee and strolled out onto the covered veranda of the eco-lodge where we were staying, looking across a lake ringed by tropical forest. Overhead came the screech of a flock of green parakeets and somewhere in the distance howler monkeys began their eerie calls.

Carmen began to sing. It was a *mulkuákve*, a prayer or religious formula that a Kogi Mama may use for meditation or counselling someone asking his advice:

iskími alúna hangu ité

iskími hába guaselgukú hangu ité

iskími mulyigába nici gataugénka

iskími hiúngulda guxa nici naugénka

Only one thought

Only one Mother

Only one single word reaches upwards

Only one single trail leads heavenward.

'That was so beautiful,' I responded. 'Thank you.'

'But now you must hear the painful part. This is what the Kogi Mama priests have told me... "We have observed great changes on our mountain, where normally everything was in equilibrium. For generations we have lived in peaceful harmony with our environment, but seeing critical changes to the water, trees and animals caused us to give a dire warning to all of you who are prepared to listen. Up to now we have ignored the Younger Brother. We have not even given him a slap for his misdeeds. But now we can no longer look after the world alone. Younger Brother is doing too much damage. He must see, understand and assume responsibility. Now we will have to work together. *Otherwise, the world will die.*"'

Once again I got a shocking message about the destruction of the world. I turned and looked sadly at Carmen. She took my hand and said, 'But *you* can tell people and do something about it!'

Indigenous Wisdom

The Kogi Elder Brothers and the Hopi together say that the imbalance in nature could cause the world to end. They do not understand why those in power fail to honour ancient Earth wisdom. Leaders of these tribes are not telling us to give up our modern world completely, but rather to do an urgent and radical rethink of how we live, finding all the ways we can to adopt sustainable and appropriate methods.

I turned to Carmen again. 'Can you as an anthropologist explain how indigenous peoples have been able to predict the outcome of our ways? How did simple mountain-dwelling people in present-day Columbia know that technology would give birth to a monstrous culture that would lead the Western nations? Why is it that our technological world, based upon science and scientific prediction, failed to predict its own faults whilst indigenous peoples continue to warn us of its consequences?'

She looked up at the lush trees around us and replied, 'For the Elder Brothers it was simple because they could easily see devastation on their mountainsides. They only had to look at the dying trees and the water drying up from their lands to see the consequences of the Younger Brothers' ways. Let me tell you what happened in 2004.

'In that year a special piece of low-lying land called La Luna, that had recently been given to the Kogi, was designated an Indigenous Reserve, a protected area within one of UNESCO's Biosphere Reserves. Fifteen days later, without warning, on 17 July, a plane from Dyncorp passed over to fumigate La Luna with chemicals, supposedly to eradicate coca-growing. It caused a complete disaster.

'Following this spraying by the plane with the illegal toxic mix Agent Green, La Luna became a tragedy. The Kogis had previously worked five years to regenerate the soil in La Luna. Now they will have to wait at least five more years to replant there. Everything is contaminated and defoliated. The streams are dry because there are no more trees to retain water.

'What are they going to eat? What are they going to drink? Where will they go?'

Carmen was in tears as she sobbed out, 'The destruction was pointless because there was no illegal coca growing in La Luna anyway.'

'Look Carmen,' I said. 'I am the eternal optimist. I can see that modern science can provide answers instead of problems. You know well enough from your studies that a great wave of environmental awareness is sweeping through the universities of Europe and the rest of the industrialized world. Politicians are coming under pressure from environmental NGOs (non-governmental organizations) that call for anti-pollution programmes to be initiated by governments and for environmental targets to be met. Perhaps the best news yet is that respected researchers like you are now speaking out in support of ageless prophetic wisdom coming from indigenous leaders.'

She managed a slight smile, squeezed my hand and walked off.

Wow, I thought, that was one of those special encounters you get as a traveller!

CHAPTER 5

The Children of Time

*It's not true that we come here only to live – we
come only in passing! We do not own all that is
given to us. On this journey we eat, sleep and dream,
and whenever you are ready, Oh Maker of Life, I'll
come home to you.*

From a Haudenosaunee (Iroquois nation) song

H ere we unravel some further details about the Maya Prophecies,
calendars and their context in our time. We shall also travel to
Nah Chan (Palenque), one of the greatest of the Maya sacred sites, a
university for cosmic education, as one Maya Elder described it.

The Eleventh Hour

I have already mentioned the gatherings of priests and elders from the
whole vast continent of the Americas. The immense logistical problems
of visas, permissions to travel, funding and support to enable elders,
who in some cases have never left their community before, goes
virtually unnoticed in the media, and we can see that these events don't
make headline news. But what the elders have to share relates directly
to all our futures on the planet. Clearly many of these priests and elders
are expert at reading the Threads of Time and occasionally they give
their insights to the wider world. During the past 60 years Kogi, Hopi
and Maya amongst others, have decided to place their messages on the
'world noticeboard'.

They have specifically referred to a number of disastrous environmental changes that are taking place worldwide. Their ability to do this demonstrates that they take a keen interest in much more than what is occurring in their local community, their tribal or national environment alone. They urge all those who hear their words, and governments in particular, to listen to their wisdom and make great efforts to reverse these ecological threats. Before the era of mass communication their voices were fragmented by sheer communication difficulties, but all that has changed and their voices sing one anthem in unison across mountains, seas, deserts and rainforests:

Now is the End Time – it is almost too late to change –
wake up! – listen to the heartbeat of Mother Earth –
hear her pain.

Once, when I sat upon Glastonbury Tor in England for a meditation, her pain became my pain, with a heartache I have never previously experienced. At first I found I could see downward, deep inside the Tor. There was a sheer edge of rock descending and, out from its side, about a third of the way down, was a rainbow of cascading water. Then the water changed into blood, the blood of the Earth. 'I am bleeding to death – please understand, please help.' Then I felt an unbelievable pain inside my body. I simply cried and cried till my emotion was exhausted.

A little shiver ran down my spine as I realized that we must be prepared for anything. No longer is the world a cosy place for people in developed countries. I needed something to restore my faith in the ability of large groups of people to take responsibility for their lives. I was looking for a different model to live by.

I found it with the elders from the Americas. Although I could be physically present only on one occasion, I was inspired as each year they met in their large bio-regional gatherings, sitting together in talking circles to share their personal and regional efforts to redress unemployment, water and land rights. At these gatherings they endeavour to speak as one unified prophetic voice. Emphasis is placed upon the recognition of their *collective* rights, as stated in the UN Draft Declaration on the Rights of Indigenous Peoples. The declaration was planned to be adopted by the UN Human Rights Council in June 2006.

Regrettably, even if adopted, the declaration will *not* be legally binding for member states. However, it is a comprehensive statement addressing issues such as collective rights, cultural rights and identity, in addition to education, health, employment and language. The declaration emphasizes the right of indigenous peoples to maintain and strengthen their own institutions, cultures and traditions and to pursue their development in accordance with their aspirations and needs. The impact of international recognition, with many countries being signatories to such a declaration, means greater credibility and respect for the voices of the indigenous peoples.

My journeys so far had taken me across parts of North and Central America. I had attended one of the bio-regional gatherings as an observer and had discovered a number of prophecies, but nothing was to prepare me emotionally for the effect that the range and depth of the Hopi and Maya prophecies had upon me. For the first time, my quest really hit home. It hit my core beliefs about what I was doing with my life. The words of the Hopi Nation elders of Oraibi, Arizona, released at the end of 2001, are heart-rending in effect.

You have been telling the people that this is the eleventh hour. Now you must go back and tell the people that this is *the* hour, and there are things to be considered. Where are you living? What are you doing? What are your relationships? Where is your water? It is time to speak your truth. Create your community. Be good to each other. And do not look outside yourself for the leader. This could be a good time!

There is a river flowing now very fast. It is so great and swift that there are those who will be afraid. They will try to hold on to the shore. They will feel they are being torn apart, and they will suffer greatly. Know that the river has its destination. The elders say, we must let go of the shore, push off into the middle of the river. Keep your eyes open and your heads above the water. See who is there with you, and celebrate.

[There are various versions of this statement dating from 1998 to 2001. This comes from www.matrixmasters.com.]

I recall how very downhearted I felt when I first heard about the Hopi prophecies many years ago and, more recently, the Maya prophecies. I felt I was alone and misunderstood in wanting to bring them to a wider audience – to people who could perhaps do something about the warnings. I threw myself into antinuclear and environmental protests. But Great Spirit works in many ways and on many levels. I realize now that I was going to be given the strength to make a difference, that something extraordinary was about to be revealed to me – something that I could never have anticipated.

Nah Chan – Palenque

I take a deep breath, excitement leaping in me, as we near Nah Chan in Chiapas, Mexico, for this wonderful place will always be my spiritual home. The road from Mérida, 590km (365 miles) away, has passed through the dry Puuc hills around Uxmal and across flat, wet ranching areas with vast fields, once rainforest, which are now home to gaunt beef cattle.

Now the view is of lush virgin rainforest and, as we drive the last few kilometres into the Biosphere Reserve of the Lacandón people, the *halach uinik* or 'real people' of the forest, I cannot wait to step out into their welcoming green paradise. The rush of humidity as I open the car door is like a promise of things to come – here an elusive fragrance, there a strange sound carried on the all-pervasive, hot, moisture-laden air.

I quickly make my way past the tourist stalls where the proud Lacandón, in their white tunics and long dark hair, sit carving arrows or stringing bead necklaces of bright red seeds, ready for the morning crowds of chattering foreign tourists. I reach a certain point on the path into the sacred city and stop.

It is a habit of mine, and part of the teaching I have received from many wise ones, that I should acknowledge an energetic 'gateway' upon entering a special place. It enables me to make a subtle transition between this everyday world and the mysterious world of the forest dwellers, as if I am stepping from my *tonal* (usual self) into my *nagual* (dreaming, magical or energy body). As well as asking to be allowed to enter into resonance with the energies of the place, I also give a little offering, usually a flower, a crystal or a pinch of tobacco (a customary Native American offering).

Passing the modern tomb of Alberto Ruz Lhuillier, the archaeologist who did so much to bring the wonders of Palenque to the world, I call upon the spirit guardians of Nah Chan to guide me well. I am not disappointed. Their messengers, chattering flocks of green parakeets, call out as I enter their domain. My first sight of the temples, set like jewels amidst the grassy hillocks with a backdrop of the *Yemal-K'uk-Lakam-Witz*, or Descending Quetzal-bird Big Mountain, sets my heart pounding with a passion, as it has every time I have visited.

Of all the places where I could have imagined something extraordinary happening to me, this city of Nah Chan is the place. But *los aluxes*, the nature spirits who looked down from the mighty tall ceiba trees, and the ancestors whose memories were locked in the stones, had other plans. This was not the place where an amazing gift was to be given to me. The Maya gods, in their wisdom, had passed this responsibility to those in the Lands of the Eagle, North America.

Now I rest, thankful to be at Nah Chan again. Something about the place shouts 'You are home!' From a seat under the trees I can see the stunningly beautiful Temple of the Inscriptions. This particular temple, the largest of four in a row at the entrance, is set upon a white-stepped pyramid that shines as it reflects the midday power of Father Sun. Sometimes it seems to me that the pyramid just hovers there, somewhere between this world and the next.

The Temple of the Inscriptions, as well as being the burial place of shaman-priest-king Pakal Votan, houses three massive stone tablets recording the now almost completely deciphered Maya history of creation and royal lineages. The story, written in Maya hieroglyphs – a Greek word meaning 'holy carvings' – tells of Pakal Votan and cleverly substantiates his claim to rulership by linking his birth to the primal goddess, First Mother. The commencement date of this current Fourth Creation of the Maya was established upon another carved stone tablet in the Temple of the Cross, also at Nah Chan. The date given equates in our calendar to 11 August 3114 BCE.

In the Temple of the Inscriptions Alberto Ruz Lhuillier and his team found an unusual stone set into the floor of the upper room. On removing it and digging down into the staircases below for 75ft (23m) they finally revealed, in the year 1952, a moist stone chamber that sparkled with calcite crystals in their flashlights. They gasped as they saw a large stone sarcophagus in the centre of the chamber. With great effort, and the assistance of several car jacks, the elaborately carved lid, weighing more than five tons, was prised open.

What lay within were remains of the bejewelled and masked body of Ahau Pakal Votan, honoured as Lord Shield Snake and 'Looker through the Dimensions'. He was said to have been born in 603 CE as a *Votan*, an embodiment of a Snake God, with a foot like a snake's head! The tomb had been undisturbed for almost 1,300 years.

My personal reason for going to Nah Chan again was to reconnect with the energetic imprint of Pakal Votan. Some revere him as a Maya avatar, an enlightened being who returns to Earth to help humanity. But for me, my visit to Nah Chan was a kind of pilgrimage to be undertaken, since it was a good place to contemplate all the powerful Maya prophecies.

At Nah Chan these prophecies are hidden within difficult-to-decipher hieroglyphic carvings, worn with time and the elements as well as Pakal Votan's tomb itself. If you look very carefully you can still see exquisite pictures that the artists chiselled into the stones. They tell a story of the gods and kings, the queens and royal lineages, to anyone who cares study them. Only in the last 50 years have epigraphers understood the complicated glyphs. What the rulers recorded for us to read in the future was incredible.

Nah Chan was a 'cosmic university' in Pakal Votan's times, and fortunately one whose secrets can still be accessed today. Maya day-keeper Hunbatz Men says (in a private communication) that many races once came from around the world to this city to learn the secrets of the universe. For example, my research has shown that three temples, the Temples of the Cross, the Foliated Cross and the Sun, are laid out in a ground plan reflecting three of the prominent stars in the constellation that we know as Orion, and the Maya know as the Turtle and the 'Hearthstones of Creation'. (More about this in my book *The Maya Shamans – Travellers in Time*, Vega, London, 2002.)

The Laws of Time

Later, I asked José Argüelles, author of a number of books including *The Mayan Factor* (Bear & Co, 1987), to comment upon the importance of the discovery of Pakal Votan's tomb in relation to prophecy. He replied with information that has become the basis of his initiative for a worldwide movement advocating change from our Gregorian calendar to a different type of calendar, which he calls natural time.

The 2012 Prophecy is very clearly coded into the facts concerning the discovery of the tomb of the Great Pakal (Pakal Votan) in the Temple of the Inscriptions, Palenque. These facts show us that this is the prophecy of the return to natural time, which is universal time, and hence the coming of cosmic consciousness on Earth.

Pakal Votan's prophecy is known as *Telektonon*, Earth Spirit Speaking Tube, which refers to the tile tube that runs from his sarcophagus beneath the pyramid to the central chamber on top of the pyramid. It was the chance finding of this tile tube in 1949 that led to the discovery of the world-famous tomb three years later in 1952.

Here are the facts of the timing of the tomb that reveal the prophecy of the return to natural time by 2012.

The great tomb was sealed off in 692 CE (9.13.0.0.0 in the Maya calendar) when the Temple of the Inscriptions was dedicated. The difference in years from the discovery of the tomb to its dedication was 1952 - 692 = 1,260.

This refers to the number of years in the Hell of Materialism. This number is found in the Book of Revelation, referring to the exile of the woman, clothed in the sun, crowned with the 12 stars and seated on the moon (13th moon). 1,260 is the number of the artificial timing frequency 12:60 – the irregular 12-month

Gregorian calendar and the 60-minute mechanical hour
– the two timing devices which enslaved humanity to
materialism by the advent of the Thirteenth Baktun in
1618 CE.

The difference in years from 2012, the end of the
cycle, and the dedication of the tomb is 2012 - 692 =
1,320.

This is the number of the natural timing frequency
13:20, encoded in the *Tzolk'in* – 13 galactic tones and 20
solar seals.' (This refers to numbers and day signs in
Argüelles' *Dreamspell Calendar*).

From a private communication, 2006

José Argüelles went on to point out that the prophecy hidden in the
symbology of the tomb meant, 'when the tomb was finally to be
opened and revealed to the world (this occurred in 1952), 60 years from
the closing of the cycle, humanity would be suffocating in the artificial
timing frequency of 12:60 materialism'. This brings us right up to the
year 2012. His thoughts about our present-day Gregorian calendar
with its 12:60 symbolism of an illogical 12 months to a year (with
differing months of an arbitrary numbers of days that are a hangover
of the whims of Roman emperors), and 60 minutes to an hour, certainly
links in many ways to the concept of the Matrix that I have previously
explained.

In the Matrix 'time is money' and the feminine cycle of the moon
is disregarded as nature is trashed, courtesy of the controlling 'gods' of
materialism. Argüelles' proposal hinges on the concept that a change
to a 13:20 way of counting, that is, 13 lunar cycles each year and 20
aspects of the sun (as used in the Maya *Tzolk'in* calendar and adopted
for his Dreamspell calendar) is a more natural way of counting time. I
suggest that if we regarded time in a different way we might not be so
tied to counting the hours that we work. Instead we could labour with
the ethos that 'work is love made manifest', an ideal proposed by Eileen
Caddy, cofounder of the Findhorn Foundation, Scotland.

The world of science too, now gives us astronomical evidence that, upon the molten, moving surface of the sun, an area comes into direct alignment with the Earth in a complex rotational pattern of almost exactly 260 days. Thus, as the Ancient Maya inexplicably knew, in the days before powerful telescopes, a different little piece of the sun is presented to us every 260 days. Presumably they could *feel* the different energy, or observe its effects, each day. (These 260 days are called *kin*, being formed from the 13 x 20 days that make up the traditional *Tzolk'in* calendar cycle.)

Perhaps a practical, moderate and acceptable path forward would be to follow natural lunar cycles and change to a 13-month calendar. This would go some way towards harmonizing the manner in which we in the Western world count time. As Argüelles says, referring to the tomb of Pakal Votan, 'The prophecy makes clear that this would come about through the discovery of the Law of Time (including the 12:60 and 13:20 timing frequencies). Its practical application is the 13-moon/28-day calendar intended to replace the erroneous 12-month calendar of artificial time.'

It is important for you the reader to know the background to this theory of the laws of time. Argüelles is named 'The Closer of the Cycle'. It means that the final closing of this chapter of human history which culminates at the end of 2012 is now being undertaken. Argüelles is a man with such a brilliant mind that I could liken him to a Michelangelo of our present era. Often misunderstood, with ideas way out of time, his integrity shines through inspired writings and art. He has now gone into a period of quietness and introspection in order to fulfil this role. Believe me, not everything is what it seems to be on the surface of this world: many unseen factors are at work on dimensional levels we overlook because daily life holds us back from seeing them. We might call them energies or influences but, whatever they are, we humans are receptive to them because we are all, everywhere, and all at once, part of Great Spirit.

Someone else appears to have a vested interest in the ending of the cycle too, or else there is an unlikely 'tourist' walking through the ruins of sacred Maya cities, or archaeological sites as the authorities insist on calling them. In 2006 George Bush, the US President, spent a day at Chichen Itzá. The whole place was cleared of tourists for his private visit. More recently he went to Uxmal in Yucatán and Iximché, 30 miles west of Guatemala City. Iximché, from the words Ixim (maize) and ché (tree), or 'Place of the Maize Tree' was the main city of the Cakchiquel Maya people, reaching its zenith at a post-Classic time when the Maya culture was very much in decline. The visit took place on 12 March 2007, on the day that falls almost in the centre of the *Tzolk'in* calendar. Named Twelve *Toj* in Kiché Maya language, it is interpreted by their day-keepers as related to the element of water, the power of the moon and *the day to make payment of karmic debts.*

Concomitant with these little-publicized, to the point of secret, visits to key Maya places, President Bush, seen by some as upholder and figurehead of the Matrix myth, spearheads a visible force fighting to hold on to the supremacy of the Matrix over a number of Central and South American nations. A great upwelling of political power is occurring at grassroots level in those countries. The Western media try to have us believe otherwise by focusing on specific names, such as that of President Chavez of Venezuela, as extremist leaders. But the peoples of *Abya Yala* or Turtle Island are stirring as we approach the ending of this cycle of time. By waking up they are acting as a key part of the prophecies. Indeed they *have* to wake up in order for the prophecies to be fulfilled.

I was intrigued by the possibility of these two figureheads, Argüelles and Bush, fighting it out at other levels of reality. Perhaps you will understand that this is not such a crazy comment if I tell you that the CIA infiltrated at least one of our Maya conferences held in recent years in Mexico. It's time for some of us to lose our naivety and start to sharpen up on our real reasons for being here on Earth at this crucial point in history.

I resolved to be more careful in my travels seeking the meaning of prophecy, and to be *much* more careful about whom I would talk to. It's not a question of fear – for fear feeds the Matrix – but of adopting other means to negotiate our way through the tangled Threads of Time. Great Spirit moves in many ways to combat a future world where terror could reign.

I, like others who have moved from the control of the Gregorian calendar to an understanding of the traditional Maya calendar, a lunar-based calendar, or of the Dreamspell calendar, am quickly unlocked and opened up to other possibilities beyond the professed 'normal' reality. It is one way that the Lords of Time prod us and prompt us to open our eyes and awaken from cultural hypnosis. Their avowed adversaries, the forces behind the Matrix, like the gods of death in the stories of the *Popul Vuh*, the 'council book' of the Kiché Maya, will stop at nothing to try to achieve their ends.

An episode in the *Popul Vuh* recounts a ball game between the Hero Twins and the Lords of the Underworld, in which the twins achieved a staggering defeat over the masters of hell. Historians tell us that, on occasions of immense political importance, Maya rulers would take on the role of the Hero Twins and their opponents would play the role of the Underworld rulers. It was ordained in those times that the Maya rulers would win the ball game, thus symbolically defeating the forces of darkness, sickness, famine and death. The *Xibalba* Underworld gods, graphically named One Death and Seven Death, Skull Scepter, Scab Stripper, Blood Gatherer, Pus Face and Demon of Filth, all resplendent in their terrifying costumes, were nothing compared to the present-day seen and unseen opposing forces now lined up at the end of *this* cycle time, culminating at the end of 2012. The stakes are now high. Matters are moving rapidly to their conclusion.

Suddenly a little shiver ran down my spine for, as I write, I have just heard that Pakal Votan's tomb at Nah Chan (Palenque) is to be permanently closed to the public and the media. There will instead be an expensive replica in the nearby museum devoid of any energetic link to Pakal Votan.

This was disturbing news. Nah Chan and the Temple of the Inscriptions have always been special places for me. My heart soars whenever I am there. In the cool palace courtyard, in the chamber of the unknown enigmatic 'Red Queen', or atop the stepped pyramid with Pakal's tomb hidden in the depths below me, I leap through all the timelines of the past into the present or future, moving effortlessly through the dimensions. I feel like one of *los aluxes*, the little fairy-like nature spirit guardians to whom the ancient Maya entrusted their temples when they left so many years ago.

The End Times

Sitting outside their stone palaces just over 1,000 years ago, the astronomer-shamans looked at the stars – pinpoints of light stretched from horizon to horizon in the unpolluted air. Dreaming of the myths that told of wise ones who came from the stars to Earth, they honoured the 'Four Balaams' – intergalactic travellers. They enacted especially painful rituals of self-sacrifice, personal bloodlettings to induce visions of their guiding ancestors. Their blood dripped onto the Earth and onto fine bark paper that was burnt in offering.

As the jaguars stalked the dark forest all around and the ordinary people bent over their cooking fires, a profound realization came to them. This realization was so vast that they needed all their skills to track it with their calendar counts. They consulted with day-keepers and, at the command of the *Ahau* 'kings', instructed the stonemasons to leave a message for the End Times. The glyphs they drew indicated a date equivalent to 21 December 2012 CE, as the ending of a precise cycle of time, as well as the predicted finale to this Fourth Creation.

The astronomer-shamans knew the beginning date of the present Creation and they knew its end. Can we really comprehend what this must have been like during Pakal Votan's reign? Those people way back in history were thinking, planning and calculating a huge time period of 5,125.36 years, beginning in 3114 BCE, and translating it into a mythic message that had meaning, not only then, but now in the End Times.

The astronomer-shamans envisioned our future on the Threads of Time. Together with skilled day-keepers they teased out the threads to see us in the final 144,000 days (the last of the Thirteen Baktuns) at the end of this 5,125-year period.

This is the Maya Prophecy that brings ominous portents, for somehow they knew that we were to be thrown into a survival challenge.

Then those people, with their hopes and dreams, their wars and struggles to survive, became lost in time. Only their memories were preserved on the stones, eventually to tell Westerners, once quick to laugh at the myths and superstitions of 'natives', the truth about the ending of this Creation.

Today's Maya calendar day-keepers repeatedly tell us that what happens at the end of a cycle of time sets the scene for the next time cycle. Presently an important sub-cycle is the 13 years up to the December Solstice in 2012, counting from December Solstice in 1999. They call it the Seating or Preparation years. In these few remaining years they caution us to learn how to pull positive and life-enhancing Threads of Time toward the human race, containing the strands of a coming golden age. Those golden strands, I believe, are ready and waiting to be woven together.

We stand at a cosmic crossroads, with the fate of Earth in the balance. We now know that, if humanity continues on its present course in the last few years of this Maya Creation, up to and beyond 2012, we are likely to see more of the horrors described in their prophecies. Almost daily, news items appear in which scientists unwittingly confirm predictions originating from the indigenous peoples of the Americas, ranging from impending volcanic eruptions to climate change. Astrophysicists are even suggesting a possible magnetic pole-reversal in our sun, with unknown consequences, due in the year 2012.

Here is a prophetic teaching about the Earth and climate change from Dan Evehema, a Hopi elder.

> At each pole there are two water serpents, each with a warrior sitting on his head and tail. These command nature to warn us by her activities that time is getting short, and we must correct ourselves. If we refuse to heed these warnings, the warriors will let go of the serpents. They will rise up, and all will perish.
>
> **From *The Hopi Survival Kit* by Thomas E Mails & Chief Dan Evehema (Steward, Tabori & Chang, 1996). Respected elder Dan Evehema died in 1999, aged 108.**

This elder went on to express concern for climate changes that he sees all around. He said that, although his people know the proper time to plant seeds, in recent springs unprecedented snow and cold weather have delayed planting. His people fear that shorter summers will cause their traditional food crop, corn, to stand unripened. The harvesting of this, their staple food, together with beans and squashes, is in danger. An ancient prophecy says: 'One day we will plant wearing finger sacks (gloves), clearing away snow with our feet before planting.'

Speaking as if his eyes could gaze into time future, Dan Evehema stated that the result of these changes was anybody's guess. The question I put is, *will this occur the world over*? The elders tell us that this would depend on geographical areas. In regions with different climates, different things will happen in different ways. Tropical land could become a land of ice, and the Arctic region could become tropical. They stress that this need not happen if we, the people, together with our leaders, do something about the harm being done to the environment.

I thought about this elder's words, knowing that my task and yours is, through the sheer strength of our will, to transmute human-made negativity to avert dire predictions on the Threads of Time. Instead we can draw towards us precious life-enhancing qualities. Those are the golden strands that humanity much needs if we are to travel beyond that predicted end date to a better future for all. Those are the qualities that constitute the Sacred Hoop of Native Americans and the WorldWideWeb of Life and Light envisioned in dreams of a better world. In those dreams, in our light-bodies as we sleep, we can also ask to connect with the Beings of Light, who guide the evolution of humanity from other worlds and dimensions.

Beings of Light? Surely they can't be real? Remember, I have talked of a fractal world where all is not what it seems. It's a bit like gazing out across the still surface of the sea, thinking the surface is solid and that there couldn't possibly be another world of life going on below it. As a child you don't know you can swim under the sea until you first dip your toe into the water! But your toe is not particularly intelligent and certainly cannot see, so it's not till you summon up courage to put your head in the sea that a whole new world emerges. This is the unseen part, the part where you are required to use courage and trust as your inner guide.

What worlds are there still to be explored? Are they within us or beyond? Where do the mysterious beings that I have encountered come from? Maybe you, like me, will think that they are beneficial extra-terrestrials and transdimensionals.

In places with a vibrant spirit of the land, such beings occasionally break through into our awareness, especially when consciousness has been raised to superconsciousness level. Could it be that these mysterious encounters have something to do with the prophecies? As I pondered these questions I began to realize that, in the words of the elders, 'They are those that we have been waiting for'.

I began the arduous climb up the steep steps to the top of the Temple of the Inscriptions and gazed across the land, just as Pakal Votan, Serpent Lord, must have done. The forest stretched as a great viridian sea of vegetation, hiding decaying temples within its depths. Far off in the hazy distance, dominating the tallest trees, male howler monkeys were calling to one another, announcing coming rain. I was now high enough to see another flock of noisy parakeets whisk below me in a blur of lemon-green.

Turning, I walked reverently into Pakal Votan's Temple, built over the steps leading down to his tomb. I sat down on some mossy stones in a dark corner and drifted into a vision of the future. In my vision I was shown a beautiful flowering Earth with many white-columned temples set within gardens, where people of all races walked together in peace. I knew for certain that, if we work with wise indigenous elders who have already had centuries of contact with beneficent beings and extraterrestrials, we can change the future.

All day I walked the well-trodden paths and cool palace terraces of Nah Chan, pausing here and there to make sketches of special stone carvings. I climbed to each of the temples in this cosmic university, very aware of different vibrational energies alive within each one.

Then, sitting in a shady spot on the time-smoothed rocks by the little river that flows through the ancient city, the afternoon drew to a close and, with a tiny flame of hope for humanity burning in my heart, I remembered the following prophetic words.

Upon suffering beyond suffering: the Red Nation shall
rise again and it shall be a blessing for a sick world.
A world filled with broken promises, selfishness and
separations. A world longing for Light again.
I see a time of seven generations when all the colours

of mankind will gather under the Sacred Tree of Life and
the whole Earth will become one circle again.

In that day, there will be those among the Lakota who
will carry knowledge and understanding of unity
among all living things, and the young white ones will
come to those of my people and ask for this wisdom.

I salute the Light within your eyes where the whole
Universe dwells. For when you are at that centre within
you and I am in that place within me, we shall be One.

This statement was taken from Oglala Sioux Chief Crazy Horse (b.
1840s, d. 1877), as he sat smoking the sacred pipe with Sitting Bull for
thelast time, four days before he was assassinated. For more details see
www.legendsofamerica.com.

The Origins of Prophecy

In this world where so much is speculation, one thing is certain to me
– that the Maya temple builders, the astronomer-shamans and rulers
understood the Threads of Time and had the ability to 'read' prophecy
upon them. Either through shamanic vision or accessing our superconsciousness, we too can travel in non-ordinary realities. We all have the
ability to develop superconsciousness, which in turn provides the
focal lens through which we are able to see into the WorldWideWeb of
Light upon which prophecy travels.

A friend described to me how he looked up at the night sky and saw
all the stars connected by tiny threads of light. He saw how this
normally invisible light was swirling constantly around our planet. But
if these are the threads of the WorldWideWeb, we still may wonder who
actually bears the messages of prophecy to us. From a shamanic or
traditional teacher's perspective we can glean some understandings
from the following words of Don Isidro, a Kekchi Maya of Guatemala.

He refers to strange kinds of creatures that feature in the *Popul Vuh*
as the bringers of prophecy. They are also to be seen in Maya art such
as the folded book known as the *Dresden Codex*, a copy of which dates
from the 15th century. In it a great horned owl appears as a bird of

omen. Apparently the lords of *Xibalba* (*Xibalbay* in Kiché) had a well-known tactic of despatching such creatures to give their messages. The exploits of the characters in the *Popul Vuh* are well known to all followers of Maya tradition and hence it is not surprising that Don Isidro tells us about these messengers. Most likely a number of key people in his community would have received similar visions. (*See Popol Vuh*, translated by Dennis Tedlock, Touchstone, New York, 1985.)

Before the start of the war (in Iraq in 2003), the visionaries and prophets had begun to talk because we received the messenger from *Xibalbay*, known as the Underworld. *Xibalbay* is not like a Christian inferno. Some that are still deeply hidden in dimensions of this underworld of *Xibalbay* have sent a strange creature called *Cablicot* as a messenger.

Its origin is as ancient as the night of time and it has as its companion *Camalzotz*. *Cablicot* is an owl with two heads and *Camalzotz* is a bat with two heads. Today, *Cablicot* has come and its words are a warning. It is a prophetic memory for these times, during which various prophecies converge, be they from Maya or other traditions. Because of its own dualistic nature, *Cablicot's* words came with the war, like a preamble. This is a special messenger that looks towards the darkness. Its head turns 360 degrees. Each of its faces looks with equanimity towards the two polarities. Its words bring a call without charge, almost like a recording. Its own essence of polarity is the message.

Don Isidro goes on to remind us of the changes we can anticipate as we approach the fifth *Ajaw* (his Kekchi word for *Ahau*, the Fifth Sun or Creation). He points out that 21 December 2012 begins a new period of 5,125 years. He says that it will be a cycle of wisdom, harmony, peace, love and consciousness, and a return to natural order. He stresses it is not the end of the world, as many from outside the Maya tradition have interpreted it.

He describes the previous Creations, stating that the first was of a feminine energy and its element was fire. The second cycle was of a masculine energy, and its element was earth. The third cycle was of a feminine energy and its element was air. The fourth cycle, our present time, is of a masculine energy and its element is water.

He indicates that the fifth cycle will come with the power of transmutation. It will bring us a time of transition where confrontations between duality, represented by the polarities of feminine and masculine energies, will be balanced. As we balance these energies they will support each other. This is why this cycle will be called one of harmony, the kingdom of love and the return of superconsciousness. Its element will be the ether.

Explaining further, Don Isidro said, 'To reach this state of supreme harmony, it will be necessary to create a balance of the forces of light and dark. This is where the importance of the call of the elders comes into place – the quest for unity, for the return of natural order. This call is urgent in the face of the prophetic times in which we are living, principally for spiritual guides and conscious people.' He also tells us that the peoples of Earth urgently need to unite to create a 'belt of light that will contrast with the negativity'. (I tried unsuccessfully on a number of occasions to contact Don Isidro personally to discuss this prophecy. You can read it for yourself on www.sacredroad.org.)

As I left Nah Chan, with the sun casting long shadows through the trees, and birds beginning to awake from their afternoon slumbers, I thanked the guardians of the place, the parakeets and the little nature spirits, the Maya *aluxes*, and headed back to our lodging in a *palapa*, a palm-thatched hut on the road from the sacred city.

That evening we listened to Alonso Mendez, a Mexican archaeo-astronomer, who explained the specific alignments of sacred buildings and the different light phenomena he had discovered within the temples of Palenque (Nah Chan). For example, a shaft of sunlight from the rising sun on 21 June enters the Temple of the Sun at an oblique angle and goes right through the centre, the very heart of the temple. He described his discoveries as examples of *hierophanies*, or as evidence of the sacred in the mundane, as coined by M Eliade (*see* Mendez' article on www.mayaexploration.org).

With a surge of excitement I realized that the ancients were still able to communicate the purpose for which the temples were designed – for the enlightenment of humanity and as a 'cosmic university'. I now also had my answers about stone markers and light phenomena left in many sacred sites throughout the world, ready for the End Times. This was a great realization. If archaeologists continue to chart the progression of such light phenomena, those who wish to study Earth's orbital changes at any time in the future will now have some very clear ground-level measurements by which to monitor them.

Part Two

The Song
of the Skulls

CHAPTER 6

Harvest of the Gourd of Ashes

Here is the oldest continuous record of human habitation on the continent outside of Mesoamerica, a habitation that has fashioned this region into a humanized landscape suffused with ancient meanings, myths and mysteries.

Anthropologist and Pueblo Indian, Alfonso Ortiz, 1939–97, *New Perspectives on the Pueblos* (University of New Mexico Press, 1972)

I n search of further insights into the Maya prophecies, I went to southwestern USA to see what I could find out about the Anasazi and the Hopi prophecies, which are not dissimilar to those of the Maya. There, to my surprise, I was given a gift, and charged with an awe-inspiring mission. After this, I returned to Mexico to visit the ancient city of Teotihuacán, where another surprise lay in wait for me.

The Plains Indians

A typical Western education teaches us to think of the 'Indians', those who lived on the wide open grassy plains of the United States, as war braves riding bareback on wild ponies, complete with feather head-dresses, bows and arrows. These outdated images, usually from the white man's viewpoint, depicted the colonizing forces as civilizing influences. Nothing could be further from the truth, since the Native American peoples were consistently and cruelly persecuted and killed by the intruders into their lands. Pictures like this, still engrained in Western consciousness, give little honour to an indigenous way of life that has survived for thousands of years; wise elders, such as Chief Sonne Reyna, Yaqui-Carrizo Coahuilteka Nations, call for them to be urgently and radically changed in order for reconciliation to begin to take place. He said in 2007, 'People are in major denial. We must redress this trauma. Healing of the modern world is determined by reconciliation of the Indian holocaust – then we can say that in our life we Spoke the Truth.' Today there are approximately 1 million Native Americans left in Canada and 2 million in the USA. Before Columbus arrived there were 5 to 10 million people, speaking over 500 languages, living in North America. Whilst war or massacres amounting to genocide killed large numbers, what mostly decimated them was the spread of European diseases, to which they had little immunity. It is estimated that a staggering 90 per cent of the indigenous population died following early contact with Europeans, sometimes even before Europeans reached them.

By and large, in the face of terrible suffering, they have managed to retain just a small fraction of their original lands, despite bribery, corruption and compromise. In the 21st century, far from further dying out, small groups of indigenous peoples carefully keep to their traditions. Once again their voices are calling out to us to heed warnings about the possible fate of Mother Earth.

Our consciences are stirred when we hear of continuing oppression. We are told by Adrian Beckingham, writing for Survival International in *Stories that Crafted the Earth* (Gothic Image, Glastonbury, UK, 2005) that 'The Indians (of North America) continue to suffer persistent racism and persecution. Conditions on most reservations and reserves are appalling. In USA, American Indians are eight times more likely to contract tuberculosis than other US citizens, and 37 per cent of all Indians die before the age of 45'. He adds that, in Canada, the suicide rate among Indian youths is five to six times the national average. Indian infant mortality, once much higher than other Canadians, is now slowly declining.

One group of Plains Indians in the southwestern USA, the Anasazi people, developed from nomadic tribes who found benefit from settling on fertile land. By 100 BCE they were cultivating corn, beans and squash. An abundance of food, together with different weather patterns from those of the present day, led to their culture and its spiritual beliefs evolving rapidly.

Some say the original Anasazi living in Chaco Canyon were early Maya people who had left their homeland in a great migration. This might explain why the Anasazi seem to have appeared from nowhere, with no traceable roots. They flourished successfully and peacefully in the canyon for around a thousand years, and then they disappeared from the area when a prolonged drought gripped Chaco Canyon from 1130 to 1180 CE. Their descendants, today's Pueblo peoples, include the Hopi, Zuni and Tewa, now numbering more than 50,000, speaking 6 languages and living in Arizona and New Mexico.

I left the lands of the Maya and travelled north into the USA. I then undertook the long scorching journey to Chaco Canyon, a gorge about 22 miles (35km) long and several miles wide. It was well worth the arduous journey and the lengthy walk, for in places the sandstone cliffs rise majestically more than 150ft (50m), with hot wind-sculpted natural 'temples' shimmering in the sunlight.

Suddenly, in what seemed a vision from the past, the fascinating ancient dwellings at Pueblo Bonito came into view. More than 650 cave-like rooms were cut, one above the other, into the copper-coloured sandstone of the cliffs in the canyon. These were once home to the mysterious Anasazi people. It was appropriate, in this time-worn landscape of burning sun and windy peaks, that an unusual story should emerge from the Threads of Time Past, that was to take me far into the future.

The Anasazi built special places for healing and communal ceremonies. Called *kivas*, they were made of a circular stone and mud wall that was roofed over, sometimes as much as 45ft (16m) in diameter. Each pueblo (village) in the canyon has numerous *kivas* within it, now in ruins, that were ceremonially used over 1,000 years ago. Today's Hopi people of Oraibi, Arizona, still use *kivas*, giving us a living link to the past on the Threads of Time. It is clear from the birth and creation ceremonies they enact within *kivas* that the *kiva* itself is representative of the Earth Mother.

The Hopi say that we are living in the fourth of seven ages, the Fourth World. Their wise ones recall traditional stories which teach that the First World ended by fire, the Second ended with floods and ice when the Earth became unbalanced and rolled over twice, and the Third World ended in a great flood. They describe the changeover from one world to another as an 'emergence' and it is symbolized by a labyrinth/spiral pattern and also by the *kiva* itself. Every *kiva* has a hole in the floor that is revered as the emergence point (called *sipapu*) into the Third World. The ladder to the hole in the roof is the emergence point into the present Fourth World.

Each year in November a special New Fire Ceremony is still enacted by modern Hopi, along with an emergence ceremony called *Wuwuchim* that takes initiates through a kind of spiritual rebirth. Many people gather for the ceremonies, packed into the *kiva* like a flock of colourful birds at a waterhole in a desert. Their traditional dresses are resplendent with feathers, turquoise and bone jewellery.

Everyone is watching and waiting for a special moment. Peering up through the hole in the roof they study the display of stars in the cold night sky, spread above them like a diamond-studded dark cloak. As soon as a very special cluster of stars, the Pleiades, appears and stands directly overhead in the velvety blackness, encircled by the roof hole, the ceremony culminates with everyone rushing and trying to get up the *kiva's* ladder to the outside – being reborn, before the world symbolically ends.

I wondered how many years these ceremonies had been enacted. How did the ancestors really live? How did they speak to the gods and the stars that they said had birthed them? How did they cope with adversity in their simple lives? We know for certain that times past were hard and there were good and bad years. The rains did not always come. In our 21st-century comfort we have little understanding of the effects of drought and disease in such circumstances but, from what is known of them, here is a little cameo of their daily life.

Each year Anasazi people prepared to plant their special coloured corn, of which the blue is the most prized. To assist its growth they undertook ceremonies and painted symbolic pictures on the walls of the *kivas* as auspicious signs of abundance. In the pueblo, in little plazas, people sold or exchanged their leatherwork, turkeys and beans, with prized macaw feathers and shells brought by traders from the south.

Alongside their mud-brick houses they cut out a patchwork of vegetable plots in the sandy soil. They covered these plots with gravel to retain moisture and repel the grey-green mass of sage, tumbleweed and cholla cactus, ever ready to take hold.

Women and children made frequent treks to the river to fill their water jars. Each evening, when the vermilion sun cast long shadows and dipped below the canyon walls, dusk softened the hard land into silence and families gathered around their cooking fires, as they had for centuries. Stories were told late into the night of Turkey and Owl, Rattlesnake and Opossum and the children's favourite Rabbit. Rabbit is the Trickster and perhaps the only one who really knows how *this* world will end.

The *Kiva*

The Pueblo peoples see themselves as being inextricably woven into the natural scheme of the entire universe. They are not simply pieces of bone and flesh, not simply possessors of certain faculties. They are those things, but they are also of the sands, the winds, the stars, the plants and grasses, the thunder, lightning, rain, the Sun and the Moon and the seasons – everything that is born and lives and dies in the eternal cycle of life.

Historian John Upton Terrell, ***American Indian Almanac,***
(Ty Crowell Co., USA, 1971)

I sat inside an old *kiva* with a broken-down roof, enjoying its soft coolness, a shady respite from the ruthless flaming sun of this treeless landscape. I tried to imagine how the Anasazi survived. It is known that there was a system for collecting rainwater running off the cliffs and that the priests tracked the solstices, keeping accurate calendars for plantings and ceremonies. At one time, researchers tell us, there would have been much more rainfall than at present.

Relaxing my back against the dry mud wall, memories held in the timeless sacred space of the *kiva* began seeping into my bones. Images passed across my mind's eye and I remembered a Zuni myth about rain, originally recorded at the end of the 19th century. It tells why the Anasazi abandoned their high cliff dwellings in Chaco Canyon.

A terrible giant called Cloud Swallower devoured the poor men, women and children, consuming the cloud breaths of the beloved gods and the souls of the dead, whence descend the rains. From all the directions of their sacred medicine wheel came change; the welcome snows ceased in the north and the west, rain ceased in the south and the east; the mists on the mountains above were drunk up and the waters of the valleys below were sucked dry.

Fortunately other beneficial and powerful supernatural spirits, the twin gods of war and Grandmother Spider, destroyed the dread Swallower of Clouds, but fearing that never again would the waters refresh their canyons and fill their pitchers, the ancient peoples who dwelt in the cliffs fled southward and eastward – all save those who had perished aforetime. They are dead in their homes in the cliff towns, desiccated, dried up like their cornstalks that shrivelled and died when the rain stopped long, long ago, when all things were new.

As I moved my position and become more comfortable I got a sense, a shamanic form of 'second attention' or *seeing*, of those ancient ones still sitting unseen in tiny cliff houses – the dead abandoned by the living. In the unbearable skin-drying heat, I imagined what their shrunken, starved bodies and gaunt skin-taut faces would look like; hands set in grim torturous positions with fingers pointing accusingly at the fortunate ones who had left.

A sudden wind stirring a bunch of tumbleweed outside startled me and caused me to look up to where part of the *kiva* roof was broken away. I saw a face silhouetted against the brilliant turquoise blue of the sky. No ghost had slipped through the Threads of Time – instead it was a friendly, living face looking down on me.

An elderly woman, traditionally dressed in white and red, came slowly down the ladder into the *kiva*, lowering her old bones carefully, rung by rung. Smiling, I indicated I would welcome her to sit beside me on the earthen floor, joining me in meditation. Time passed, the afternoon wore on and, apart from each of us taking a drop of water, we continued to be in silent reflection. Then just as the sky began changing into the colour of fresh blood the woman turned to me, asking if I knew about the White Buffalo. I replied that I knew a little, about the constellation of Orion's belt being known to the Sioux people as the Heart of the White Buffalo.

At this point she took up my words with: 'In August 1994 a white buffalo was born in Wisconsin, USA. Two more were born in May 1996 in South Dakota. One died but the other lived. I have spoken to many wise men and women of my tribe about this and what it could mean. The Sioux holy men have told me that, as we move into the future, it will be very difficult for all humanity. Many have foretold of disaster, few of hope. Black Elk, a great Sioux visionary who died over 50 summers ago, foresaw the joining together of the world's nations, into what he called the Sacred Hoop – a reference to the thousand years of peace that is to follow the third "world shaking".'

I looked puzzled, not sure what she meant by 'world shaking', but she continued, looking deep into my eyes. 'The Legend of the White Buffalo says that a beautiful sacred young maiden brought a holy pipe to be used by the Sioux in ceremony. Although she looked human she was really a space sister, an interdimensional traveller, and because of this she could not stay long in the human world. So she soon prepared to leave, saying that she would return again when needed to help the people, if they were in trouble and turmoil. As she walked away she miraculously changed. First she turned into a black buffalo, then a red buffalo, then a yellow buffalo and finally into a white buffalo. Immediately after this, people watched as she disappeared back up into the clouds. Since that time the old and wise ones in the pueblos, knowing that we are indeed in turbulent times, have watched for prophetic signs and awaited her rebirth in the form of a white buffalo.'

The woman turned to me, barely visible, her eyes as pools of light in the darkening *kiva*, saying, 'I think you understand this now.' I thought about the colours of the buffaloes and those miraculous happenings. I knew that this account fitted in perfectly with Medicine Wheel and Sacred Hoop teachings. It was a clever way of teaching that the buffalo and the people of the four human races, the black, red, yellow and white are one, just as all the colours are part of Buffalo Calf Woman.

Really, nothing is separate in the Sacred Hoop of life. We are all connected within it, for what we do to one has an effect on the many. We are all one in the One Heart of the WorldWideWeb, woven from light, becoming ever more apparent on a global level through individual spiritual awakenings, positive communication, global health policies, disaster relief and many other things.

The old woman gently took my pale hands in her leathery wrinkled palms, turning them over, peering deeply and examining them carefully. She said, 'I foresee a long and interesting life for you, and I know that you love the Earth upon which we walk. When I smoke the pipe of peace and part the tangled strands of time I can see that we have been together in the past. Now, my time here is nearly over. When I leave I want you to look after something that is in my medicine bundle.' She pointed to a tattered old bag on the ground across the other side of the *kiva*.

'It is something that you need to treasure, for you are the one who will take it to the End of Time.' I reached across and squeezed her bony hand in thanks.

Lifting up the heavy, tattered, old brown hide bag, pulled together with string, I was very curious, wondering what could possibly be within. I began to untie it. Just as I finished, a sudden cooling rush of wind spiralled down into the *kiva* from above. Looking up, through the birth hole, I sensed that the woman had gone, just disappeared, and I was left holding ... a crystal skull!

Amazed, I held the heavy, clear quartz skull in my hands, marvelling at its coolness and the play of light within it. I was quite bemused. It was one of those moments when time itself seemed to stand still. Then, suddenly aware of the lateness of the hour, I hurriedly put the crystal skull back into the bag and rushed from the *kiva* into the ever-darkening night sky.

The Hopi Prophecies and the Harvest of the Gourd of Ashes

War will exist until that day when the conscientious
objector enjoys the same reputation and prestige that
the warrior does today.

J F Kennedy, US president, 1960–63

Leaving Chaco Canyon with the crystal skull I was somewhat mystified
as to how this heavy old object might help me in my quest to
understand prophecy, the End of Time and the year 2012 predictions.
I needed to know more. So I began to seek more information about
crystal skulls, but all the while I kept the existence of the skull I had
completely secret.

I would take myself off to any quiet place I could find. Away from
family and friends back home, I sometimes sat for hours. But nothing
seemed to be revealed to me. So I began to assume there might be some
connection for me in the creation myths of the Maya which, as I have
already mentioned, record how humanity was blinded. Blindness was
imposed on us when we became too clever for our own good and forgot
to honour the ancient creator gods.

The whole story is recounted in the fourth part of the Kiché Maya
book of creation myths, the *Popul Vuh*, which said 'They were blinded
as the face of a mirror is breathed upon'. Of course this blindness is not
a blindness of our physical eyes but of our inner eye and our
connection to our spiritual selves. At or after year 2012 the Maya
prophesy that we will lose the blindness that the old gods imposed
upon humanity.

Was it because I was 'blinded' that I couldn't feel anything of
value in the skull? I needed a formula to enable me to lose this
blindness! I decided to research and carefully cross-reference the alternative history of the world – the stories not explored in schoolbooks.

I chose to heed the wise words of living indigenous people who
have kept true to their own prophetic traditions. So the next source of
wisdom I turned to was that of the Hopi of Oraibi, Arizona, known

throughout their lands as 'the peaceful people'. They too recognize that the natural world is at a fragile moment of truth. Their elders speak with integrity and sincerity, asking us to listen to messages coming directly from Mother Earth.

In the process of losing my own 'blindness' I realized that there is an importance in acting with passion – the kind of passion for life that will secure a precious future on Earth in the way that the elders express it, 'To make a world fit for our grandchildren's children'.

So my quest next took me to the Four Corners area of Arizona, as it seemed important to meet the peaceful Hopi. Perhaps they would have more information for me, especially about prophecies. I had a strong calling to go there since the most famous and most discussed of all the prophecies that have been given in the last 50 years or so are those originating from them. Searching amongst all the distractions of modern living I found the Hopi people.

They continue to live upon their own lands, resolutely defending their traditions and language after centuries of oppression. More recently they have suffered the polluting effects of coal mining and government schooling policies that took children away from their homes and families. In the presence of great adversity the Hopis' determination and independence have become an example to inspire other Native American nations.

Fortunately *Maasaw* their god, both a creator and destroyer of all things, enjoys continuing celebration in their stories, songs and ceremonial dance. At the beginning of time he instructed the people to maintain simple lives. *Maasaw* taught that when we die all our ancestors are waiting in a lower world to greet us. They regularly leave their spirit home below to visit us as raindrops. They float up into the sky and become clouds whose rain restores the fertility of the Earth.

I saw how the uncomplicated Hopi cycle of life and death has been disrupted by the invading white man. Elders continue to predict that, when the heart of the Hopi Land Trust (their reservation) is dug up, with mining or oil extraction, then great disturbances will develop in the balance of nature. 'Because Hopi land is holy land, it is a microcosmic image of the entire planet, and any violations of nature in the Hopi Oraibi Four Corners region of the US will be reflected and amplified all over the Earth.'

This teaching has the meaning of *what we do to the Earth we do to ourselves*. Furthermore, if the movement of the Earth is displaced and Oraibi disappears, the cycle of Hopi life will be broken – as *Maasaw* warned, the oceans will swallow all the lands like a sea of dead souls. If all the ice of Antarctica and the Arctic melts, worldwide sea levels will rise 70ft (25m). Impossible? At the end of the Ice Age the sea rose 600ft (200m) in three bursts or floods, around 12000 BCE, 9000 BCE and 5000 BCE and, in the final flood, not so long ago in human history, it rose 60ft (20m).

Reading indigenous prophecies is not always easy – they are sometimes couched in symbolic language and are difficult to comprehend. On the Hopi Reservation in Arizona there is a sandstone cliff, near Second Mesa (a flat-topped mountain), and upon it is carved a picture of their people's past, present and future history. This sacred site is more commonly known as Hopi Prophecy Rock.

One stone carving or petroglyph pictures the Hopi people emerging from underground, up to the surface of the Earth, like ants, at the beginning of this Fourth Creation. This is why the emergence ceremony that I previously described takes place in a *kiva*, a symbolic womb. The exact location where this event is said to have happened at the beginning of this Fourth World is in the Grand Canyon.

The story on Prophecy Rock continues by showing how the leading clans of the Hopi migrated in four directions, east, west, north and south. After many years of journeying, they were destined to return to the centre. Only one group completed their journey – to the North Pole and back – under the guidance of a brilliant 'star' in which Great Spirit *Massaw* travelled, now transformed into a man.

Upon landing, he drew that petroglyph picture on Second Mesa, showing a maiden riding in a wingless, dome-shaped craft and signifying the coming Day of Purification. *Massaw* called the land where he landed Oraibi, saying, 'It shall be your home, and your name will be Hopi.' When all the people who had scattered in the four directions finally reach the real spiritual centre, it is prophesied that it will be the end of this Fourth Creation.

The Sioux Nation bring attention to their creation stories by saying that, at the beginning, they emerged from underground at a place in the Black Hills known today as Wind Cave. Like the Hopi, they travelled in four directions after emerging. Their tradition records that humanity has evolved through four ages – the Age of Fire, Age of Rock, Age of the Bow and the Age of the Pipe. Although the length of each age is unknown, the prophecy states that toward the end of each age, humanity would gradually become 'two-heart'.

Hopi Prophecy Rock also, interestingly, draws our attention to three 'two-heart' individuals. Interpreting petroglyphs and, for that matter, all glyphs is not solely the prerogative of academic experts. Reaching back through the timelines as a 'sensitive' I believe they have another message: the two-hearted person organizes his or her life through the head rather than the heart, relying heavily on analytical thinking. Put simply, their heart is ruled by their head, hence they become 'two-hearted'. This is symbolic of the effects of cultural hypnosis on modern humanity, where our largely left-brained society is out of balance. The drawings of 'two heart' people are a warning to care for our intuitive side and adopt a one-hearted, centred mode.

Prophecy Rock shows a point where two-hearted people have a choice: to choose whether to think with their hearts or to continue to think solely with their heads. If they choose their heads, it will lead to self-destruction. If they choose to think with their hearts they will return gradually to natural ways and their own survival.

On Prophecy Rock three circles represent three 'world-shakings'. The Hopi say the majority of people have lost their ancient understanding of how we are all related. Because of this the Creator, Great Spirit, will cause three major 'world-shakings', to remind everyone on the planet of our relatedness and how we are codependent.

They profess that the first world-shaking would be recognized 'when a bug on ribbon is tossed into the air'. This is interpreted as an airplane or glider. The time when airplanes were first used in war was World War I, so that shocking event was interpreted as the first world-shaking.

They told that the second world-shaking would be recognized when man used the Hopi migration symbol in war (a swastika, but reversed). This occurred during World War II. Next, a mysterious object called a 'gourd full of ashes', was referred to in the Hopi prophecies.

Many believe this was the detonation of the first atomic bomb on Japan, or perhaps its testing in the American Southwest. A respected Oglala Sioux holy man, Nicholas Black Elk, also foresaw and prophesied the coming of World Wars I and II.

But, according to the prophecies, all is not yet ended. The coming third world-shaking will be recognized by a red cover or cloak. When collecting the prophecies I was clearly told that Westerners should not speculate upon their meanings. The Hopi Prophecy also indicates that the following signs would foretell the impending third world-shaking:

1. Trees die;

2. Man builds a house in the sky;

3. Cold places will become hot. Hot places will become cold;

4. Lands will sink into the ocean and lands will rise out of the sea;

5. There will be an appearance of the Blue Star Kachina.

> Sourced from *The Book of the Hopi*, Frank Waters
> (Ballantine Books, 1963).
> These are Thomas Banyacya's (1910–99) words. Also from
> www.welcomehome.org/rainbow/prophecy/bayanaca.html.

The final stage of the Hopi Prophecy, called the 'Day of Purification', is described as the hatching of a 'mystery egg'. No one really seems to know what this can mean. But it is said the Hopi are alert and watching for certain signs to indicate that this day is about to arrive.

One such example, thought to be a signal, was on 7 August 1970, when a spectacular UFO sighting was witnessed by dozens of people and photographed by Chuck Roberts of the *Prescott Courier*, USA. This occurred after a 'UFO calling' by several Hopi and was interpreted by some of them as being a partial fulfilment of the message of an inscribed stone on Second Mesa. It warns of a coming 'Purification Day', when true Hopi will be flown to other planets in 'ships without wings'.

I was told that elders loyal to the Oraibi covenant should be consulted if I wanted to know more about the Hopi Way.

That evening I sat on a rocky outcrop in the desert, watching the sunset changing the sands to flaming orange, with rocks casting deep violet shadows. Reading a little, but mostly deep in thought, I found I needed caution as I read the following Native American teaching:

Do not put one foot in the red man's canoe and one foot in the white man's boat since the ancestors foretold that a great wind would arise and tear the canoe and boat away from each other. Those people who have one foot in the canoe and one foot in the boat are going to fall into the river and no power this side of Creation can save them.

Nine Prophetic Signs

I sat in a breakfast diner sipping coffee as an old Native American, grey hair pulled back to reveal still fine features, slapped a leaflet on my table. 'The Nine Prophetic Signs of the Hopi', I read.

This is the First Sign: we were told of the coming of the white-skinned men, like our great being *Pahana*, but not living like *Pahana* – men who took the land that was not theirs and who struck their enemies with thunder (guns).

This is the Second Sign: our lands will see the coming of spinning wheels filled with voices (covered wagons).

This is the Third Sign: a strange beast like a buffalo but with great long horns, will overrun the land in large numbers (longhorn cattle).

This is the Fourth Sign: the land will be crossed by snakes of iron (railroad tracks).

This is the Fifth Sign: the land shall be criss-crossed by a giant spider's web (power and telephone lines).

This is the Sixth Sign: the land shall be criss-crossed

with rivers of stone that make pictures in the sun
(concrete roads, with their mirage-producing effects).

This is the Seventh Sign: you will hear of the sea turning
black, and many living things dying because of it (oil
spills).

This is the Eighth Sign: you will see many youths, who
wear their hair long like our people, who come and join
the tribal nations, to learn our ways and wisdom
(spiritual seekers).

This is the Ninth and Last Sign: you will hear of a
dwelling-place in the heavens, above the Earth, that
shall fall with a great crash. It will appear as a blue star.
Very soon after this, the ceremonies of the Hopi people
will cease.

My hands were shaking as I realized what this foretells.

The leaflet went on to say: 'These are the signs that great destruction is here: the world shall rock to and fro. The white man will battle people in other lands – those who possessed the first light of wisdom. There will be many columns of smoke and fire such as the white man has made in the deserts not far from here.'

A shiver ran down my spine as I thought of the atomic weapons testing that has been hidden in the deserts of the American Southwest. But I read on: 'Those who stay and live in the places of the Hopi shall be safe. Then there will be much to rebuild.'

I ordered another long, strong coffee. 'After the great destruction *Pahana* is expected to return, bringing with him the dawn of the Fifth World. Even now he is planting seeds of wisdom in our hearts that will smooth the way to the emergence into the Fifth World.'

Here the leaflet ended, making a recommendation that the best way to understand these signs would be to read them through and, if you were so inclined, prepare yourself to undertake a series of profound meditations over the course of nine days.

Understanding prophecy is a lifetime journey of traditional study by those of the red races. Indigenous peoples believe they have a sacred duty to preserve their spirituality – it must never be bought or sold. They are custodians, inheriting spiritual teachings from their ancestors and holding them in trust for their descendants. Therefore many Plains Indian peoples are both saddened and angry that white man is again taking from them, even trying to steal their spirituality.

Yet others are speaking out openly and sharing their prophecies with the world, hence this call to awaken from the cultural hypnosis of materialism. The release to the public of the nine signs may not be the wish of all traditional Hopi, but since they are freely available on the internet and they are of great importance to understand, I included them in this section.

Prophecy of the Return of Great White Brother

The entire Hopi Prophecy, which I have related in part, is said to take many days to tell and many lifetimes to understand. I first heard about the Prophecy of the Return of the Great White Brother years ago in England. It was by chance – and what is chance? – that I met someone whose mission while she lived in USA was to assist Hopi elders to find him.

She told me, 'The Great White Brother is the teacher of the new time. It has long been said that life-and-death matters will be determined when this White Brother, *Pahana*, appears from the east. Theories abound as to who he will be. There are a number of tests that this White Brother will need to pass in order to satisfy the Hopi people that he is the true White Brother *Pahana*.'

Continuing, she said, 'The story takes us back to the end of the last and the beginning of this world (from a Hopi perspective). Many thousands of years ago, a small number of Hopi, survivors of the Great Deluge, had managed to live almost completely in accordance with the Divine Plan. Whilst Earth was settling into a more balanced pattern, these people, who numbered amongst them the ancestors of the present-day Hopi, set off on a long migration to find lands in which to settle.'

'They split up into four groups, didn't they?,' I asked.

She replied in detail, 'Before their migration commenced special rocks, called Hopi Clan Rocks, were given out to each of the groups who comprised the four races of humanity.' I realized that these races, with skins of the colours of red, white, black and yellow, are the same people that the Maya talk about in their teachings.

'The four groups then set off in all four directions seeking good lands in which to live.'

'But where are the Clan Rocks now?' I questioned.

Lowering her voice so that other people in the room would not hear, she replied, looking cautiously around as she spoke, 'They are in safe keeping within the following locations: those of the red race are in the Hopi land of Oraibi; those of the white race are in Switzerland; those of the black race are in the Kilimanjaro mountain area of Africa and those of the yellow race are in Tibet.'

Becoming quite agitated now, and her voice dropping even more she told me, 'Each rock had a plus sign and a minus sign on it, with a circle. These symbols represent positive, negative and neutral forces in a magnetic field, and where they cross over is a vortex – like a stargate – into the next dimension.'

She continued to recount the prophecy, 'A light-skinned Hopi, called *Pahana* the True White Brother, went off into the direction of the rising sun, promising to return. He had a very special stone tablet which would help to identify him in the future. It matched one still held by present-day Hopi. Up until a few years ago this Hopi tablet was in the safekeeping of respected Elder Grandfather Titus Lambson, who then gave two pieces of a tablet to his son in a ceremony.'

Her voice lowered to a whisper, 'I have heard recently that the tablets were taken from him.'

I thought, 'Let's hope that they are still in good hands.'

Then she would say no more. 'I have said too much already,' she told me, again looking around nervously to check that we had not been overheard.

Before embarking on my next journey I delved further into this prophecy. Part of it told of a whole race of white-skinned people that would arrive from the east, causing danger to the Hopi – this sounds remarkably like the invading white settlers and present-day corporations that threaten the Hopi partition lands. However, their elders were to watch and wait patiently, for the True White Brother carrying the stone tablet would give proof that he had not left the traditional spiritual path.

Hopi of past centuries wondered whether he could have been a Spaniard or an Anglo-Saxon. They devised tests for determining his true identity. These tests included knowledge of the special greeting of brotherhood, similarities of religious beliefs and possession of the missing piece(s) of the stone tablet(s). Over the years many people were tested, including Catholics, Baptists and Mormons, but none has yet passed to the satisfaction of traditional Hopi.

Sometime after leaving the Hopi region I pulled my car off the road, screeching to a sudden stop. I just had to get out and walk into the desert. Something out there was calling me. I rushed off, almost tripping over in my haste. Finally I stopped my wild directionless dash across the rough terrain. I sat down and decided to take the crystal skull from my day sack. It felt old, worn and very heavy. *Why, it's heavy with information*, I realized, and held it up to the setting sun. The crystalline matrix lit up as I recalled the words of one elder: 'The whole world will shake and turn red, turning against those who are hindering the Hopi.'

Many people I have spoken to say that the Hopi play a key role in the survival of the human race, through their vital communion with unseen forces that hold nature in balance. I felt it was about time to begin working in some way with my crystal skull, now positively glowing with a strong crimson light.

Far from alleviating any fears that I had about coming times, this strangely glowing skull was scary. My meditation was short and intense as, with a heavy heart, I was hoping against hope that the True White Brother would return one day soon and in some way restore peace to this troubled Earth.

Something caused me to look up as I walked back across the edge of the desert to my car, to continue my journey to fulfil the request of the old woman who had left me the skull in the *kiva*. One would think that a desert would be quiet, but even here there were sounds of animals foraging, merging almost imperceptibly into the cool approaching night. A soft movement of air swept past and, seemingly from nowhere, a large owl swooped over my head. The owl called out and, ever watchful of nature, I knew that this was a sure sign from the ancestors.

Black Elk Speaks

At this juncture I was reminded of the famous prophetic words of Black Elk, an Oglala Sioux, describing the vision he had at Harney Peak:

> Then I was standing on the highest mountain of them all, and round about beneath me was the whole hoop of the world. While I stood there I saw more than I can tell and I understood more than I saw; for I was seeing in a sacred manner the shapes of all things in the spirit, and the shape of all shapes as they must live together like one being.
>
> I saw that the sacred hoop of my people was one of many hoops that made one circle, wide as daylight and as starlight, and in the centre grew one mighty flowering tree to shelter all the children of one mother and one father, and I saw that it was holy.

Black Elk was an Oglala Sioux medicine man, born in 1862. He became known to many people in 1932 through the book *Black Elk Speaks – the Life Story of a Holy Man of the Oglala Sioux*, by John G Neihardt (University of Nebraska Press, reprinted 2000). Black Elk personally knew the old days when his people still freely rode the open plains and hunted bison. He was a great warrior who fought against the white men at the battles of Little Bighorn and Wounded Knee Creek, before he came to Europe as part of Buffalo Bill's travelling show.

But Black Elk was not cut out to be an entertainer. He was a wise elder who received many prophetic visions that he used for the good of his people. Shortly before his death in 1950 Black Elk shared the Seven Rites, given to the Sioux through visions, with J E Brown, who recorded them in the book *The Sacred Pipe* (Penguin, 1971), in order that 'They will realize that we Indians know the One true God, and that we pray to Him continually'.

Lembal

After I left the Hopi and whilst researching their prophecies I hardly looked again at the crystal skull. It remained wrapped in the old leather bag in which it had been gifted to me, stuffed into the bottom of my rucksack.

Travelling back to Mexico on a long-distance coach I decided to read more about the skulls (*see* Appendix 5). I found that a few have been discovered in the lands of the Maya. The most famous is a quartz skull called the Anna Mitchell-Hedges Skull. Others have almost certainly been hidden safely away by tradition-keepers and only brought out for special ceremonies and initiations. Maya people, and others such as the Navajo and Seneca, all say that crystal skulls are sacred, figuring prominently in their myths and ancient traditions.

The *heyoehkah* (shamans) of the Cherokee nation recount stories of the times when a number of crystal skulls were kept together in an 'Ark'. They believed it had been kept within a cave in Teotihuacán, Mexico, reputed to be the first city built in the Americas. Stories tell that the skulls were there right up until the time when Cortés landed. Upon hearing word that the Spanish Conquistadors were about to seize them, together with all the gold they could lay their hands upon, indigenous leaders took the skulls away. Shamans say they were hidden until such time as their *lembal* (the knowledge encoded within them) would be needed. Givers of ancestral prophecy would agree that time is now!

The Prophecy of the Crystal Skulls

I read that life-size crystal skulls, most often miraculously hand-carved from one piece of quartz, and less commonly from amethyst or other hard natural crystal, possess very special properties. Extraordinary claims are made about them. Sometimes the crystal skull has a separate moveable jawbone of crystal. These are considered by the elders to be very ancient skulls that can 'sing', because the lower jaw opens.

At last I was finding a real connection, a resonance, between these ancient artefacts, the bringers of prophecy, and us! After all, it is in our skull that higher centres of perception are housed, not to mention the pineal gland, master orchestrator of our hormonal and immune balance.

My research suggested that Maya shamans were aware of the symbolism of skulls right from the beginning of their grand culture, as if it was an important mythic memory for them. Indeed, I heard claims the crystal skulls are 100,000 years old! Thirteen original crystal skulls are thought to exist. I was told that the last time all of them were together was in the 15th century, in a secret location in the mountains of Oaxaca, Mexico. When placed together in a circle, the 13th skull in some unknown way activates the others.

Wow, I thought, perhaps my crystal skull is that powerful too. As this idea came, I suddenly got a direct communication from it. My head exploded with a burst of stars. I saw the face of the Indian brave that I had met in the mirror. The skull (or was it the Indian?) communicated to me the huge and weighty responsibility that I now carried – as a guardian of a crystal skull.

I was 'told' that if you are fortunate enough to be the keeper of a crystal 'singing skull' it is not only a great responsibility but you must know that it is extremely powerful when used as a tool to activate super-consciousness. As the years went by I did realize its power and understood the reason many keepers of skulls use them as meditation devices, placed in the centre of a meditation circle. Only occasionally would they allow them to be held by individuals who wished to go deeper into their symbolism and hidden powers.

A number of mysterious stories exist connecting crystal skulls with the original unknown people who built the great city of Teotihuacán, in an arid valley in central Mexico. Travel the 30 miles (48km) northeast from Mexico City and even today you will see more lizards and clumps of cacti than people. The Teotihuacános, numbering some 100,000 to 200,000, appeared for a short span of history, constructed huge pyramids and temples, accurately aligning them as solar 'clocks' and pointers to the positions of the planets. Around 750 CE, like the Maya at a later date, they just disappeared from the Threads of Time. Unlike the Maya, they left no stones with language or hieroglyphs upon them. So the original name or detailed history of those who were named Teotihuacános by the Aztecs is not known.

The end of their 500-year civilization was precipitated by a great fire that swept through the vast city, causing the collapse of elegant buildings decorated with accomplished artwork. What was left for the future was evidence of their peaceful and religious way of life – spacious dwelling compounds with drainage systems, temples and enormous pyramid monuments. Under the massive main pyramid, as high as a 20-storey building, made of earth faced with adobe mud and stone and dedicated to the sun, lies a natural cave.

Perhaps it is that same cave that Cherokee *heyoehkahs* talk about. I wondered what yet-to-be-uncovered secret this cave holds. Was it the real reason for building the pyramid? A sun mask in the form of a skull faces out toward the two-mile long Avenue of the Dead which passes it and, in turn, guards the way into this cave. It has survived to this present day.

I began to question people I met. Was this cave a secret 'place of the skulls'? Did all 13 skulls manifest into earthly existence there, sent from other life forms in the galaxy, as the myths relate? Is it possible that the 13 skulls alternate between being visible and invisible, and is that why people on Earth keep searching for all of them but can't find them?

Because skull images have associations with death, I asked whether the Avenue of the Dead was really the Avenue of the Skulls. And will we have a final realization about them in December 2012?

In answer, I was told that the astronomers of old, who worked closely with architects to map out the city of Teotihuacán, although they were not Maya, were aware of a particular cosmic significance that Maya sages once knew about. They arranged the avenue so that it was precisely orientated to the rising point of the Pleiades on 13 August 3114 BCE, the start date of the Maya calendar and the beginning of the current Fourth Creation.

In addition they had placed the carving of a skull like a pointer. Looking across the Avenue of the Dead, it indicated the place on the horizon where the Pleiades stars set. The whole length of the avenue is a reminder of this Maya cosmology, which connects the Pleiades to *T'zeb*, the Tail of the Rattlesnake or, as more often graphically depicted in this region of present-day Mexico, the Feathered Serpent Quetzalcoatl.

Significantly, this same 3114 BCE alignment of the Pleiades does not occur again until that familiar day of 21 December 2012 CE. This date marks the end of 144,000 days of the Thirteenth Baktun in the Long Count calendar and prophesies the end of this Fourth Maya Creation.

Now it was vitally important for me to get to Teotihuacán, named by the later Aztecs 'the abode of the gods'. I was sure, in my excitement for the quest, that I would discover more about my heavy old crystal skull there.

The Place of the Skull – Teotihuacán, Mexico

I arrived at the excavated remains of the vast sacred city just as a group of white-clad people, dancers, musicians and brightly dressed shamans ceremonially walked the long Avenue of the Dead to the Pyramid of the Sun. Others were joining them as they approached the steps leading up. A smile and a wave from one of the throng of participants encouraged my husband and me to join in. The ceremony progressed on to the flat platform atop the long sweep of steps.

Then a woman shaman motioned for me to step forward, saying, 'You have something for us'. With a jolt I realized she meant the crystal skull that I had only that morning transferred to my day sack, preferring not to leave it in my hotel room. She told me to put my skull on an altar that had been set up on the pyramid.

'We have been waiting for you,' she said mysteriously. How could she know I was coming? Only my husband knew my travel plans. As I drew closer I saw that on the altar were a number of other crystal skulls – two were clear quartz and others, that were smaller, were in all kinds of different coloured crystal. I was asked to place my skull with the two large clear ones. A fire priestess, dressed in red traditional clothes, approached the altar and began wafting fragrant copal incense over the skulls.

The woman shaman continued the ceremony, calling on the powers of the four directions and then presenting my skull to the other two larger skulls. That was a surprise! Clearly she valued it highly. I couldn't tell you what happened the rest of the time, for I seemed to go into a kind of a trance. I was transfixed to the spot.

As the ceremony ended, the group I was standing with became very excited, talking quickly and pointing in the sky to the east. They were repeatedly saying a Spanish word – *ovnis* – that I didn't understand. Feeling rather left out, I made my way carefully down the uneven stone steps.

Afterwards I spoke to the two people who were guardians of the chief crystal skulls used in the ceremony. I was told, 'The crystal skulls have many esoteric properties. When placed together in the darkness and interacting with human psychic energy, a coherent energy field of light manifests around the skulls. It means that they shine with light created by photons in an ordered, coherent pattern. This manner of creating light within darkness or, more properly, within the absence of light, is similar to the abilities of ancient yogis sitting in their dark caves. Experienced interdimensional travellers use this light to access other realities and fields of consciousness.'

I remembered that recent investigations of 'bioluminescence' have demonstrated the unique therapeutic properties of coherent polarized light. In pioneering work, a type of energy generator is used, producing a particular light field that has healing qualities, as well as unaccountable time anomalies in the Threads of Time, held within the light field. Without technical knowledge of the energy generator, I questioned my new-found friends, 'Could a crystal skull be capable of being programmed, to create a similar effect?'

They answered, 'Traditional inhabitants of Turtle Island believe that crystal skulls were programmed by the ancients under the guidance of extraterrestrials. They used light, much in the way scientists now program the very small, clear and perfect silicon quartz chips used in all our modern technology.' I could just imagine the quantity of information that could be held within a 'chip' the size of a skull!

Modern ways to access information in crystal skulls include using meditation. Sensitive people have found they have spontaneously begun to channel a particular type of language, unknown on this planet. Some sounds within it are similar to a few present-day Mayan words and its frequency causes a resonance to be set up between a person's own bones and the crystal skull.

Star Johnsen-Moser (USA), keeper of a crystal skull called *Xamuk'u*, says, 'The Sacred Languages of Light contain words of power, mantras, encoded keys that unlock and activate circuitries or ancient pathways of consciousness that have been programmed inside certain sacred objects and within the ruins of ceremonial sites by our ancestors, ancient records for reawakening and re-establishing communion with the higher evolution' (from an unpublished, undated publication and private discussions).

Other people with psychic abilities have alleged that another beautiful crystal skull named Max is around 36,000 years old. They say that all the genuine ancient crystal skulls are 'record keepers' that will enable us to retrace our way back to our 'home' in the stars.

Ovnis

Crowds were gathering around a troupe of Aztec dancers performing a lively dance. They all wore feathers in their hair and bunches of seashells on their ankles that rattled as they jumped around to the beat of a tall traditional drum.

Another group of ceremonialists, dressed totally in white and gold, had come all the way from Argentina to be here at Teotihuacán. With them was a leader they obviously found charismatic; young, slim and, to some, handsome with his dark hair bleached blonde and, I could swear, baby-blue contact lenses. Not surprisingly most of his group were women!

He gathered them in a circle, swaying like lilies, at the foot of the Pyramid of the Sun. Standing in the centre of his admirers, then looking intensely at each person in turn, he went up to them, whispered a few words – a mixture of Spanish and a language I didn't know – and repeated the word 'ovnis' over and over again. Then with his forefinger he touched the person's head at the third eye chakra and, at that moment, one after another, each fell back into the waiting arms of a helper who laid them gently on the dusty ground.

A few minutes before this started happening he had called me into the group. I was really curious to find out what was going on. It came to my turn, but no way was I going to fall into the energy trap being spun by this guy. His blue eyes probed mine as he whispered *ovni, ovni,*

ovni to me. Apart from feeling slightly dizzy, I managed to remain standing upright.

Later, when I went to my dictionary to discover just what the hypnotic leader had been saying, I found that *ovni* (*objeto volador no identificado*) is the Spanish word for a UFO!

Things were getting more and more curious. I had heard that some wisdom teachers working with crystal skulls appear to access mysterious realms that are different to our usual third dimension – but UFOs and ETs!? I needed to know more and approached the woman shaman who was by now sitting alone on a stone step. 'May I join you?' I asked.

She told me, 'Following the descent of humanity from spirit into matter, we lost the ability to know our spiritual paths. We forgot how to see the luminous fibres connecting us from part of our spiritual body, that we call the assemblage point, to the energetic pathways and the WorldWideWebs of Life and Light. We forgot how to talk to those that guide us – those other beings and the helping ETs.'

'What can I do to understand more of this?' I asked.

'If you want to strengthen your abilities in other dimensions, one way is to work with the physical and subtle energy circuits of your body – your aura, chakras and meridians. You can do this with t'ai ch'i or yoga, and some complementary medicines that work on vibrational energy.'

This didn't seem like shamanic talk. I wanted to know more about the ETs and how to use my crystal skull.

'Look,' she said. 'Like a baby you want to run before you can walk. Are you a mouse or a great golden eagle? Before you can fly you must build up your auric bodies of Light, you must strengthen your energy field so that luminous fibres emanating from your assemblage point will stretch and link firmly into a deeper appreciation of the Web of Life.'

'But what about *ovnis* and ETs? And why did you want my old crystal skull in the ceremony?' I probed.

She cast a quick look at the white-and-gold robed, hypnotic Argentinian leader – still the centre of attention. Turning to face me directly she held her finger to her lips and whispered 'Take care.'

CHAPTER 7

Evolution and our Return to the Stars

The ancestors are alive and their vision
lives through us.

Ingrid Washinawatok El-Issa,* Menominee nation

I was finding out that there was much more to these crystal skulls, and to the task of caring for one, than I could have foreseen. This was becoming a compelling mystery, now with immense personal implications for me. I couldn't just get rid of the skull, and didn't want to. It was leading me over a threshold, and I could sense that this was going to be no small matter. But there wasn't much choice in this matter – I had made the choice already by starting on my quest into the Maya prophecies, and the skull was both a gift and a challenge.

Bonampak, Mexico

Something unknown, deep in my past, was calling me back to the Lacandón forest on the border between Mexico and Guatemala. It had always felt like home to me, and my intuition was telling me to find a way to contact the ancestors. I sensed that the crystal skull in my care somehow wanted me to go to Bonampak to reconnect with some

* A social justice activist, born 1957, who helped found the Indigenous Women's Network. Taken hostage and murdered in March 2002 whilst helping the U'wa people in Columbia (quoted on a Survival International leaflet).

kind of ancestral wisdom awaiting me there. Complete with crystal skull in my backpack, Mikhail and I were driven the last few miles through the jungle in a bumpy old bus into the heart of the Selva Lacandón.

Have you ever dreamt of a hidden city lost in the midst of dense, humid jungle? Here, brilliantly coloured parakeets flock overhead and solitary macaws provide a flash of scarlet amongst viridian vegetation. It is a place where sudden sounds tear the silence. The deep, eerie warning cries of howler monkeys, as one family group confronts another, echo from distant mountains, playing havoc with anyone's sense of direction and space. This is the magical picture in sound and colour that presents itself upon reaching Bonampak, a city dating from the Maya Early Classic period.

As in many other great Maya ceremonial centres the stonemasons recorded the lives of the rulers, the dates of their births, their ascent to power and their deaths. All this was immortalized on the stones of the buildings as if they wished for some godly permanence in an ever-changing world. At Bonampak today, some of the surrounding jungle-like trees and strangler vines have been cleared away, leaving its great plaza, astounding in its sheer size of over 340ft (100m), easier to view. In front lie steps and terraces, together with a number of temples and large standing stele stones, looking like grey ancestral sentinels.

Most of the buildings' exteriors were once brightly painted, bringing to life a passion for colour in the midst of the greenness. This once vast city has not yet been fully excavated or restored, with many treasures still covered by the clawing fingers of the all-embracing rainforest. Meagre resources allocated by the government in this area means treasures still find their way onto the illegal markets to augment the equally illegal narcotics trade.

By the afternoon, moisture was visibly rising from the grassy plaza and the few visitors sought the shade of three ruined but splendid temples. A visit to their interiors reveals some of the most beautiful wall murals ever to be found in the Mayalands.

In 1946 American explorers, led by Giles Healey and guided by local Lacandón Indians – descendants of the ancient Maya – eventually reached the city ruins. Wielding sharp, shiny machetes they cleared an area of undergrowth and in due course discovered three small temples facing onto the plaza. To their astonishment the interior walls were covered in highly coloured paintings that recorded in complex detail a number of elegant scenes from the everyday life of the rulers. They include unique pictures of a lively musical procession, with dancing and rival warriors who had been captured in battle.

The paint was applied direct to the interior plaster and, over the years, high humidity resulted in calcite salts rapidly coating the walls and almost destroying the rich colours. In 1984 the Mexican government undertook a three-year programme to clean the murals and, although some of the paint is still visible, a layer of salts has again permeated the stonework, making the scenes barely visible, irreparably damaging parts of them.

The remoteness of Bonampak made any long-term conservation work, such as a temperature and humidity controlled environment, impossible. Our best images of the wall paintings are now available only on computer-enhanced pictures, as well as an impressive replica in the National Museum of Anthropology, Mexico City.

It had long been my desire to visit Bonampak to see these amazing murals. So it was that in March 2003 I finally walked into the steamy jungle-rimmed central plaza, after having paused to read the plaque placed nearby by INAH, the government organization with responsibility for ancient monuments, that says, *nuestra memoria al alcance del mundo*, 'our memory made available to the world'. Despite the poor condition of many of the paintings I was not disappointed.

Stepping into the central plaza, once-dormant energies of times past wove threads of understanding for me. Pausing to make an offering of Lacandón-grown tobacco at the 'guardian' stele, I walked in silence and reached the first of the three famous temples. Once inside, I gazed in awe at the still visible details in image after image. In all, more than 200 figures are depicted. I marvelled at the intensity of the blue paint since, unlike other colours, it had not faded.

I realized why my heart was pounding: my superconsciousness was resonating with the little details of everyday courtly life captured by the skilled artists of long ago. It was like opening a picture book into time itself, as my eyes became accustomed to the dim light and strange shamanic ceremonial scenes lit up before me. Here a king in a jaguar-skin cape, named in the accompanying glyphs as *Chaan Muan*, and there a servant holding the baby heir apparent.

I noticed assembled nobles decorated with special red spondylus shell necklaces and lavish headdresses, showing their shamanic power animals in all their glory. Little details like the nobles' precious jade necklaces that adorned their strong, proud bodies gleamed with an unearthly green-blue tint. An entourage of musicians and shamans dressed as a fierce caiman, a green crayfish, and the maize god played on through the strings of the Threads of Time.

All these images from the past still breathed life. But in the midst of the celebrations was death, for as I entered the second temple I saw a battle raging, captives being tortured and dying, *Chaan Muan* holding his prisoner by the hair. Then the third temple acknowledges the dignity of royal women as they let their own blood by piercing their tongues, a bowl ready to collect the offerings, to be burnt and in turn offered up to the gods. Clearly, bloodletting ritualistically honoured the presentation of the heir on this special occasion. Strangely, the murals in the three temples were not completed – something happened in that royal city to cause the young heir never to ascend the throne.

Overawed by the power of the temples I went outside to rest. I was not alone sitting under the trees surrounding the plaza, for I had with me my very precious travelling companion – the crystal skull safely wrapped in a Mexican blanket in my backpack. Every so often I felt compelled to take it out, hold it up to the light and marvel as the sun illuminated what seemed to be circuits of consciousness shining within its crystalline matrix. One moment they appeared as formless points of light in a spatial void, next they turned into a million stars whose message almost shouted to me, 'What's in your *own* skull, Patricia? Look within.'

I already knew that we humans have a very special relationship with crystals since our bodies resonate with them and we are formed from similar chemical elements. I marvelled that we are composed of approximately 30 of these elements, and those very same elements can be identified in starlight, using spectrographs which analyse them in bands of colour correlating to each element, according to the periodic table of chemical elements. So I was reminded of old teachings that say:

'We are beings who have come from the stars; we were created from star matter and to the stars one day we return.'

The ancient Egyptians knew this and, equally, many contemporary Maya teachers in our day say that human consciousness came from beyond our planet. They name the Pleiades group of stars as the place of origin of the first intergalactic voyagers who came to Earth to educate people in their ways. Incredibly realistic Maya temple carvings that I had visited at Ek' Balaam in southern Mexico, show humanoid life-size beings with extremely elongated skulls. They look as if they could step down at any moment to greet you, so realistically are they posed and sculpted.

Modern Maya call these beings of light the 'Four Balaams from the Pleiades'. They have clearly visible wings, just like angels are shown in Christian paintings, but predating the Conquistadors and Christian teachings by more than 700 years. This whole recently discovered frieze, including the beings with wings, had been carefully covered by the façade of a later Maya building, itself hundreds of years old, as if the stonemasons wanted to preserve the Balaams' energetic presence and their message for later generations.

When I was at Ek' Balaam I was drawn towards a towering ceiba tree close to the winged 'beings' carved in stone, and I thought it time to sit quietly in the sunlight with my crystal skull. Gently, with half-closed eyes, I allowed my mind to find the deep centre of calm within. All was calm within and without.

Focusing attention on the light patterns within the crystal skull before me, my brain started to buzz, rather like the kind of noise one gets when inadvertently dialling a fax line. I reached out, compelled to touch the forehead of the skull before me. It was like a light switch turning on in my own skull. The incoherent 'singing' I had been experiencing turned into clear words, as if an interpreter had suddenly started to translate. The words flowed as question after question...

Is the light pulsating in this skull before me coming
from beyond our sun, because our sun is acting as an
amplifier for a cosmic vibrational song?
How can I find the light switch in my own skull to

connect me with the destiny of the ancient crystal
singing skulls?

Are crystal skulls the reason why references to the
'place of the skull' appear in esoteric Western
mysticism?

How much more wisdom can I unlock that is already
in my own skull, if I prepare myself correctly?

I must have fallen asleep, for I awoke several hours later, disturbed by
the site guards wanting me to leave. It was sunset. Deep within, I somehow knew that the answers to these questions were the reasons that the
ancients went to such lengths to carve the singing skulls. The Four Balaams
stood as a gentle reminder to future generations, lest we forget their importance. The skull was pulsating in my hands as I left Ek' Balaam. It seemed
to be wanting to communicate something to me.

Crystal Encodements

The mystery of these very ancient, human-sized skulls has caught
many people's imagination. The purity of the natural crystal causes
anyone who comes near a crystal skull to become entranced by its sheer
beauty and otherworldly nature. Maya elders and other indigenous
peoples hold them in high regard because of their connection with
other worlds, and because they are channels or storage devices for occult
information.

I will recount the story of one of the best-known skulls, the Mitchell-
Hedges skull. In the 1920s, in an archaeological dig in the Maya city of
Lubaantún, in present-day southern Belize, Anna, the daughter of an
eccentric explorer, found the crystal skull. Upon its discovery inside a
crumbling temple, her father held it up for all the Maya labourers to see.
For them it was an amazing and overawing sight. They fell on their
knees in joyful prayer.

Apparently Frederick Mitchell-Hedges decided that the skull was so
sacred to the Maya that he could not possibly take it away from them,
and he planned to leave it behind when he left. By 1927 excavations
were finished and the archaeologists prepared to leave, but the Maya

leader stepped forward and handed back to Frederick Mitchell-Hedges a bundle containing the skull. When he examined it closely he could see that the skull had a separate moveable carved crystal jawbone. Upon asking the Maya leader about this he was told that it was an extremely precious and unusual skull, called by them a 'singing skull'.

So, the skull began to travel the world, being an item of interest at Frederick's dinner parties and finally being inherited by his daughter Anna, who allowed psychics and mediums to work with it. Many years later, in 1970, it was subjected to a number of scientific tests by a team from the electronics manufacturer Hewlett-Packard in California. They confirmed that it was made from a very pure type of natural rock quartz crystal, silicon dioxide, only slightly softer than diamond, identical to the material used for silicon chips in computers. Such crystal has a piezo-electric effect, meaning that when it is put under pressure it gives a positive and negative polarity, like a battery, and generates electricity.

They said that making such a carved skull, even with modern cutting techniques, would be well nigh impossible – the crystal skull and the jaw carved from the same material would be prone to shatter. The investigating team was unable to find evidence of any modern instruments having been used to make it, even under great magnification. As it is impossible to carbon-date quartz, since it does not decay or change with time, they were at a loss to explain its origins. They concluded that it must have been made by hand over a very long period of time, requiring at least 300 man-years of work.

During these tests the Mitchell-Hedges skull was found to have unusual optical properties, for it is able to focus light from below, out through the eye sockets. This happens because quartz crystal has an optical as well as an electronic axis and the originators of the skull realized this.

Another property of quartz crystal is that it is able to hold electrical energy under control and oscillate any current at a measurably constant frequency – hence quartz is used in timepieces. So it is not beyond the bounds of possibility that this skull, and others like it, can hold or process information in the form of electronic pulses, just as silicon chips in computers, radios and telecommunication satellites do.

Here's a brief explanatory digression. Human life beneficially uses vibrational energy from the lowest audible sound through infrared and the rainbow colours to ultraviolet light. It has recently been discovered that light travels as messages within the DNA in every cell of our bodies. The visible light spectrum is called the 49th octave of vibration. Beyond that range of vibration, we are currently protected by Earth's atmosphere from the harsh, incredibly fast vibrations of X-rays, gamma and unspecified cosmic rays that scientists consider are harmful to the physical body.

It is relevant that our bodies, comprised mainly of water, have blood and body fluids, acting rather like liquid crystals. There are also vibrational patterns locked into the minerals that form our bones. Such vibrations are within all crystals, rocks and stones too.

This causes me to wonder whether we crack some code or break the light barrier when we die. If our life is a preparation for something beyond, then it is surely important for us to learn to bring ourselves up to the speed of light, if our destiny is with the Creator. So how can we learn to bring our living bodies to the speed of light?

When we use crystals in meditation, we increase our bodies' vibrational rate by a process of harmonization or resonance. This clears out embedded social conditioning that traps us in illness and death. Crystals give us a clue that, in the future, we will learn how to realign the light-encoded filaments of our DNA in accordance with the Divine Plan of Creation.

Suddenly I made another connection, to strange experiences that were triggered whenever I was close to carved glyphs and stelae in these old Maya cities. Of course! They contained the intentionally implanted vibration from all that took place in the far-off times of the ancestral Maya. I imagined the winged Balaams (who look like space travellers) carved upon the large frieze at Ek' Balaam coming to life. The stones literally hold the 'programs' or memories of these presences, rather like silicon chips. Thus the sacred sites themselves are 'portals' to other vibrational dimensions. Within the stones of the temples are embedded centuries of mythic ritual and shamanic practice that have maintained strong ancestral connections.

Over the months that I had been the caretaker of the crystal skull

I had meditated with it many times. Now I realized that this is the message the crystal skulls remind us of: *we came from the stars and to the stars we will return.*

One meditation with the crystal skull took me into an understanding of light and superconsciousness. This is what I 'received':

> Superconsciousness involves allowing yourself to sink into deeper, heightened consciousness.
>
> It involves letting go of all that is immediate, tuning to the pulse of your life, breathing and listening to the beat of your heart, then rising through your energy field into the depths of your mind. Its forbidden secrets creep out of its dark corners, for the mind is expansive. Above and below – within you and beyond.
>
> It opens, unfolding, falling, sinking, lifting, rising into superconsciousness. For you *are* superconsciousness. You are this light that you are feeling.
>
> Every cell is linked to every filament of your rainbow body. Radiant colours move you from violet to green and back to violet. Golden light rushes into the top of your head. It came from the space where there is no thing.
>
> Merging, it devours the magenta coming from the Earth and, expanding, it blasts its golden effulgence to the crown. It glows a halo that rises, falls, sinks and heightens.
>
> It totally enwraps a peach-coloured life-light within its glow, drawing into your essence the reason for being, your soul purpose, your opening to wonder and your superconsciousness field.
>
> No void, no angels, just divine light, a radiance beyond radiance, beyond the void, passing through the tunnel of light, faster, faster, through the WorldWideWeb of Light, merging with the stars.
>
> You star-born, crystal-formed, sons and daughters of Earth laugh at the ease of moving effortlessly. You move

further away and then further in. Falling out of time, seeing into spatial realms of light, held in the embrace of prophecy, lightness, radiance.

No thoughts in this superconsciousness. No doing. No being. Just merging, through time, beyond time, opening to the effulgence of starry drops of dew, falling into the cosmic ocean. Absorbed, consumed superconsciousness.

Dedications and Dangers

I was drawn to a particular carved stone stele in a remote corner of the plaza at Bonampak. Placing the crystal skull before it, I felt the need to undertake a dedication ritual. I made a little impromptu altar with a ring around the skull of natural local obsidian pieces, lit a joss stick and, resting my head upon the cold crystal, I said with genuine conviction, 'I would give my life to protect you, skull.'

I knew that, in some strange way, this enigmatic object was now part of my consciousness, every moment of my waking hours. At night I was dreaming of strange journeys to distant stars and of rose quartz crystal planets. It was really impressing itself upon me in a very strange way. Sometimes the dreams turned into nightmares. Mostly I was in situations were I was being pursued by something unbelievably evil.

Leaving the temples of Bonampak, I carefully rewrapped the crystal skull. Sitting at Bonampak with it had certainly revived my interest in vibrational energy. Although I had had a few more realizations whilst meditating, nothing very unusual occurred, and for this I was a little sad. I had perhaps had too many expectations of Bonampak.

Despite its remote and special location within the Lacandón Forest, I wondered if something terrible had happened there that caused the ancestors such pain that they could not communicate with me clearly through the skull. It was a beautiful place, but I sensed an abrupt ending to the ruling dynasties who had held the true cosmic wisdom. Perhaps they had not had sufficient time to transfer the guardianship of the place ceremonially to the beings who would remain behind, *los aluxes*, as had happened in other cities. *Los aluxes* continue to keep a pure energy within the ancient cities wherever they have been charged to do so.

Mikhail and I left Bonampak and journeyed on, wishing to stop at a riverside restaurant we knew. The whole journey there gave me a very uneasy feeling. I repeatedly visualized a protective circle of light around our car and the crystal skull as we drove. I felt I had picked up some sort of unpleasant energy at Bonampak. Also I noticed that a white car had pulled out of a side turning as we left Bonampak and followed us for some distance.

Arriving at our destination we sat down in the restaurant, built out over the river on a kind of floating wooden platform. We had just ordered our meal when suddenly I felt myself being thrown to the floor. A sound like bullets rattled on the tin roof. The old sheets of tin gave way, dropping down to where I had just been sitting.

Mikhail, seeing what was happening, had pushed me to the floor, saving my life. The platform sank down into the fast flowing river and I scrambled, somewhat shaken, onto the riverbank, safe but scared.

What had happened? My husband pointed to a tree that had crashed down on the roof, making the sound of gunshots as its branches rasped on the corrugated tin panels. Why would the tree suddenly fall? I had an uneasy feeling again as I sat quietly, having a cold drink to restore myself.

Walking over to the base of the tree I saw it had cracked exactly at the point where there was a deep saw cut. I began to wonder if the white car driver had anything to do with this. It was so strange: I had just dedicated my life to the crystal skull!

I ran quickly to the side of the restaurant, only to see the white car pulling away rapidly and causing a cloud of red dust.

Continuing the Journey

After a while my fears calmed down and my husband and I continued on our long, exciting journey through some of the most remote areas of Mexico, travelling from Bonampak towards Yaxchilán, close to the Guatemalan border. Now we felt we had put many miles between us and the scary incident at the river restaurant. We were hoping to make Frontera de Corazal before nightfall, which in tropical regions is a very swift transition from sunset to darkness. We would have little time in which to find overnight accommodation.

Both of us gave a sigh of relief when the river came into view, together with a little cluster of wooden shacks comprising the village. Beyond the scrappy grass that serves the village ragamuffins as a football pitch, the wide deep River Usumascinta flows like a sinuous green serpent from the interior of Guatemala to the Gulf of Campeche, Mexico, forming the border at Frontera de Corazal, dividing the two countries. Along this particular stretch it becomes rather like a rainforest motorway and most of the commercial movement of foodstuff crops gathered from the forest are moved along it in narrow outboard motor-propelled craft.

We arrived tired and thirsty at our destination, checking every so often to be sure no one was following us. By the riverside a family was harvesting coconuts from a tree beside their *palapa*, or palm-thatched hut. Cutting the top of the coconuts with a long machete, one of the children handed a heavy, milk-filled fruit to each of us. Their mother's and father's gold-capped teeth were sparkling (something of a status symbol in Mexico) as they smiled widely, and the little ones, not yet proficient at wielding a sharp machete, giggled at our thanks, muttered in inadequate Spanish. Such simple people, but generous as ever, for they would take no money for their very welcome gifts of sweet milky juice.

The Destiny of the World

That evening Mikhail and I sat down to a simple dinner and discussed the destiny of the world from the perspective of the prophecies.

The Hopi prophecies foretell events expected to occur within the next decade. Maya prophecies complement them. For example, Carlos Barrios is a Maya historian of Guatemalan Mam Maya descent who has been speaking to audiences worldwide about the times leading up to the critical date of 21 December 2012. Señor Barrios confirms what many prophecies tell us, that our present time period leading up to 2012 is crucial for humanity. In his teachings he advises that the choices each of us makes are important, 'for if your personal timelines have caused you to be incarnated into this era, you have great spiritual work to do in balancing the planet'.

Since the late 1980s and with a particular focus in the spring of 1995, many Maya elders have ceremonially reawakened the sacred spiritual energies that had lain dormant for millennia within their temples, in ancient cities scattered across the Mayalands. They also welcomed people from other countries into some of their ceremonies.

We had taken part in such ceremonies, at Uxmal for example, when crystal skulls were used in initiations and activating memories from the ancestors. It was an opportunity to 'reopen the doors' psychically so that women and men from across the planet could come to the Maya world to receive initiation into their traditions, as they did in times long past.

The Maya have always appreciated and respected that there are other colours, other races and other spiritual systems. 'They know,'said Señor Barrios, 'that the destiny of the Maya world is related to the destiny of the whole world.'

Countering Prophecies of Destruction

While I had been sitting on the cool moss-covered stones of the Bonampak temples, cradling the crystal skull carefully in my hands, I had found myself reflecting that we are already in the midst of the prophecies of destruction. Daily we hear of environmental changes, natural disasters or wars. Indigenous prophecies all agree and indicate that the world will undergo severe changes. It is important to realize that, from the indigenous world-view, it is the Earth herself who reacts to war, aggression and greed because Earth is a living entity, with feelings, thoughts and imperatives of her own.

So elders such as Roberta Blackgoat, 1918–2002, an elder of the Independent Dineh (Navajo) nation at Big Mountain, USA, said, 'All the suffering going on in this country with the tornadoes, floods and earthquakes is carried on the breath of Mother Earth because she is in pain.'

She explained that the Four Corners area (of which Hopi lands are part), is particularly sacred because it literally holds Mother Earth's internal organs – coal and uranium that the Bureau of Indian Affairs has allowed the Peabody Coal Mine to excavate. Now however, both Hopi and Navajo traditionalists are legally fighting the mining.

'They are trying to take her precious guts out for money,' declared Roberta Blackgoat. 'My grandfather told me that coal is like the liver, and uranium is both the heart and lungs of Mother Earth.' (*See* www.wisdomkeepers.com/blackgt.html.)

Thus, *what we do to the Earth, we do to ourselves.*

The more I heard words like this, the more I really started to feel that Earth's pain was my pain. However, in contrast, the following piece of wisdom from the Dalai Lama made me optimistic for the future. It is just another way of expressing the similar sentiments of caring people from many lands.

If we unbalance nature, humankind will suffer. Furthermore, as people alive today, we must consider future generations. A clean environment is a human right like any other. It is therefore part of our responsibility towards others to ensure that the world we pass on is as healthy as, if not healthier than when we found it.

Tenzin Gyatso, the Fourteenth Dalai Lama, from *Freedom in Exile* (Hodder & Stoughton, UK, 1990)

Mystics the world over speak about the anchoring of a new consciousness. It can be thought of as numerous points of spiritual light shining out, one here and one there, multiplying up through acts of compassion, kindness and love. This represents a new spirit, an illumination from within – potentially it lies in every one of us.

With the wisdom truths of indigenous peoples, we need to allow into our hearts the simple message that in these truths we can change the world. The world's present-day predicament is of a spiritual nature, caused not by the failure of religions, but simply because the next stage of spiritual evolution must grow from individual responsibility, which first has to recognize the need for a unifying force in our spiritual hearts. Some prophecies, notably those from the Hopi, say 144,000 enlightened beings are needed. Maybe everyone won't shine at the same moment, but as we progress towards superconsciousness some spiritual lights will shine brighter.

This path toward a unifying force or prescience for the good of humanity does not always manifest in an overtly spiritual way. For example, environmental support action, natural healthcare and ethical trading are all outward manifestations of the same impulse in action. Sometimes these initiatives are challenged and seemingly threaten established ways with which we are accustomed, but there has always been a cutting edge for change in society. The cutting edge has its place.

It is also prophesied that the direction we are seeking will enable us to grow into something new, something never seen before in the history of humanity. Humanity is evolving – and not in a Darwinian way!

From diverse parts of the planet there is a great 'wake-up call'. The Maya Fourth Creation is ending – and many people are responding to it, whether or not they are aware of the Maya prophecies. If we each listen to our hearts as well as our heads, using the power of silence, of meditation, of prayer, we let our spiritual lights shine.

So many of us have forgotten just how powerful we are when working on non-physical levels of reality. By these means we change the course of history as set out upon the loom of the Threads of Time. It has been done many times in the past. Notably, the power of prayer and focused positive intent in the daily 'Silent Minute' carried out by much of the population in Britain during World War II changed the course of the war when the powers of darkness were at their most extreme. Now, as in those times, humanity can weave together *positive* aspects of End Times prophecies, but it requires our conscious choice.

Alongside this awakening something extraordinary is happening. Thousands of people are undertaking journeys to ancient places, perhaps not even knowing why they are going. Many times I heard Maya elder Hunbatz Men say that we need to go and 'be woken up' by the energy of old, particularly powerful, sacred places in our own countries. He affirms that we can assist the transition to the next age by using inner guidance. As if we are remembering the words of an ancient song, we can choose to meld our superconsciousness with the past, or sing out our future.

Often we find hallowed buildings lie in ruins, druid groves are overgrown, stone markers and monoliths have tumbled down, holy springs and mountaintops sing out for recognition. Hunbatz Men urges us to be spiritual guardians of the special locations in our own lands that he names 'magnetic places'. He says that if we call upon our own gods or goddesses, upon Great Spirit or upon *Hunab K'u*, the 'One Giver of Movement and Measure', we can wake up good energies that have lain dormant in them for so long.

Once again, in our own lands or in concert with the indigenous peoples of the lands we visit, we are learning how to sing old songs of love for the Earth as we weave the Threads of Time Future. For now *we* are the voices of the singing skulls.

> *Hunab K'u*, who can see and understand everything, knows that the time for the great change has come. The word for us to return to the ancient temples has been received from the cosmos. It is here and now that Great Spirit is beginning to call us back to the magnetic sites. The incarnated masters are beginning to raise their voice of knowledge in the ancient sites so their teachings can be heard. It is in the ancient sites that the cosmic word to attain wisdom in a gradual manner has been received.

> **Elder Hunbatz Men, Itzá Maya Tradition**
> **(private communication, 1998)**

CHAPTER 8

The Cloud People

Follow your own footsteps. Learn from the rivers, the trees and the rocks. Honour the Christ, the Buddha, your brothers and sisters. Honour the Earth Mother and the Great Spirit. Honour yourself and all of Creation.

These are the teachings of the Q'ero,* the last of the Incas.

Having visited USA to find verification of the Maya prophecies and an understanding of the commonalities and differences between their prophetic perspectives, I needed to visit another of the great civilizations of the Americas. It seemed as if the crystal skull in my care sought this too, for reasons I could not yet understand but nevertheless accepted.

Lands of the Inca

My journey now took me to the lands of the Inca, carried into the high mountains by the condor and the wistful music of panpipes. Some months had passed since I had travelled in the Americas and it was time to take the crystal skull to Peru. Sheltered by the eerie magnificence of wind-worn purple and white snow-capped mountains, almost hidden from sight, lies a fertile, lush emerald-green land.

* They sought refuge in the mountains above 14,000ft (4,260m) to escape the Conquistadors, and their villages were not 'discovered' until 1949. (See www.labyrinthina.com/prophecy.htm.)

In this earthly paradise deep in the Andes, the Inca Empire built strongholds and vantage points, mainly set high above the valleys, patchworked by patterned fields and rimmed by vast areas of rock terracing. Their cities and citadels overlooked magnificent panoramas, fed by irrigation channels and water systems cut out of solid rock.

Travel in these mountains today and you will see still unexcavated sun temples within ruined cities that match anything at Machu Picchu, the better-known tourist destination. Amongst higher crevices and rocky overhangs ancient burial sites are hidden. Narrow tracks, vital to the Inca, snake their way, sometimes precipitously, across a challenging primal landscape of mountains, canyons and jungle.

The Sacred Valley, a fertile region filled with beauty in its own right, was the route to the jungle, providing access to fruits and plants from the tropical lowlands. It protected the ancient sacred city of Cusco, whose original name *Quispicanchis* means 'navel of the world', from incursions of the Antis, fierce jungle tribes who from time to time raided the highlands.

Pre-Inca and Inca farmers developed hundreds of varieties of potatoes, high-protein grains and beans, corn and many other carefully bred crops, able to feed millions of people. They were such skilled agriculturists that over half the types of food eaten in the world today are historically traceable to them.

Systems of mountain agriculture included automatic irrigation and climate control to prevent freezing. They invented the freeze-drying of potatoes in order to preserve them. Minimal work was required in the no-plough method used in their terraced fields.

Years before, I had met an Inca man when he visited my home in the United Kingdom to give a talk to a group of people. Willaru Huayta was a descendant of the Quechua nation, a *Chasqui*, or a sincere spiritual messenger. He travels the world giving his message that we need to heal the spiritual sicknesses within our societies, caused by the domination of our egos over Spirit. This is another aspect of the cultural hypnosis of humanity.

From strands of time that have come from his ancestors, he prophesies that the year 2013 will mark the end of the Inca calendar and that there will be a huge cataclysm caused by a magnetic asteroid three times larger than Jupiter. His prediction makes chilling reading: 'Most of the world's population will perish. Just a few people will survive and become the "seed people" of the Sixth Generation.' I wondered why this prophecy transmitted through him mentions the year 2013 instead of 2012. When asked, his inscrutable response was that only the Shining Ones could answer this question.

Such predictions leave me feeling powerless. So instead of dwelling too long upon it, I researched the 'alternative' history of Peru and, in the process, discovered other, quite different and more positive predictions from those magical lands.

I had become intrigued with a legend about something extraordinary that the original inhabitants of Sacred Valley possessed. They left behind many secrets for those prepared to go beyond the usual tourist trails. I knew that, hidden within the Peruvian high mountains, is a race of indigenous people, the *Chachapoya*, known to some as the Cloud People. A fascinating legend states that they are the present-day guardians of a precious object, one of the treasures of the ancient world.

The legend tells of a solid gold disc, more than 6ft (1.75m) in diameter, known as the Golden Sun Disc of Koricancha. It was believed to have come from Mu, a large inhabited landmass said to have once existed in the Pacific in the Creation prior to Atlantis. The disc was passed to the Atlanteans who, realizing its importance, then handed it on to the predecessors of either the Incas or Aztecs. This treasure has the reputation of being a kind of secret key able to unlock prophetic messages within the calendars of the three highly developed civilizations of the Inca, Aztec and Maya.

I believed my crystal skull could reveal something about these incredible secrets. So I felt impelled to take it to the lands of the Cloud People, though I knew not why. Originally I had no intention to take myself higher into the Andes, being content with Machu Picchu. But my plans were to change. *Who's calling the shots? The crystal skull or me?* Have you ever been in a situation where something seems to cause you to completely change direction from what you intended? This was one of those moments for me!

Seeking guidance, I went first to the old church of Santo Domingo in Cusco, dating from the 17th century, built on the walls of an Inca Sun temple. Throughout these lands many temples were deliberately destroyed and Christian churches placed upon them. The original temple on which the church was built was called *Koricancha*. Whilst primarily a Sun temple, it is still to this day the centre point of a system of 41 alignments to sacred places specifically connected to the moon. A central egg-shaped stone survives, feminine in nature, from which these alignments were probably taken. However, it is said that the enigmatic Golden Sun Disc, whilst still in its original position of importance, was the centrepiece of all solar and cosmic alignments.

I could see that a large section of the church cloisters had been gutted in order to reveal four of the original chambers of the great Sun temple. Some of the finest Inca stonework in existence is to be found at the curved wall beneath the west end of the church. How stunning it must have looked when the walls of the Koricancha were lined with 700 solid gold sheets, each weighing two kilos. There were life-size gold and silver replicas of corn, golden llamas, figurines and jars.

But today all that remains are stones. The Conquistadors, with a mission to plunder treasures of gold, took it all. We will never see these treasures, for they were totally melted down. Nothing survived except, as mystery tales have it, the Sun Disc! At some point it was moved from Koricancha and held in the personal keeping of the Aztec ruler Montezuma II. Upon the rapid and bloody destruction of his Aztec empire by the Spanish forces, legend has it that it was quickly taken away for safety.

Maybe it was hidden in the black depths of Lake Titicaca or in the lost city of Paytiti. Possibly it passed into the safekeeping of the Cloud People, who still keep it securely concealed. So the enigmatic Golden Sun Disc, supposedly possessing special powers, has disappeared from human sight. In the ensuing years since the 1400s, many questors have searched for it in vain, travelling deep into inhospitable regions of the high mountains of Peru. It seems this quest is particularly dangerous, for it is said that no one is known to have returned from the Lands of the Cloud People or to have been successful in their quest for pre-Columbian gold.

Modern day travellers' tales also say that no one can go to their lands and come back, for the mountains inhabited by the Cloud People are a mysteriously dangerous area, constantly hidden in dense mists and snow-capped peaks 'on the top of the world'. It is whispered that, to this day, there are white-clothed priests and priestesses of an unknown white-skinned race who guard the Sun Disc.

While in Mexico I had listened enthralled to incredible stories told by an American, now living near Palenque. He was the living image of a buccaneer and eccentric explorer rolled into one portly personage, who had got part of the way into the lands of the Cloud People seeking the Sun Disc. Fortunately he did come back – probably since he was unable to find it.

Surprisingly tourists fare better. If you go to the Museum of Anthropology in Lima, Peru, you can see a replica of the Golden Sun Disc of Koricancha there. Upon it is the 'face' of the sun (representing a world age), and numerous undeciphered symbols around the outside. We cannot be certain how accurate it is to the original.

Inca Prophecy

The Spirit of the Land of the Condor was honoured in Inca cosmological beliefs. They held large rocky outcrops in reverence, as if they possessed some hidden spiritual force. I had seen the Q'enko (zig-zag) near Cusco, one such place. It is a fine example of a rock that has been artfully carved *in situ*, creating complex patterns of steps, seats, geometric reliefs and a puma design. It is an excellent example of Inca 'rock worship'.

On top of the rock are zig-zag channels which served to course *chicha* (local maize beer) or sacrificed llama blood for purposes of divination. The speed and route of the liquid through the channels, with the patterns it made in the rock, gave answers to the priest's invocations. Inside the rock are large niches and an altar where the dried mummies of lesser royalty were perhaps kept, along with gold and precious objects.

When the Golden Sun Disc was in place in Koricancha it was aligned with the sun in such a way that it reflected the morning sunlight onto the mummies of the Inca rulers. When I was in the temple I felt an urge to place the crystal skull at the same centre point and watch the play of early morning light upon it. Parts of the cranium of the skull came alive and seemed to light up with additional pinpoints of brilliance. I needed to ask the skull to tell me more about the Golden Sun Disc, and this is what I came to understand.

'Yes, the Sun Disc was here,' I heard in my head. 'It represents the fulfilment of an Inca prophecy. The power of the disc will be reactivated during the period of the tenth *pachakuti* (meaning "to turn upside down"), a kind of cosmic transmutation which began in 1992 (some say 1993) and involving Earth and Time.'

I was shown pictures in my mind's eye of earthquakes and, rising above them side by side, the Golden Sun Disc and the Ollin, the central symbol on the Aztec Sunstone, that calendrically represent our present times.

I went on to hear the message, 'From 1992 to approximately 2012 will come the merging of our three realms, Upper, Earth and Underworld (*hanaq pacha*, *kay pacha* and *ukhu pacha*). This time period is called the *Taripay Pacha* which, translated, means "the age when we meet ourselves again". During this cycle we urge you to prepare your bodies with work to both clear and strengthen your vibrational energy fields.'

I was warned, 'It will not be easy, since it is prophesied that Earth will turn upside down.' Whether this meant a geophysical phenomenon such as a magnetic pole reversal, or that our lives will be metaphorically turned upside down I could not ascertain.

Again the skull spoke to me, 'We are the Q'ero, the last of the Inca, and we ask you to look with the eyes of your soul and to engage with the essential. Regaining your luminous nature is a possibility today for all who dare to take the leap.'

The crystal skull continued to sparkle with light and, shifting my gaze, I became aware that I was not alone. A young Inca man in Western clothes stood waiting quietly beside me and whispered to me in clear English, 'The year 2012 is predicted by the Inca wise ones as the time when humanity will spiritually evolve. You must go to our yearly festival of the Snow Star, *Qoyllur Riti*. It is held just below the glacier on Mount Ausangate here in Peru. It is a long, long, walk. You will not be alone because many pilgrims flock there to await the emergence of three "luminous Shining Ones" who will lead Peru and the world into a new era of peace. You must bring the crystal skull with you.'

Puzzled, I looked closely at him. Yet something told me it was a journey I would have to undertake another year. I had read the book *Beyond 2012* by Geoff Stray (Vital Signs, UK, 2005) and, according to his review of the *Qoyllur Riti* prophecy, something will happen to time, or our perception of it. Our present time period of *Taripay Pacha* will somehow merge or become the golden age. I asked the young man about this and he immediately smiled knowingly at me.

'I am just a *chasqui*, a messenger. I have spoken and now I must go.' In that instant he walked quickly away, his long black hair almost dancing in the wind, and he disappeared from my sight.

Once I was back in my lodging room I started thinking about the messenger and the extraordinary story in the book *The Four Winds – a Shaman's Odyssey into the Amazon,* by psychologist and medical anthropologist Alberto Villoldo and Erik Jendresen (Harper & Row, 1990). He has studied with leading Inca shamans of Peru and says that they believe the world faces a period of extreme upheaval and renewal. Then, sometime after 2012, time as we know it will end and *a new species of human will emerge.*

I shivered with excitement as I thought about this and began avidly studying other papers I had with me, reading more about the Inca prophecies. Apparently the three Shining Ones who will 'emerge' from the Snow Star Festival will eventually meet up with others at specific predestined places, until there are six women priestesses called *nust'a* and six male fifth-level priests called *inca mallku*. The fifth level is a level of consciousness that enables the priests to have miraculous healing abilities. The sixth level is presently beyond our comprehension.

Eventually these 12 Shining Ones will return to the Temple of Wiraqocha to perform what is described as a coronation ritual. This will initiate the supreme Inca ruler and his sister wife, who will be the first beings to achieve sixth-level consciousness. They will have shining auras visible to everyone who beholds them. At that point it is prophesied that a hidden city called Paytiti will materialize, rather like the legendary mysterious city of Shambhala, signalling the start of a golden age. During the golden age it will be possible for the seventh and highest level of consciousness to arise in humanity. This potentially high spiritual evolution is referred to by the Inca priests as *titantis ramji*, or deity incarnate.

Of course I, like others, sometimes doubt the possibility of such an evolution taking place, but then a voice started saying in my head 'Remember… remember…' So many of the prophecies of the Americas that I had studied speak of a new humanity. This is awesome, I thought, since all these civilizations are separated by thousands of kilometres of often harsh land, with no cars and no Internet and yet with their prophecies coinciding.

Suddenly I realized what a mission I was on, gathering these strands of time together. The new humanity could actually become a reality. It was as if a searchlight was switched on. Within my head I felt a great expansion of light through my crown chakra into infinite starry space. Having the crystal skull before me was such a great gift towards my realization.

I placed my hand carefully upon it, offering a prayer of thanks to Great Spirit. I finally understood that the Inca prophecy, originating from the Q'ero priests and shamans, says that it will not be long before we emerge into the age of an earthly paradise. The distant tolling of bells and wistful melodies of panpipes accompanying unknown songs were carried like an omen on the wind as I made a promise to myself to go to the Snow Star Festival the following May.

Sacsayhuaman

The next day I went to Sacsayhuaman, a magnificent Inca fortress over-looking the city of Cusco, impressive in its stark beauty and monumental scale. Sacsayhuaman can be variously translated as 'speckled falcon' or 'speckled head'. The last interpretation refers to the belief that the whole city of Cusco was planned by the shaman priests who set it out in the form of a puma, whose head was the hill of Sacsayhuaman. The exact date of the fortress is uncertain but is generally attributed to the period of Inca Pachacuti, the man who founded the empire.

Sitting on the rocks and ruins of Sacsayhuaman, gazing towards the sun, I mused about the importance of the Golden Sun Disc. I had heard all the legends about it and wondered if it would be revealed to human eyes again before the end of the present age. I turned a question over and over in my mind: in what way could it be connected to the Inca prophecies of the three worlds merging? Was it able to give us information about the predicted coming age of 'No Time' or was it in reality a calendrical device similar to the better-known Aztec Sun Stone from central Mexico?

The Aztec Sun Stone, 12ft (3m) in diameter, was uncovered in the centre of Mexico City in 1790. According to archaeologists it was carved in 1479 CE, only 40 years before the arrival of the Spanish. There have been several interpretations of the symbols upon it but there is now general agreement that the central design shows four previous eras, or suns, and that the central face is *Tonatiuh* the sun god, ruler of our present fifth Aztec era.

The Maya say we are currently in the fourth era, and preparing to go into the fifth. This is not a contradiction. The Maya counted from zero and the Aztecs from the number one. Aztec tradition says that the first of the four previous suns ended in a flood, the second with an eclipse, the third with hot volcanic dust and rocks raining from the sky, and the fourth with strong winds.

In Geoff Stray's book *Beyond 2012*, he suggests that the Aztecs had knowledge of the same Long Count Calendar that the Maya possessed but that, by 1479, when the Sun Stone was carved, they had forgotten this extended count of time. If we accept this idea, it means that they could give every day its own unique day-name and date position over a period of 10,250 years (two Thirteen Baktun cycles of the Maya).

He states that all the civilizations of Mesoamerica used a 365-day calendar (the Maya *haab*) alongside their 260-day sacred calendar (Maya *tzolk'in*) and also, in the case of the Maya, the 360-day *tun* (part of the Long Count calendar). If this is the case, then clearly the Aztecs also knew of the current End Time predictions concerning the year 2012.

Portals

I returned to Europe from South America and began a further round of research. I needed long periods of quiet in order to sort out my thoughts and feelings about the prophecies and everything that I had learnt in Peru. Calendars were crucial to it all and, here I was, a writer and artist, having to centre my attention upon complicated charts and numbers!

As I focused attention on the complexities of the different calendars recorded so long ago, my brain started to become quite confused! I try as much as possible to keep away from 'mind stuff', especially those tricky numbers; but sometimes something just switches on and I have so many questions. I pulled myself determinedly into a meditative mode, as my training had taught me, and I began to consider a teaching that Maya elder and day-keeper Hunbatz Men had given me some years previously. I recalled being told that the Q'ero believe doorways between the worlds are opening again, like holes in time that we can step through and beyond. They are places where we can explore our human capabilities in luminous bodies.

Once when I was sitting in a remote part of the ruins at Nah Chan, hidden within the forest foliage, and with few other people around, I placed my old crystal skull on the stone in front of me and gave 'his' head a friendly polish with my scarf. He seemed to glow a little brighter as I read Hunbatz Men's words about interdimensional doorways, or portals.

> When you have the knowledge, when you walk inside
> the intuition, so the doors will be very easy to open.
> There exist natural doors in many places but you need
> to be very sensitive to see and touch those doors. First,
> what you feel; in the physical aspect it is very
> complicated because you need more discipline to be
> able to go up to the door.
>
> Mantras (sacred sounds used in meditation), help you
> to go inside that door. There exist dangerous situations
> – some people go inside and it is difficult to come back.
> Some use marijuana, peyote or tobacco to help open

and then close the door, which you must do when returning to everyday consciousness.

But there are other ways. If you know the vibration of your body, which is slow, and of Spirit, which is fast, then you accelerate your body. Then you have, let us say, 5,000 vibrations of your body and 5,000 vibrations of your Spirit, and then you are equal.

Your body will not be heavy any more and at that moment you become 'winged'. Therefore only the body can get old, never the Spirit, for Spirit is a vibration of the cosmos.

Hunbatz Men, Itzá Maya Tradition, March 1998
(private sacred study document)

This Maya perspective states that doorways or portals may be opened at will, but it is vitally important to know the code of conduct not only to open, but also to close them. Those people who are trained in meditation or shamanic techniques have an advantage here. When attempting to give oneself over to unusual energies it is prudent to know the way to handle them.

For most people, hallucinogenic drugs, exotic plants or mushrooms are not the answer. Old Don Pedro Bravo, sitting in his desert shack, had once told me, '*Peyote* is for the Mexican desert. *Ayahuasca* is for the Amazon. If you want an uncontrolled fantasy "trip", take them. If you want lasting enlightenment, don't.'

He went on to say, 'You people just don't know how to work with these things, and you are barely able to cope with the effect they have upon your body. You don't realize that these are sacred plants that are used for raising a person's spiritual vibration during ceremony.'

I asked, 'Can this vibrational energy of the drugs make you "shape-shift" to predetermined locations or travel into otherworldly states of consciousness?'

I remember him banging his fist on the table, looking angrily at me and saying firmly, 'Señora, you ask too many questions!'

Clearly the lesson was that I hadn't gone into a more intuitive mode myself. I still had too much 'mind stuff' going on!

As I finished reading Hunbatz's words I looked across at my crystal skull, and looked and looked again. Right in its centre a picture seemed to be forming. Not an ordinary picture but one made of tiny shafts of silvery light.

Something was drawing me deeper into that picture. I found the lights were pulling me closer to what appeared to be a huge swathe of stars – thousands and thousands of them.

As I stared at the lights that were forming, appearing and disappearing before my eyes I recalled Maya teachers instructing me that within specific parts of the cosmos are crucial portals. One area in particular is relevant to their predictions – the Milky Way stars. At dawn on 21 December 2012 there will be a convergence of the Galactic Centre, that is, the point (a black hole) around which our galaxy revolves, with the rising sun. On that date, as seen from Earth, the sun will rise exactly through the Dark Rift of the Milky Way, although the bright light of the sun will make the surrounding stars invisible.

We know, according to Maya astronomical predictions, that because of precessional 'movement' of the Milky Way, the sun and Earth will be in alignment with the Galactic Centre. Although this event happens over a number of years the evidence at Maya sites clearly points to the 2012 date as the nexus point. In the next chapter we will see how Maya researcher John Major Jenkins describes relevant evidence that he found carved on stones at the old ceremonial city of Izapa at the foot of the Sierra Madre range in southern Mexico.

What the event means, according to Maya thought, is that a new event of cosmic importance occurs at the *end* of a period – hence at the end of the 13.0.0.0.0 Baktun date (21 December 2012). So a new birth is anticipated, but what exactly it will be is the subject of much debate. Some say it will be a completion of human spiritual development, others a pole shift in our collective psyche and yet others suggest a more 'physical' birth complete with drastic planetary changes, due to a field effect energy reversal that will allow all life on Earth to resonate with the 'source' at the Galactic Centre.

Day by day the crystal skull sitting on my meditation table at home was becoming increasingly energized. Thoughts and ideas kept flooding into me, and questions and more questions caused me to ask what the implications of all this knowledge were. I could only guess. But for some 2,300 years this Dark Rift region of the Milky Way has been considered a portal or doorway into another dimension or state of being. It was known by the ancient Maya and present-day wisdom-keepers as 'White-bone Snake' (or *Ek'Way*) meaning the 'black transformer' or 'black dreamplace'.

As I continued looking into the crystal skull all the chatter in my mind suddenly ceased and I did indeed go into a dream-like state. The mass of stars cleared. I saw the central dark cleft in the Milky Way that the Maya and perhaps the earlier Olmec once termed the birth canal of the Milky Way, or the Great Mother Goddess, while modern astronomers call it the Dark Rift. I realized that the cleft equates to the birth canal of the Cosmic Mother through which the Cosmic Father, the Sun, rises to impregnate her. I wondered what would be birthed as a result. I heard the words: 'Look, the black portal is moving. Beware the twisting white-bone snake.' Then a few moments later, 'The Threads of Time are parting. The day is coming very soon when the Heart of Heaven is ready to be opened.'

My impromptu meditation drew to a close as I started to rational-ize what I had seen. Again I began asking myself what this could possibly mean, whether it was all symbolic or whether it really will affect us on a physical level, down here on planet Earth. I knew by now the portents for Earth were critical, and heeded these enigmatic words that came from the crystal skull.

The Maya elders accord great reverence to the Heart of Heaven, which I believe is the black hole at the centre of our galaxy. I was fortunate to have been shown it has an actual location and direction in the sky – and that it was shortly to come into alignment with Earth. That night I stepped out into the garden of my house. I looked up at the faint mass of Milky Way stars, trying to identify the precise place where the Threads of Time would open to reveal the Heart of Heaven, also called the Heart of the Universe. I recited a Maya prayer I knew:

May the Heart of the Universe be in my heart,

May my heart be in the Heart of the Earth,

May the Heart of the Earth be in my heart,

May my heart be in the Heart of the Universe.

I was also beginning to gain insight into End Times cosmology by studying the dynamics preserved in creation mythology. In the Maya creation myth a vain and false ruler, Seven *Macaw*, has to be revealed and killed by The Hero Twins. This enables their father, One *Hunahpu*, to be reborn from Great Mother, the Milky Way. On an astronomical level Seven *Macaw* are the stars we know as the Great Bear or Big Dipper, whilst One *Hunahpu*, known as *Hunab K'u* in Mexico, is the deity of the Galactic Centre – the Heart of Heaven. With a sudden jolt I realized that the black-and-white *Hunab K'u* symbol does indeed look like a vortex, a meeting of matter and antimatter, a black hole.

Mirroring this mythic story, we have been 'blinded', in a period of spiritual darkness, led by vain and false rulers. Maya researcher John M Jenkins said in 1999 (at the commencement of the 13 'seating years'), 'The solstice-galaxy alignment, that the Maya intended their 2012 date to target, is the end of humanity's descent into deepening illusion and confusion. We are about to turn the corner and begin an ascending 13,000-year cycle, toward a new golden age of light and truth revealed. However, at this critical juncture all the control systems and delusion-generating propaganda will be making a final effort to destroy life and consciousness on the planet.'

This is our challenge.

I gazed longingly and contemplatively at the stars, mentally preparing myself for the next part of my quest.

The Festival of the Snow Star

Returning alone to Peru at the end of April, I booked a long trek that would take me to Cusco and then on to Apu Ausangate, an imposing 20,594ft (6,277m) ice peak. I had a mission to fulfil – what, I knew not – but the Inca messenger had been insistent. I had long since forgotten the attempt on my life in Mexico. The mountains and beautiful people in Peru gave me a deep sense of security.

Now I was struggling to keep up with the group of hikers. I could understand why the Incas worshipped these stunning mountains. We crossed spectacular passes, explored a chilly landscape below ice-clad peaks and enormous glaciers, hiked among herds of tasselled llamas and alpacas, and stayed in little huts provided by traditional Quechua families or camped on the edge of brilliant blue-glass mountain lakes.

As I got closer to Apu Ausangate (*apu* means 'spirit'), I started to mingle with crowds of other people on their way to the Festival of the Snow Star. Ausangate is the highest snow-covered peak in southern Peru. Its reputation as the place where the enigmatic Snow Star would be found caused the annual pilgrimage of many thousands of people to follow the herders' trails upwards. Crossing high grasslands, our group passed glacial moraines and walked alongside lakes of unbeliev- ably vivid blues, ringed with jagged snow-capped mountains in every direction. This magical world of snow, ice and glaciers is home to Quechua highlanders, who herd alpacas and llamas, relying on them for wool, food, transport and fuel.

At one of the campsites I was able to treat my sore feet to a refreshing soak in a natural hot spring! My shamanic training had taught me that the spiritual warrior always struggles to overcome personal weakness and limitations, against the forces that oppose his or her growth in knowledge and shamanic power. It is necessary to choose the strongest and most authentic way of carrying out each and every action. The warrior understands the importance of giving the best in everything. This implies optimum use of individual energy with the aim to increase perception of the *nagual*, the mysterious or the numinous.

So, next day, it was on again into the wilderness, enjoying the tough hike, looking out for wild llama (*vicunas*) and the spectacular sight of high-flying condors, the largest land-bird in the world. Along with my hiking group and all the other pilgrims, I was making my way to the foot of Apu Ausangate, to around 15,400ft (4,700m) of altitude, where temperatures are often below freezing.

In modern times the festival starts off with the day of the Holy Trinity and, although christianized, it is still clear to see that it is intended to bring the people closer to nature. *Apus*, who are the spirits of the mountains, still manage to call their people to the greatest festival of indigenous Indian nations in South America, the Festival of *Qoyllur Rit'i*.

Crowds were flocking to the area where the image of the Lord of *Qoyllur Rit'i* appeared on a stone. They continued on up the trails, a distant ribbon of moving colour. More than 10,000 pilgrims were climbing to the snowline, accompanied by all sorts of dancers in full costume (*chauchos*, *qollas*, *pabluchas* or *ukukus*) who portray various mythical characters. The *ukukus*, or bears, are the guardians of the lord, the *Apu* mountain spirits and *apachetas* (stone cairns).

Everyone is hoping that this will be the year for the fulfilment of the prophesied appearance of three Shining Ones, who will emerge from the Snow Star. As mentioned earlier, the *Qoyllur Rit'i* prophecy says that something will happen to the way we experience time – our present time period of *Taripay Pacha* will somehow merge into or become the golden age. I was encouraged to go on, despite tiredness.

I walked on with a great throng of happy people, struggling and almost gasping for breath in the cold air, with the dull weight of the crystal skull in my backpack. There seemed to be no particular reason for me to be on the mountain, but I had an overwhelming feeling that the skull simply needed to be there.

At first I was an onlooker, then the energy of the event swept me up into the dances and festivities. All around me the ordinary people seemed to be in a happy mood, moving in the dances like one huge body bedecked in robes of many colours. Then special dancers dressed up as mythical characters took over, enacting all sorts of weird and wonderful ceremonial dances that I couldn't even begin to understand.

I felt I was a little child again, for it was like a picture book with pages unfolding before my eyes. A magical kind of reverie came over me, as I partook of a feast spiced with all manner of sights and sounds. Some had Christian meanings, others told of something much more ancient and solid yet mysterious. Here a dancer twirling with a brightly plumed hat, there someone stomping around dressed as a strange gremlin-like figure.

People gathered in tight little knots around wizened old Q'ero prophets as they chanted about the *Taripay Pacha*, saying that, as well as being our present time up to 2012, it means 'The Age of Meeting Ourselves Again'. Plaintive songs on the panpipes accompanied many of the dancers as they moved to primeval rhythms. Later, young and old all joined in and, on occasions, I had to make a great effort in order to stay standing upright after my long walk up the mountain.

A condor circled over the highest peak. Was it a sign, an omen? Could this be the very day when the Shining Ones of legend would appear? Every so often excitement in the crowd seemed to rise to unprecedented levels – were they coming? What could I manage to see through all the masses of people if I stood on tiptoe? Some said that there were more than 40,000 pilgrims here this year – and the thought even crossed my mind that I should get out my camera, ready to record the momentous occasion. But no, it was just the ceremonies dedicated to the A*pus* reaching a climax.

Hugging my backpack containing the crystal skull tight to my chest, I was sure that the Shining Ones would grace the mountain and the waiting pilgrims another day soon. Enchantment was carried on the cool air and the sun brightened momentarily. At that moment I was convinced that, as the Inca shamans say, something could quite easily happen to the fabric of Time itself, such was the magic that the Festival of the Snow Star swept down upon the crowds; just like the soft flurries of snow that sparkled in our hair for a moment, and were then gone.

All too quickly the colourful dances, festivities and ceremonies were over. I was beginning to get chilled to the bone. On my way back down I watched in amazement as people hacked out huge blocks of ice that they hauled down the mountainside on their backs, for the symbolic irrigation of their lands with holy ice water from Apu Ausangate. The ethereal sounds of lone panpipes calling out from the mountains accompanied my downward trek.

It was with a heavy heart that I said my goodbyes, eventually reaching the airport to begin my long flight back to England. Images of the beautiful mountains and people of the high Andes imprinted themselves in my memory banks, as I made ready to enter into a dream state as my 'silver condor' flew me across the Atlantic, even higher than the mighty mountain I had just visited. This led me to think of a teaching given by Willaru Huayta, an Inca *chasqui*, at a private gathering in 1993 (it is quoted on several websites, one being www.indigenouspeople.net/southam.htm):

> We have been waiting 500 years. The Inca prophecies
> say that now, in this age, when the eagle of the North
> and the condor of the South fly together, the Earth will
> awaken. The eagles of the North cannot be free without
> the condors of the South. Now it's happening. Now is
> the time.

Back Home

Talk of ancient wise Beings of Light, the golden age of the Inca and Maya prophecies, new dimensions and worlds to explore, and all before 2012, was to be a big challenge for me. Yet I had been entrusted to carry the crystal skull 'to the End of Time', so I presumed that I would be given all I needed to know to help me in this mission.

Again and again I wondered what the End of Time really meant. Will life as we know it end, or can a golden age become a reality? Settling down to write my experiences, I sometimes had to pinch myself to know whether they had really happened. Returning to one's home country after time away always enables reflection and gives a certain sense of security derived from surrounding oneself with the familiar things of home. However, my complacency was to be shattered by turning on the television!

There on my television screen was a programme called *End Day, Apocalypses*. (BBC3, 12 November 2005). It proposed five different scenarios happening in quick succession that could totally destroy or severely limit our life on Earth. These were to be: a mega-tsunami striking New York, a dead comet annihilating Berlin, a super-volcano devastating the USA, Britain becoming a viral prison camp, and scientists destroying the Earth. Like a magnet the television drew me into the story, leaving me despairing.

The high sacred mountains of Peru and the enigmatic Cloud People seemed very distant as, with a heavy, saddened heart, I turned off my television and prepared to meditate before sleeping. Unlike many other people I am fortunate to be able to 'switch off' the negativity induced by such a programme. One way is to light a joss-stick or burn some herbs to dispel such a cloud of potential doom and gloom.

Once again I set the crystal skull before me, going deep into the intricacies of the crystalline structure through its eye sockets. I was immediately propelled into the stars of the Milky Way, travelling through them at great speed to a completely dark place in the sky. Time and distance had no meaning and I believe I saw the luminescence of the Great Central Sun around which all Creation turns, before I was brought sharply back into my room by the telephone ringing.

CHAPTER 9

The Singing Skulls

All was mystery; dark, impenetrable mystery. *

John Lloyd Stephens

My quest in the Americas was becoming like a detective story or treasure hunt, except that I wasn't sure what I was looking for or what the extent of the territory was. I was simply on a quest, and disparate pieces were slotting into place – to a great extent prompted by the crystal skull and its own seeming needs and intentions. This was now to lead me through the realms of history, astronomy, prophecy, extraterrestrial intelligence and crystallography, and to a major post-Classical sacred city in Mexico called Chichén Itzá.

Back to Mexico

The phone call disturbing my meditation was from the Yucatán. An old friend was telling me of the preparations for ceremonies being planned for the spring equinox at Chichén Itzá. She was sure I should be there. *Here we go again*, I thought. Only just recovering from jetlag! Why didn't *los aluxes* plug me into going straight up to Mexico from Lima? But, trusting her intuition, and my own on receiving her call, I made plans to return to my beloved Mexico.

* Comment by explorer John Lloyd Stephens upon his arrival at the ruined Maya city of Copán, Honduras, in 1839. He later purchased the extensive ruins for 50 dollars. It is now a UNESCO World Heritage Site.

As I sat in the aircraft for the long flight I had plenty of time to consider how prophecy has guided people worldwide throughout the ages. I specially choose that word *consider* when referring to taking my thoughts deep, because its meaning is based on the Latin *considerare* – 'to study with the stars'.

I thought about the crystal skull in the cabin locker above me. Even in the aircraft, it was able to make an energetic link with me. Every time I closed my eyes I received a violet burst of light in my head, causing me to question deeper and deeper the destiny of the crystal skulls and how they might 'sing' in some vibrational way to make a profound connection or revelation between the past and what is yet to come.

Are the shamans really able to understand the Threads of Time coming from the future? To answer this question we need to look closer at the stars.

The display of stars in tropical night skies is particularly brilliant – every night revealing a tapestry of fine points of light piercing the velvety, deep blue sky. I particularly remember an occasion when I was sitting together with Hunbatz Men under this awesome star canopy. He was explaining how the Pleiades figure in both the ancient as well as present-day wisdom-keeper teachings.

Looking up and pointing at the small hazy group of stars, he said, 'We Mayas call the Pleiades *Tzek'eb*, the tail of the rattlesnake, or sometimes the "four hundred boys". Every 52 years the movement of these stars in the cosmos causes them to come back to the same apparent position in the night sky. In Classical times (300–900 CE) our ancestors recognized these 52-year cycles of the Pleiades and celebrated a New Fire Ceremony at the end of each cycle by rebuilding temples. With great ceremony, all fires were extinguished, pottery was smashed and then new fires were lit from the rays of the Sun.'

I asked if he thought the ancestors of the present-day Maya were obsessed with the stars and time. He replied knowingly, 'They were watching for prophetic signs in the night sky about this very time in which we live, the final years up to 2012.'

Hunbatz Men described how their art of astrology was not solely about the obvious movement of stars and planets. More especially it was a mystical science, a *cosmovision*, to understand Spiritual Light. The

Maya recorded their memories in their folded books – a glyphic written record of earlier happenings, once retold orally or carved on stone monuments and later written down, rather like stories in the Christian Bible.

We know for certain that, over aeons of time, they charted their calendars, recorded astrological and astronomical details and waited for prophesied changes to occur. Hunbatz Men showed us places in the ceremonial cities of Chichén Itzá and Uxmal where astronomer-priests had constructed observatories and 'star platforms' upon which to take star measurements. It enabled the shaman-priest-astrologers to accurately calculate and record cosmic movements.

In Chichén Itzá the original observatory is named the Caracol (snail), because of its labyrinthine-like spiralling passages. I am fascinated when I look up to its roof and see statuettes of little extra-terrestrial-like people – perhaps evidence of the inhabitants' contact with living entities from other planets. Within the twists and turns of the Caracol's narrow interior passages a number of spyholes once enabled precise night-time astronomical measurements to be taken.

Archaeologists have discovered some observations consistently recorded by the Maya. Among them, the setting moon on 21 March, setting sun on the 21 March and 21 September equinoxes, on the 21 June solstice, and also the rising points of Venus. It is estimated that it would have taken 384 years to establish the accuracy of the Venusian cycle. Quite extraordinarily they calculated it to be 584 days, whereas modern astronomers fix it at 583.92 days.

Similarly, the name of 'Four Hundred Boys' given to the Pleiades is interesting, since modern astronomy identifies around 500 stars in the cluster, when only up to 14 are visible to the naked eye – so somehow the Maya possessed astronomical knowledge that modern people acquired only relatively recently.

By observing the stunningly beautiful nightly vista, the astronomer-priests were aware of the effects of the precession of the equinoxes upon the positions of the stars in our sky. They devised the Long Count calendar in order to track it. How else could they have predicted the end of the Fourth Creation, coinciding with the end of the Thirteenth Baktun of time (each Baktun being a period of 144,000 days), and then have it corresponding exactly to the northern winter solstice on 21 December in our coming year 2012?

They accurately accomplished all this from their stone-built observatories using, as far as we know, only the simplest of instruments. But just how did the old astronomer-priests, with their primitive methods, manage to predict so accurate a date, so far into the future? First, they fixed the start point of the present Fourth Creation as (in Gregorian dating) 11 August 3114 BCE. This was the beginning of Baktun One, or the beginning of the first 144,000 days. Then they counted forwards 13 Baktuns. Now we are nearing the end of that 13th Baktun, thus completing 13 x 144,000 days, totalling 1,872,000 days or one Great Cycle of Time, up to our date of 2012.

The Maya Long Count calendar worked like this:

		1 kin	= 1 day
20 kins	=	1 uinal	= 20 days
18 uinals	=	1 tun	= 360 days
20 tuns	=	1 katun	= 7,200 days
20 katuns	=	1 baktun	= 144,000 days
13 baktuns	=	1 Great Cycle	= 5,200 tuns
	=	1,872,000 days	

I asked Maya researcher John Major Jenkins, who wrote *Maya Cosmogenesis 2012* (Bear & Co., Boulder, 1998), to explain the origins and significance of the 2012 date. His response was this:

Izapa is an early Maya ceremonial centre in southern Mexico. It was the ceremonial centre of the Izapan civilization, which flourished between 400 BCE and 100 CE. As such, it was the transitional culture between the older Olmec civilization and the emerging Maya. Izapa is unique because many carved monuments are preserved at the site, and they depict the earliest version of the Maya creation myth (the Hero Twin myth). Izapa is very important for understanding the nature of the 2012 end-date in the Long Count calendar, for the

Izapan civilization invented this 2012 calendar.

The carved monuments depict mythology that encodes astronomy, and the monuments themselves are oriented to the horizons, which highlight the movements of the Big Dipper and the December solstice sun – both key players in the creation myth. As a deity, the December solstice sun is One *Hunahpu*, father of the Hero Twins in the creation myth. He is shown being reborn on Stelas 11, 22 and 67 at Izapa. This is the event that occurs at the 'end of the age' – on the end date of the Thirteen Baktun cycle in the Long Count calendar, 21 December 2012.

Izapa was an astronomical observatory that calibrated the future alignment of the December solstice sun and the Dark Rift in the Milky Way, which is the birthplace of Great Mother. Such an alignment occurs only once every 26,000 years (in connection with the cycle of precession of the equinoxes, of that length). This Dark Rift is a well-known feature of the Milky Way, viewed in the nuclear bulge of our galaxy's centre, between the constellations Sagittarius and Scorpio. This Galactic Centre location is also targeted by the Maya Sacred Tree, which is the cross in the sky formed where the Milky Way crosses over the ecliptic (the path followed by sun and planets). All of these astronomical features are deeply encoded into Maya traditions, such as the sacred ballgame, the king-making ceremonies and the creation myth.

The 2012 alignment of sun and galaxy, of cosmic father and cosmic mother, is preserved on the monuments of Izapa, which also served as initiatory teaching devices. In order to understand the original Maya revelation about the transformative alignment era of 2012, we can read the monuments of Izapa on several levels, as they preserve mythology, astronomy, spiritual teachings and a prophecy.

John Major Jenkins, website: http://alignment2012.com

Prophecies and Extraterrestrial Intelligence

Following an intuition to go back to the Yucatán, my husband and I arrived in Mexico City then flew on to Mérida. A cool air-conditioned coach swiftly took us to the heart of the Yucatán peninsula. We stayed in Pisté near the modern entrance to Chichén Itzá, sacred city of the Itzá Maya. That evening we sat upon the terrace of our *palapa*, looking out into dense dry jungle, lit by the occasional firefly. Countless toads croaked their night-time symphony. Distant dogs began to howl at the full moon. As ever, my crystal skull was nearby, so that it would imbibe as many experiences of sacred places as possible. Sitting in the cool silvery night, a welcome release from the heat of the day, a conversation with my husband began.

With the crystal skull between my hands, I asked him, 'Why do you think so many people in diverse parts of the world, over such long periods of time, have all observed the night sky, and some have even recorded visits by beings from other planets? You know, people such as the Dogon of Mali in West Africa developed a complex mythology indicating they had contact with extraterrestrial beings.'

'Yes,' replied Mikhail. 'As skilled astronomers, the Dogon observed Sirius and gave it special significance as a double star, centuries before modern astronomers confirmed that it was a double star.'

'And,' I said, 'in Egypt, mummified Pharaohs prepared themselves for rebirth from their elaborate tombs, because they believed they would be reborn as a star in a location in the sky called *duat*. This is the selfsame place in the night sky known to the Maya as "Eight-Partition Place". Curiously, the Egyptian symbol of rebirth was an eight-petalled lotus flower, still able to be seen in tomb wall paintings and carvings.

'What could have been the connection between these different groups of people?,' I asked him.

'Don't you remember?' Mikhail said. 'Hunbatz Men told us that Maya ancestors appeared in many places on Earth: the Naga Maya in India, Cara Maya in Greece and Mayax in Egypt. Couldn't that be the connection? Couldn't they have all been visited by extraterrestrial intelligences – for example, the Four Balaams, the people with wings and elongated skulls, that we saw carved at Ek' Balaam in Mexico?'

I replied, 'All of those countries you named are known for their great knowledge, for their astronomy and astrology, and they are places where prophecies originated or oracles were consulted. You are right – they must have all had a common origin. Do you recall the words "starseeds", that some people talk about?'

'Yes,' he agreed. 'Some teachings say that humans were "seeded" from the stars. Myths about creation and rebirth were very important to the Maya. The stars that figure most prominently in Maya mythology are those of Orion, called the Turtle of Rebirth, which was the fertile seeding place of rebirth for First Father, Creator God of this present age.'

Mikhail went on, 'Even today, the Maya refer to an area in deep space known to us as the Crab Nebula, M42, in the constellation of Orion. Creation myths tell us that it was connected with the birth of the first humans.'

'Perhaps they were the stars where those humans came from who "seeded" planet Earth in ancestral times?' I commented excitedly.

This conversation was getting really interesting. I got up to find my notes. This is what I read:

Astrophysicists reported in 1997 that there was an unusual type of ultraviolet light emanating from the M42 Nebula. Ancient myths are oftimes confirmed by science, for this is the very same part of the cosmos that the Kiché Maya of Guatemala name 'the Smoking Fire of Creation' (Q'aq), and the Mexican Itzá Maya call 'The House of *Hunab K'u*, the One Giver of Movement and Measure'. The astrophysicists confirmed that cosmic sources of ultraviolet light are very unusual. They said that coming from the very place of the Smoking Fire of Creation is polarized ultraviolet light, a governing factor in determining the left-handed spin of amino acids – the building blocks of all life forms on Earth; a crucial component in the formation of our DNA.

I wondered what other people in the Lands of the Turtle, the Americas, could tell us about our starry origins. Who better to consult than the Hopi, known as the Record Keepers, who are credited with having extensive knowledge of the past history of the world? As we have already seen they are also highly respected for their complex and detailed prophecies for the future.

I was becoming really excited as I pictured the Hopi people I had met sitting around smoking fires beneath starlit skies, telling stories of their ancestors, whom they say came from the Pleiades.

'Don't you remember?' I asked Mikhail. 'They told us a lot of stories, but the one I remember most is that their visionaries can go into altered states of consciousness, remembering even before Pleiadian times, when they came from Lyra. This is the Ring Nebula that they call the "Eye of God".'

The full moon was very bright now, spreading an almost golden glow upon the little streams of water running past our jungle *palapa*. An aquatic symphony of croaking toads was rising in a crescendo and my crystal skull, standing on the table before us, was scintillatingly alive.

The Hopi have named our present time 'The Fourth Age of Man'. According to Hopi sacred teachings, we are about to enter the Fifth Age or 'the World of Illumination'. Their wise ones predict two more worlds after this: the Sixth Age, which is 'the World of Prophecy and Revelation' and the Seventh Age, named 'the World of Completion'. So, clearly, if we can all heed their warnings, survive prophesied tumultuous changes and learn to respect and care for the Earth, they do not anticipate the world will end in 2012.

I sighed with relief as I realized that the world would not actually end. But I said to Mikhail, 'Times are going to be difficult for many people as we adapt to change, forced upon us by our constant overconsumption and neglect of the environment.'

'But I do believe we are waking up,' he said, taking hold of the crystal skull.

'Yes, and I am encouraged by the clearing away of old patterns that have held us imprisoned in a dark matrix. Don't you think that, little by little, like drops of dew falling into our shining ocean of superconsciousness, more of the mystery is being revealed on our quest, to understand the prophetic messages symbolized by the singing skulls?'

He nodded thoughtfully.

I reflected on the old Maya astrologers and knew that, as their bones crumbled to dust and blew across the stones of the pyramids, their souls lifted up into the stars. A lone silver thread of knowledge remained in the memory of time. For centuries records of their teachings were forgotten, lost in thick tropical jungle, just as their vast cities were lost to our sight. With the opening of Serpent Lord Pakal Votan's tomb at Nah Chan, more than treasure had been revealed.

Great leaps of understanding in archaeology and associated sciences enabled oral prophecies, handed down through the generations, to be substantiated by facts. I shivered with anticipation as I recalled that wisdom teachers say 'the Children of Time are returning'.

We are all *remembering* something very clearly – there is a sense around the world of living in End Times or times of reckoning. As we dream the Fifth Creation, waiting for it to dawn in our superconsciousness, we are also waiting for 'the time when there will be no time'.

What we learn from superconsciousness is that we can envision our possible futures just as an artist painting a picture draws from his or her creative superconsciousness to produce a finished canvas. As we picture the future, the power we have at our fingertips is virtually unlimited, so we would be advised to dream a beautiful flowering Earth.

Before we finish scratching the paint of the worn-out old canvas with the last few years of this Fourth Creation, let us take a look at the parameters for its ending. There are many predictions related to Maya calendars that describe the end and transition into the Fifth Creation or Fifth Sun. The Maya calendar day-keepers, who have kept the count of days and passed this knowledge down in family lineages, have been given the role of 'Cosmic Time Keepers'. Theirs is a reliable predictive tradition ranging from prehistory into the future – for possibly 5,000 years of continuous knowledge.

But something unique is happening: wisdom teachers, shamans and day-keepers would once have worked only for their rulers, keeping information for their ears alone and not for the mass of people. Like it or not, globalization is upon us, and they are now willing to share their prophecies and calendars more openly. I remain convinced that we can change even the direst predictions on the Threads of Time, with concentrated intention carried out by as many awakened people as possible.

Mikhail passed the crystal skull to me to hold. I thanked the indigenous elders who have said that the crystal skulls have a major, as yet unrevealed, part to play in the unfolding world scene as we approach this 'End of Time'. I stroked the clear crystal, shimmering in the moonlight. I knew that, as visionaries, co-creators, we can paint the dream of a beautiful flowering Earth – it is up to each of us to make it happen.

Chichén Itzá – City of the Seven Golden Doors

Chichén Itzá, Yucatán, Mexico, a major tourist destination, displays many aspects of the Classic Period that preceded its main construction phase, but it has a decidedly Toltec influence and archaeologists cannot agree who actually built certain parts of it. Awesome in size and grandeur, it takes many days to really see and understand the whole cos-mological picture presented to us by its skilled architect-priests within its mystical buildings and intricate stone carvings.

The main structures were given Spanish names by the Conquistadors and early explorers but, looking into the inner secrets of Chichén Itzá, we find that seven major locations (the 'Seven Golden Doors') still retain the essence of their Mayan names, forming part of an initiatory route around the city. I wonder if President Bush was aware of this during his visit, or did the site guides give their more usual erroneous blood-and-human-sacrifice versions of the Maya story?

The predictive and construction abilities of the ancient Maya come together in a remarkable way with the annual occurrence on 21 March, spring equinox, of a light-and-shadow effect down the staircase balustrade of the Great Pyramid of *Ku-kuul-kaan*. Very cleverly the pyramid was positioned in such a way that, at this time, the zig-zag shape of a great serpent appears, made of light energy emanating from Great Father Sun. At a precise moment the Serpent of Light visually and dramatically descends the pyramid, in order to renew Earth and her peoples.

Finally I am back at Chichén Itzá, standing under the trees and lingering amongst the crowds. Some say 60,000 people have trav-elled there for this most important day in the year – spring equinox.

All are waiting for the famous Serpent of Light to appear. Little groups of white-clad people sit in meditation or mingle with the masses of colourfully dressed Mexicans, here for a day's holiday. In the past the priests and shamans would have stood waiting too, lighting copal incense and praying for *Ku-kuul-kaan* to bless the Earth with his sacred serpent light.

Now though, the immediate area of the Great Pyramid and Temple of *Ku-kuul-kaan* is strictly off-limits to all but the Mexican custodian guards of the site, with barriers to keep the crowds back. As the afternoon wears on, even seasoned travellers feel the effects of the scorching sun in this shadeless place. At 4p.m. everyone starts looking skywards in anticipation. Will there be cloud cover? Will a tropical storm arrive at the critical time, to obscure the long-awaited spectacular, provided courtesy of the ancient Maya?

I see a group of my friends in the distance and go to join them, as they are engaged in some sort of ceremony with Hunbatz Men, the Itzá Maya day-keeper. I find that I am being asked to help dispel little clouds that are beginning to cluster in front of Great Father Sun, because they will obscure the serpent phenomenon. Like shamans of the past, our prayers are sent to the spirits of the rain within the clouds and, after some while, miraculously they begin to move away. Then the full power of Great Father Sun shines down onto the crowds.

Little groups of families have found shady respite under trees some distance away. At 4.30p.m. an excited cry goes up, and they rush forwards with thousands of others towards the north staircase of the pyramid to see the serpent descend to Earth. The balustrade of the pyramid presents seven triangles of light, alternating with six triangles of shadow, forming an effect like the diamond-patterned skin of a snake. This pattern culminates in the carved head of a serpent resting on the ground with a wide-open mouth.

There is great celebration, hugging and kissing, but gradually people's attention to the light-and-shadow phenomena wanes. This is my cue. With quick thinking and determination, I take the crystal skull out of my backpack, holding it carefully. In the company of two elders, I stride purposefully past the barriers at the base of the pyramid leading to the temple on top. I look skywards, up across the great expanse of tall narrow steps, seeking guidance from the burning sun. My heart is pulsing.

In my head I am hearing words, 'Feel the auric emanations of the pyramid. Go to the serpent.' The message urges me to walk quickly to the steps, to the head of the giant snake carved at the bottom, and to place the skull into its stony mouth. 'Call upon Great Father Sun. Let the encodements of Light activate the skull as you pray for the next 13 years, and for Earth's transition into the new Creation.'

The light from Great Father Sun does its miraculous work and serpent wisdom lights up the inner matrix of my crystal skull. Rainbow points of light outline something. I see energy building up inside, I see rainbow colours, I see strange, serene, part-human faces and unexpected images seemingly filled with love. Then, yes, a star system – the Pleiades. I come to understand that this, in some way, is the reason I needed to be here – indeed, the reason I incarnated on Earth at the end of this Maya Creation. This was one of those realizations of the significance of things that you usually get after the event – a feeling that 'this is why I am alive' and 'this is why things have happened as they have'.

With tears filling my eyes I turned to smile at each of the elders. We knew that our mission was now complete. Their dark eyes acknowledged mine and, within them, I saw hidden starry depths. Suddenly our timeless reverie was broken by the shrill whistle of a guard, who was waving us away from the serpent's head at the foot of the pyramid. Hurriedly I picked up the crystal skull and we merged back into the anonymity given by the crowds of people massed around this wondrous place.

Crystal Skull Prophecies

That night, after the intense daytime heat in the wide dry expanses of Chichén Itzá, Mikhail and I went outside. We rested in the cool air looking up at the stars, identifying different constellations. Suddenly we spotted an exceptionally bright light hovering over the distant pyramid. Some years before we had seen a comet, but this object didn't look like an aircraft or a comet. Watching it until it disappeared at great speed into a bank of cloud, my curiosity was suddenly aroused as to why Mexico, the land of the enigmatic Maya, has often attracted the attention of the ovnis – UFOs – that have been well documented on camera and seen by thousands of people, especially during the 1990s.

While our human life is based upon the element of carbon, some people believe that ETs want us to know about a silicon element in their DNA. Every computer and just about every complex instrument now used at home or at work contains silicon chips, to hold and transmit information through printed microcircuits. Who knows where this will lead, as we are slowly but powerfully opened up to a silicon world? Many of us spend days on end in front of computer screens. This causes me to ask, is it not strange that gipsy fortune-tellers once looked into crystal balls to see images of the future, and now here was I looking into a crystal skull?

The next night after the equinox ceremonies at Chichén Itzá, I sat with an old friend, Elmera, who is the guardian of a quartz skull called *Ebmnagine*. Naturally enough we began a conversation about crystal skulls. When I asked her about the legend of the 13 skulls she told me that Harley Swiftdeer Reagan of the Metis Society appears to be the source of that legend.

Swiftdeer asserted that there were once 12 planets with human life on them. Each planet encoded a crystal skull with all the accumulated knowledge and wisdom of their civilization, and then the skulls were brought to Earth. Subsequently Olmec priests in Mexico safeguarded them.

Swiftdeer says that the 13th skull was larger than the others, containing information of all the worlds. It was kept in an ark in Teotihuacán. These skulls were crafted in flawless pure crystal, capable of storing huge amounts of information. They had moveable jawbones like the Mitchell-Hedges skull, and for this reason they gained the reputation as 'singing skulls'.

Another wise teacher, Canocito spiritual leader Leon Secatera, has said that crystal skulls were used as a template to bring us into our physical and material form. He believes there is an entire crystal body still hidden in a cave in Belize. He also believes that the Earth is spinning through space like a spaceship – and the only 'controls' we have on this ship are the crystal skulls. They transmit a sound current, the music of the universe, or the music of the spheres, and are part of a crystalline grid that links the Earth to the rest of the universe. He states, 'The wisdom of the skulls becomes available when you open yourself to this mystery and let the sound come in.'

Hmmm, I think, as words like 'In the beginning was the Word', 'the Logos', 'sacred sound' and 'the symphony of the spheres' come into my head.

During the course of my travels I have been told many other incredible stories about the skulls. One recounts that *Itzamná*, a solar deity, taught the knowledge of crystal skulls at Izamal, Mexico, through skulls brought there from Atlantis 13,000 years ago. A strong message suddenly came to me: *many of the skulls are scattered in different places around the world and some are even in bank vaults, or hidden or undiscovered*. Perhaps they now need to be together in the Mayalands? For me the big question was, how could this make a difference? I didn't know precisely but, all the same, it just hit me as being very important.

I had to step back again through the Threads of Time to try to understand the old stories which relate that there are 13 original sacred crystal skulls. Yet others recount there are 52 ancient skulls that came from the Pleiades star system. For centuries Pleiadians have figured highly in Maya myths – they are sometimes referred to as the *mishule*. I have heard crystal skull keepers say that, held within the crystalline structures of the skulls, is their 'lembal' knowledge, undecoded holographic messages which await humanity.

They are reputed to hold secret keys for humanity's greatest leap of consciousness within a million years.

Endeavouring to understand what this could mean, we are urged to look to the not-so-distant future, to a time within our own lifetimes when superconsciousness is to be fully restored amongst a significant 'critical mass' of humans. At this point, some modern Maya teachers say, Father Sun and Earth Mother will reunite us with our brothers and sisters from the Pleiades. It would be a momentous first step on our long journey back to the stars.

Elmera, the crystal skull keeper, told me about other skulls in private collections that are being actively worked with in meditation and ceremony. She related how another crystal skull keeper, Joshua

Shapiro, received clairvoyantly transmitted knowledge that ancient people had direct contact with ETs. According to him the skulls are gifts from ETs, whom those ancient people elevated to the position of gods. He says that mysterious etheric crystal skulls are able to separate out from the physical crystal skulls, rather like the 'out-of-body' experiences that humans can have. He also confirmed that they are here now to awaken our own sense of spirituality in preparation for the coming Earth changes.

I learned about two other carved skulls, called the Mayan Crystal Skull and the Amethyst Skull. They were discovered in the early 1900s in Guatemala and Mexico, respectively, and were taken to the USA by a Maya priest. Both of them were tested at Hewlett-Packard and, like the Mitchell-Hedges skull, they too were found to be inexplicably cut against the axis of the crystal.

A number of crystal skulls are also owned by Frank Loo, who claims they were recently discovered in caves in the Himalayas. One of these Himalayan skulls, seen in ceremony by both Elmera and myself, was small, very worn and ancient looking. Most of these Himalayan skulls have large, elongated craniums, similar to the skull shapes seen in many ancient Egyptian tomb paintings.

In the past century, skulls have been newly carved in Mexico, Brazil, Germany, Nepal and China, so certainly not all of them are ancient. But any crystal skull, old or new, is a powerful object for scrying and divination because it can act as a clear channel for energy transmission between humans and their origins in the cosmos.

Crystals – Ancient Knowledge Keepers

During the period I have been on my quest to understand the prophecies I have sometimes been able to work with Elmera's crystal skull *Ebmnagine*. I contemplated this skull, finding that quartz crystal has extremely long 'memory' ability, much longer than that of humans.

All the quartz family – Amethyst, Citrine, Smoky Quartz, Rose Quartz, Ametrine, as well as Herkimers and Diamonds – have the power to hold memories encoded within them by light processes, because of their high silica content and regular crystalline structure.

At an esoteric level, quartz 'remembers' the time between lives, the period we humans spend in *Xibalba*, the principal place of existence of the soul, according to both ancient and contemporary Maya.

So it is not surprising that whoever fashioned the quartz skulls may have been trying to tell us something about our short memories. Each human life carries only a limited memory span, but quartz crystal memory is by comparison unlimited!

Over the years I have been present on numerous occasions when large sparkling quartz crystal skulls were passed to Mexican or Guatemalan elders and shamans to hold during ceremonies. In their hands, the skulls glowed with light and a kind of pent-up energy, giving the elders enhanced abilities to 'read' the Threads of Time. Clearly they increased the shaman's abilities to enter trance states to give prophecy.

I have heard elders of the Maya, who keep many ancient secrets within their families, say, 'These quartz skulls have always had communication with the living, and those who are alive should use the skulls to practise true traditions for communication with the dead.' One of the elders elaborated on this, saying, 'The skulls are teachers, containing knowledge from thousands of years ago.' To me this sounded rather familiar.

I asked Elmera to tell me about Ebmnagine. She said, 'Ebmnagine is a clear quartz Sirian skull, with the remembrance of his celestial origins. It has told me "I am Sirian and I am you". Ebmnagine is a clear channel, a conductor of information through the essence of where we have come from. He has remembrance of his starry origins, and the Earth's, as they are the same.

'This question about Ebmnagine is a very big question, very deep – where do I start? In my experience I find it difficult to explain that, to me, everyone's experience is also that of Ebmnagine. No matter who it is, there is a connection with them on whatever level and we come together as one, collectively to evolve. No matter what or whoever, he will align with your essence. So many times over the last nine years that Ebmnagine has been in my care, I have connected with many groups of people in ceremony or on a personal daily basis and have experienced their levels of shifts within myself.'

'So why is Ebmnagine here? Why has he come to you as a caretaker?,' I asked.

'I had worked with crystal skulls in the past. I knew we had to come back together to assist in realigning the damage that was done in Atlantis. So the 52 crystal skulls connect with people that were involved in this catastrophe and they know who they are *now*. Those people have been travelling the world to certain power points to heal the Earth's grid and to restructure the damaged energies, so we ourselves become more whole and less fragmented. There will be pinpoints of light that will be synchronized with the colour, light and sound spectrum, to be worked with.'

I asked, 'What song does Eb sing? And what song do the 52 crystal skulls sing?.'

She answered, 'It is beyond us and our human ability. It is a frequency. They don't actually sing together. It is more like "beaming up". What is their frequency of resonance that would actually bring them together? It is "being in love". You talked about the Earth feeling pain and sadness. Humans put conditions on "being in love". But the Earth knows exactly what it is doing, totally in love, and we can help look after it.

'The Earth *knows*. There is an energetic link between the crystal skulls and the Earth. The skulls are a conduit, a transmitter and receiver. In this instance the Pleiades act as a timepiece for triggering our solar memory. Orion will play another role and Sirius another, and Cassiopeia and all of the stars have their role to play. This is what we call the music of the spheres, a harmony. So for the activation of the 52, there needs to be a collective consciousness.'

Afterwards, I picked up my crystal skull and tumbled into bed. I was quite exhausted by the enormity of the Maya cosmovision held in the skulls. As I drifted into sleep I was reminded of the attempt on my life last time I was in Mexico. I was determined on this occasion to be vigilant. I resolved to place a protective light around my crystal skull and myself to avoid any more frightening situations. But what we intend and what actually happens can often be two very different things.

CHAPTER 10

The Call of the Cosmic Maya

As time went on, the stakes were rising. Mikhail and I were blessed with some very special experiences, but ominous events encountered on our travels and the full implications of the prophecies were also bearing down on us. Things had by now gone too far for us to pull out. If I was to carry the skull to the End of Time, what would be involved, and what would the End of Time look and feel like when we reached it? My quest had to continue, but what this was to involve was anybody's guess.

Toniná

I had returned with Mikhail to Toniná in Chiapas, Mexico, a place that had always held a great mystery for us both. The road journey there took us through the lush scenery of the Chiapas highlands, past a turning for a series of waterfalls on the Río Shumulhá in the Parque Nacional Agua Azul, and on to Ocosingo.

To all outward appearances this is a typical ranching community but, along with San Cristóbal de las Casas, it became the centre of world attention on 1 January 1994 when a mainly Maya group, the Zapatista Army of National Liberation (EZLN), occupied the town. By May local people had occupied 19 municipal centres in the region and, by June, over 300 farms had been seized from their landowners. Through their spokespersons Subcomandante Marcos and Samuel Ruiz, Bishop of San Cristóbal, the Zapatistas, like their Guatemalan counterparts, protested against debt peonage, bonded labour and erosion of indigenous land rights.

The Mexican army rapidly and furiously countered the nonviolent Zapatista rebellion with ground troops and aircraft, causing many fatalities. But worse was to come. Prolonged negotiations failed, and 45 Tzotzil Maya were massacred in church whilst attending mass in December 1997, probably by right-wing paramilitary groups who carried out a reign of terror against the indigenous population. The struggle for basic indigenous rights continues to this day.

> Capitan Insurgente Laura is a Tzotzil woman, fierce in battle and committed to learning and teaching. Laura becomes the captain of a unit composed only of men, all novices. With the same patience as the mountain that has watched her grow, Laura teaches and gives orders. When the men under her command have doubts, she sets an example. No one carries as much or walks as far as she does.
>
> After the attack on Ocosingo, she orders the retreat of her unit. It is orderly and complete. This woman with light skin says little or nothing, but she carries in her hands a carbine that she has taken from a policeman. He only saw someone to humiliate or rape as he gazed upon her, an indigenous woman. After surrendering, the policeman ran away in his shorts – he who, until that day, believed that women were useful only when pregnant or in the kitchen.
>
> **Subcomandante Insurgente Marcos, Centro de Medios**
> **Independientes, Chiapas, Mexico**
> **(http://chiapas.mediosindependientes.org)**

During a previous journey to Toniná in 1999 we encountered many army roadblocks and a huge army base being rapidly established, following the Zapatistas' demands for indigenous rights. While the recent history of the Toniná region is one of violence and struggle, historians and archaeologists like to call Toniná 'the place of the captives', since there are carvings of bound prisoners to be seen on its walls. However, my belief is that the ancient city was dedicated to the study of Time.

Upon arrival at Toniná Mikhail and I, complete with crystal skull in my backpack, walked through two partly restored ball courts and crossed the huge grassy plaza leading to a terraced hill completely covered in stone structures. Looking up, I counted 7 massive levels with 260 steps, 8 palaces and 13 temples. A stele here has the date Four *Ahau*/Eight *Cumku* carved upon it – the origin point of the Thirteen Baktun cycle.

The lower terraces have their stonework arranged in a pattern so huge that, on first glance, it is difficult to discern but, upon gazing at the whole area, it is clearly laid out in a snake-like pattern. Looking at it more intently, with the skull in my hands, I was 'told' by an inner voice that it was a large replica of the *Tzolk'in* 260-day calendar, made in stone.

I walked to the right of the calendar where corbel-arched entrances led to two vaulted rooms with hidden stairways leading up into the heart of the original construction. Stepping alone into the dank and dim interior it felt as if I was entering a secret place from mythic times. I paused for a moment as thoughts came flooding in about all the other tunnels and underground passageways I'd been told about in Maya cities.

A shiver ran down my spine. I held the crystal skull tightly and placed a protective light around us both. I climbed the slippery steps and, emerging into the sunshine on a slightly higher level, I could see all seven main terraces, most with remains of some temples and mounds still under excavation. I knew from a previous visit that on the higher levels are two of the most extraordinary vestiges of the past to be seen anywhere in the Mayalands.

Climbing the terraces' narrow stone steps zig-zag fashion, like a serpent, I arrived at a grassy platform with a covered-over, well-preserved, large stucco-plaster mural called the Mural of the Four Suns. It is a record, a huge codex, of Time. It records in its details the story of Maya cosmology – the creation and destruction of the Ages of Creation.

Different creatures are shown in each of the Four Creations. Each sun (representing each creation) is depicted by a falling head surrounded by leaves or feathers, representing the ending of the age. The suns look as if they are falling through Time. The criss-crossing body of an undulating feathered serpent, the *nagual* or alter-image of *Ku-kuul-kaan* or Quetzalcoatl depicts Time itself.

This god, unlike most other grotesque-looking beings in the Maya pantheon, is unusual in that he or she was a benevolent deity who guarded shamans when they took to shamanic 'flight'. When these master shamans went into deep trance states they could perceive luminous rainbow-like colours, and hence the god is also 'The Rainbow Feathered Serpent'.

Repeatedly shamans travelled in and beyond Time on their shamanic 'flight' to the stars, flying on the 'road to the sky,' called *Kuxan Suum*. Here at Toniná, *Ku-kuul-kaan's* image is shown overseeing the destruction at the ending of previous ages, and he will be waiting for us at the end of this Fourth Creation. A clearer prophetic message could not be imagined. I held my crystal skull aloft to connect with the spiritual light of the cosmovision that had produced it.

Again I marvelled at the ability of the Maya to track vast periods of Time. I could only guess at why they wanted to preserve their knowledge for us – the mural had been carefully hidden beneath the structure of a later building. It was only recently revealed, literally in the last years of this Fourth Age of Creation, as we ride the slippery Serpent of Time and prepare to enter into the Fifth Sun and Fifth Age.

I felt the light within my crystal skull was trying to communicate something to me. I wondered exactly what was being played out in this area of Chiapas on other levels of reality. To my mind, it is not without reason that Toniná was at the centre of an area where people, with help from the Zapatista movement, are creating a stronghold to reclaim their indigenous rights – for with their rights go their indigenous knowledge and wisdom.

Walking on, with the skull seeming to pulsate beneath my hands, I reached an enigmatic, very ancient, altar where there is a curious image of a face that some say is the 'Earth Monster'. It appears to be guarding a black stone sphere. This sphere, safely held in a womb-like cavity, must be the Earth, I thought. So Earth Monster does not mean a monster in the Dracula sense!

Mikhail came along and I handed him the crystal skull that by now was feeling very 'alive'. He asked to be left alone on the grassy slope so that he could go quietly within himself, together with the skull, near this special altar. I climbed up to a higher level of the city to sketch some details. When I returned an hour later this is what he told me:

'I went up to the altar with the crystal skull and lit an incense stick – it is less obvious to the watchful guards than the thick copal incense I bought from my Lacandón friends. I cleansed the altar and skull with the smoke, and left a small pink crystal there, tucked into a crevice of the stonework, as an offering. I sat a few metres away, from where, upon looking up, I could see the whole of the terraced ceremonial centre above me.

'It seemed to me that this little grassy spot was inviting me to put the crystal skull down. I soon became very calm, going into a meditative state, with my eyes just a little open. I had been there only for about ten minutes by my reckoning, when I heard voices nearby and thought, *Oh dear, my meditation will be disturbed*. But I kept very still, hoping these people would not notice me and would go away.

'Then, through barely open eyes, I glanced in the direction of their voices. Just five metres away from me were seven beings – humans. Well, perhaps they were humans. I knew not what they were. I wasn't surprised, just rather overawed as to what they were doing there. As I looked closer, I noted that they were dressed in long, hooded cloaks of deep red, purple and deep blue. Most surprising was that one of the figures, also in a hooded cloak, wasn't quite *there* in the physical sense.

'It was this person that had first drawn my attention, since he kept fading in and out of my vision and I thought it rather strange. Then I realized that all the beings were very tall – about three metres, I would estimate. Most surprisingly it registered that they didn't really have faces! They just had a kind of shining silvery mask. I didn't feel one bit alarmed or threatened. Indeed, they seemed not to be aware of me at all.

'As on similar occasions when I have had "messages" given me, I just kept very still. The beings kept murmuring in a language that I couldn't identify at all, pointing their arms and walking slowly around. I switched my attention to the crystal skull in front of me. It had started to develop an inner glow – just like the faces.

'Hardly knowing whether to watch the beings or the skull, I slowly moved my hands to cradle the skull. This took me deeper into the experience and my own skull began to throb energetically. In the distance I could hear the beings making sounds, low kinds of tones that gave me a feeling of deep love. By now my hands seemed stuck on the crystal skull and my head was still throbbing.

'Glancing across at the beings I could see that they were pointing to places in the distant landscape and in the sky, as if they were giving a reference for the various temples to a place in the stars, different for each. My head was getting really uncomfortable now. I decided to move my hands to get my camera from my bag, but in that moment, as I turned away and looked back towards the cloaked beings, they were gone.

'I sat very still for some time, knowing that the beings had really been there, although probably not in this dimension. Something to do with the crystal skull had enabled me to "travel" in time and dimension like the shamans of old.

'I don't usually talk about the things I see, as it can sometimes dilute the reality of them, for me. Perhaps it is a need to keep them separate from this everyday reality. But I saw you returning, climbing down the broken narrow steps, and decided to share my experience.'

Meetings with star beings are not an everyday matter. It took Mikhail some while to absorb what he had seen. We both recalled Maya elders showing us places on flat pyramid tops where strange lights had been seen and spacecraft had been observed. Tired of telling disbelieving authorities about this, the Maya now kept these accounts to themselves.

We have both been shown 'star maps' carved into stone at other ceremonial sites during our journeys. The connection to the stars was, and is, still strong in these lands. Earlier in the week we had been at Calakmul, another old city, looking at a small platform pyramid. It would be easy to imagine spacecraft landing in these out-of-the-way places, and beings coming to visit the elders, who would welcome them.

Yet Mikhail, when reflecting on his experience, was sure that, as a passive observer, he had slipped into another parallel time dimension rather than experiencing a close encounter with ETs. Could they have been the 'Cosmic Maya' that Wandering Wolf had told us about? Stranger things have happened in these lands. Were they those beings that, through the ages, had guided the Maya shaman-priest-kings and queens?

That night Mikhail and I decided to do a ceremony of gratitude with the crystal skull. We made a small altar and set the skull upon it, surrounded with red flowers. Beginning in our usual way, we 'smudged' (cleansed with herbs or incense) each other, the room and the skull with smoke from copal tree resin. It was our first opportunity to do this on our journey.

However, as we began, all was not what we had expected. Again the skull began glowing with strange lights and both of us felt our own heads pounding. Instead of seeing the cloaked beings as we might have hoped, we started seeing very disturbing things within the crystal. Pictures were being presented to us of masses of water causing flooding, people drowning and whole cities disappearing beneath the waves. Next we both saw the Earth shuddering, buildings toppling, large artillery guns firing and a strange-shaped cloud building up in slow motion in the sky.

These images came to us in a kind of hazy timelessness. Then we did see three of the ethereal beings, one in a red cloak, one in blue and one in purple. They stood staring at us and then pointed their fingers accusingly. This wasn't a good feeling. Perhaps we should stop the meditation and the ceremony. However, that wasn't so easy because the beings communicated that we should continue to watch the crystal.

We saw images of ghastly war and people howling in torment. We could take it no longer. We called upon the cloaked figures, 'Tell us what we must do. Is there anything we can do to help the Earth?'

'Tell the people to look to the stars, to remember their origins and work to stop the pain the Earth is suffering. Everything you do to one, you do to all. This is our message. We have spoken.' And with that the images in the skull disappeared in an instant, and we remained sitting in astonishment, saying not a word for at least half an hour, as our eyes filled with tears.

The Challenge

Discussing the previous night's meditation with Mikhail I recalled that the 'Day of the Year Zero' is the name of the day that ends the traditional Maya calendar. As I have already mentioned, it is predicted by some to be the day when the world will end – though it is actually the ending of a period of time, not of the world herself. In some of the prophecies there are indications that burning and darkness will envelop our planet, and the sun and the moon will change their colours. The Hopi also predict that dramatic Earth changes will be accompanied by a halo of mist around the sun and planets.

So I began to ask what the possibilities would be for a world destruction that forms part of both the scientific and indigenous prophecies. Neither makes particularly pleasant reading. Some arise as a direct result of human failings, such as global warming or nuclear devastation, while others are earthly or cosmic occurrences that happen anyway on a cyclic or 'chance' basis, throughout vast aeons of time.

Once again I held the crystal skull and peered into its crystalline depths. The words came to me, seemingly spoken by the skull itself, 'Who do you humans think you are?.' I thought of all the ancestral wisdom of humanity, amassed for us over at least 5,000 years of accepted history.

'You haven't the sense to see and act upon the indicators all around you. You aren't listening to the rain, the wind, the oceans, volcanoes, earthquakes and tsunamis.

'For over 40 years, your environmental movement has desperately struggled against modern civilization's rush to ecological destruction. People are bombarded with facts about endangered species, overfishing, pollution, but you just don't seem to hit upon the prime fact, that you are simply going to destroy yourselves. Yes, every one of you!

'The environmental movement has had only a limited effect because it is still locked into the same mindset as those who perpetrate this disaster, with their "progress", their technological fixes. Progress will be made when the free spirit of environmentalism has a broader base, linking it with spiritual aspects of life, calling on all peoples of the world to renounce war, aggression and oppression, and to replace them with peace.'

I reflected that war has grown out of greed, but as we follow our present destructive path, there will soon be nothing much to strive for. As prophesied, humans face a fateful choice: we can go on with our usual ways, even though they obviously lead toward environmental collapse, or we can strike out in an entirely new direction, developing radically different ways of being human.

Again words came into my head. 'Isn't it time for humanity to realize that its karma is embedded in ancient lands? Look to the origins of your civilization in Mesopotamia, now Iraq. Look to the origins of Christianity in today's Israel and Palestine. Look at each conflict burning out its karma as the age ends. Chinese against Tibetan, Protestant against Catholic, Muslims against Jews – and on and on the circle spins!'

I gazed into the crystal skull once more. 'There is a way of living on Earth that is far more healthy, graceful and balanced. It is a way of life so powerfully connected to the hardly noticed wonder that surrounds you that it can actually heal the devastation you have caused in your civilisation.' The skull was reiterating something the indigenous peoples have long known. I recalled the following words:

> In our prophecies it is told that we are now at the
> crossroads, either to unite spiritually as a global nation,
> or to be faced with chaos, disaster, disease and tears
> from our own relatives' eyes.

Chief Arvol Looking Horse,
19th Generation Keeper of the Sacred White Buffalo Calf Pipe,
2001 (*see* www.myhero.com, search for 'Arvol')

The Wisdom of the Hopi

Before I set out on this journey in Mexico with Mikhail, I endeavoured to collect more prophecies. Along the way I had the opportunity to speak to my friend again about the Hopi. This time I decided I would make it comfortable for her so we met in a cosy English tearoom. Over tea, scones and chocolate brownies we discussed Native Americans more than 5,000 miles (9,000km) away in *Abya Lala* – the Kuna Nation name for the Americas. Again she urged me not to give her true name, so I will call her Anne.

Talking with her again confirmed my suspicions that she had once had very scary encounters with dangerous men who were following her. Apparently they always wore dark glasses, even at night-time, However she had been so traumatized by what had happened that nothing would induce her to bring it fully to the surface of her consciousness. Despite my most compassionate attempts, she would not go into it.

We talked instead about how the Hopi prophecies tell the history of the migrations of the Red and White Brothers, sons of the Earth Mother and Great Spirit, who each had different missions when they set out in the four directions. Anne told me that in some accounts of the prophecies, Red Brother was charged to stay at home and keep the sacred traditions of the land while White Brother went abroad. Eventually forgetting the ways of Great Spirit, he made great inventions, even rockets that could take men to the moon.

At this point Anne's voice dropped to a whisper as her old anxieties surfaced. Tall and blonde, she was a fine contrast to the Hopi of whom she spoke. But today her back was bent over in pain and I noticed the first grey hairs carefully combed into her neat coiffure. Sitting there in her designer suit and high heels it was difficult for me to imagine the position of respect she said she had once held in the traditional life of the Hopi.

She continued, 'One day White Brother was destined to return to his homeland and share his inventions in a spirit of respect for his Red Brother's wisdom. It was said that his inventions would include cobwebs through which people could speak to each other from house to house, across mountains, even with all doors and windows closed. Of course, they were telephones.'

Her voice dropped lower, and I sensed a hidden fear within her as she gave the predictions, 'There would be carriages crossing the sky on invisible roads, and eventually a gourd of ashes that, when dropped, would scorch the Earth and even the fish in the sea.'

I responded, 'Yes, the Hopi have told me that if the White Brother's ego grew so large in making these inventions that he would not listen to the wisdom of Red Brother; he would be instrumental in bringing this world to an end, in a great purification of natural forces. They say there would be only a few survivors, but they would bring forth the next world, in which humans would know how to honour one another and nature, and there would again be abundance and harmony.'

Anne added, 'In this purification, wars and natural catastrophe may be involved, and it is said that the degree of violence will be determined by the degree of inequity among the peoples of the world and in the balance of nature. In this crisis, rich and poor will be forced to struggle alongside one another in order to survive.' She looked so pained by this prophecy that I wondered whether to go on with the subject.

I responded, 'But we may still lessen the violence by caring for the natural world and the rest of humanity.'

Again I held back, reluctant to discuss the final stage in the Hopi prophecies. Years before, a close friend had been so upset by the thought of world annihilation from the threat of nuclear war that she was totally broken and, until the end of her life, spent many months in mental institutions.

Gently I asked Anne, 'The final stage, the Great Day of Purification, has been described as a Mystery Egg. What do you think that could mean?'

'This is my great fear.' said Anne. 'There were all sorts of top-secret experiments way out in the desert when I lived in Arizona. I believe powerful energetic forces will be released, culminating either in total rebirth or in total annihilation. But, even now at this moment, during the Time of Warning, the Time of Preparation, *the choice is still ours.*'

I nodded in agreement. I knew that we could change. But time and again I had heard that, if no one is left to continue the 'Hopi Way', the hope for such an age is in vain. The messages coming from my crystal skull and the indigenous people were both clear: ancient, spiritually based communities such as the Hopi must especially be preserved, without being forced to abandon their ways of living and the natural resources they have vowed to protect (*see* Appendix 6.)

We finished our tea – two English women, born perhaps into the wrong culture, with a passionate desire to respect the ways of Great Spirit. As I got up to leave, Anne, knowing my interest in crystal skulls, asked me to take a look at the prophecies given by the Council of Elders of the Cherokee Nation.

The Elder of the Twisted Hairs Society

'Metis' Thomas Thunder Eagle, a Cherokee elder, made the following declaration:

In the tradition of the Cherokee secret medicine societies, the Elders of the Twisted Hairs Society, I have been moved by the secret knowledge and spirit to reveal the following words.

This sacred knowledge is from my Elder Heyoehkah, the war chief of the Twisted Hairs and a member of their council of elders.

There will be a disaster that is of great consequence. But, in essence, your disaster has already begun. You will find much death amongst your life forms upon the planet. You will find that which is grown in the ground will cause much change and you will see that which feeds upon the ground will end up with much death.

You will see much destruction due to what you call 'radiation', caused by your self-destructive tendencies. You will find much pestilence in that which now flies aloft upon your planet. There will be eruptions and disruptions of weather patterns, and much separating of atmospheres. You will have much surface wind, and your livestock will die in very great numbers.

Your waters will rise where they should not rise and your land will be sinking underneath the waves. Landmasses will disappear and seas and oceans will rise. There will be a great splitting of the Earth from deep within the Earth. The magnetic field will shift and is already shifting now.

The Earth will split asunder and the discharge will wander through the Earth and into the outer atmosphere. The atmosphere is already entering a state of negative pollution – your oxygen content and biosphere cannot cleanse itself completely anymore.

This is what you, the beings of the Earth, are causing with your disruptive, negative thoughts and actions. And this is why we left these receptacles (crystal skulls) for you to find, in your time, from over 750,000 of your Earth years ago, very long, long ago, in times far past.

When we realized that so many had forgotten the original purpose of your incarnation into this physical dimension, when we realized that the mind of separation would take hold and that there would be a great catastrophe on this Earth, we chose to return to our own original dimension. But we left behind the legacy of our minds.

We knew there would be those whose knowledge, seeking and spiritual progression would turn them towards this path. We knew that, because of the disaster that would befall this planet, there would be those who would be needed to call upon their reincarnation memories to heal, to counsel and to love a world gone mad, a world without knowledge, a world without hope, where the fires of destruction would reign. But when the time comes, it will be the duty of all those who seek spiritual knowledge to instruct others when the Earth moves from its axis.

Within this receptacle and the others we have left you lies that which you will need. Our imparted knowledge, here crystallized, will be imparted when the right time arrives. It was determined that, through these receptacles, the minds of oneness would be activated and would present themselves when your Earth was in need. And this is now beginning to happen, as you say, 'at this time' and 'in this place'.

full version to be found at
www.redelk.net/website/CrystalSkullMsg.htm

The Journey Onwards

We had so much to think about when discussing all these prophecies. Our minds were dwelling upon world-shattering events, so we gave little thought to our own protection – physically or psychically. Mikhail and I walked around the small town where we wanted to stop overnight after leaving Toniná. It was clearly a truckers' stopover, as everywhere huge articulated diesel monsters were drawn up at dusty roadside cafés and dubious-looking lodging places.

We were searching for a reasonable hotel and somewhere to eat. We sat at a little bar and asked for bottled water and beer. All they had was Coca-Cola. Then, to our surprise, the bar owner went out, dashed across the busy highway and returned ten minutes later with our water and beer.

We sensed something was not energetically right. It seemed as if I had fallen through a crack into a different alien world. The feeling we had about this town wasn't good. We reluctantly took a room in a small hotel, knowing that it would otherwise be a long drive to find other possibilities. We settled for the night but were disturbed by voices. Looking out towards the parking lot, we saw the shadowy silhouettes of two people who were arguing loudly. Even in the poor light I was surprised to see that they were wearing sunglasses.

'Mikhail,' I said, 'That's the car that followed us before.' I felt agitated and explained to him that I had memorized the first part of the number plate. It was the same white car that had followed us when the tree fell upon the riverside restaurant over a year previously. Now the identical car was parked opposite ours.

Since that incident we had always tried to take great care of the crystal skull. My rucksack virtually never left my sight when we were travelling. We decided to leave this strange place as soon as possible. When the two men had gone we would creep down to our car and leave. We took turns to sleep, waiting until we thought our pursuer would be asleep too.

Finally, as the moon rose, casting her long eerie shadows across the parking lot, we quietly got into our car, placing the skull between my feet, carefully wrapped in a Mexican blanket, and we drove away. Once on the main road we speeded up, putting as many miles as possible between us and the hotel. We decided it would be safest to head off for the border to Guatemala, passing through San Cristóbal. Arriving in the early hours of the morning on the Mexican side we dozed in the car until the sleepy customs post at La Mesilla woke up demanding an extortionate *inspeccion aduanal*. Would they search us, find the skull and confiscate it? On other occasions we had even had our Mexican oranges confiscated!

Armed police strutted in high leather boots and an army post, bristling with arms, lurked behind a towering wall of sandbags. There were scary consequences of being caught with an ancient artefact in one's possession. Would they think we had been digging in the ruins and throw us into prison? We smiled sweetly at the customs officer as we reluctantly handed over our dollars, just thankful to be getting out of Mexico without further incidents.

We spent the rest of our time on that journey reflecting upon the dangers that had crossed our path and deciding whether in future it would be best to just stay safely at home with the crystal skull. After all, it could be put to good use for meditation and scrying. But then, would I fulfil the mission I had agreed to in the *kiva?*

As the years sped by, my decision was clear. All my shamanic training urged me on. A spiritual warrior does not flinch when things become tough. My *nagual* self spoke clearly to me on many occasions when I 'communed' with the skull. It became imperative that I should take the skull to the 'End of Time'.

Part Three

Time – After Time

I take you forward in time in these last three chapters into an allegory about just one future possibility on the Threads of Time. Once 2012 has actually passed, it might not be possible to tell you the story of how I reached the End of Time!

Whether or not things will work out in this way I do not know. Parting the strands of Time and then weaving them into a whole vision for the future is never easy, even for those masters, the Keepers of Time.

If I ask you to dare to peer into the future under their starry cloaks, you may perhaps see a picture you might never have imagined – not even in the most colourful of your dreams. For wisdom may be found, without struggle or effort, when you access superconsciousness and the WorldWideWeb of Light. By engaging with possibilities held there, perhaps we actually call them into our world. Perhaps our intuitions can be tweaked to help us clarify what we need to do *now*, in the present – and this is the most important thing.

I believe the ancient Maya want us to complete our mission in the present, to secure our future. So I invite you to walk with me on this path over the edge of Time, where there is no knowing what may happen, or where, or when.

Some years have passed, and we start in the year 2011. Mikhail and I have returned to Guatemala City, eager to escape the spreading hand of relative poverty that is now taking its grip in Europe, following a time of disaster. I am aware also that, if my mission to carry the crystal skull to the End of Time is to be fulfilled, I must act quickly. I must do something to return the skull to the lands of the Maya, where intuitively I just know it needs to be.

CHAPTER 11

Jaguar Paw Stone

Guatemala City, Spring 2011

S pending a day walking the streets of Guatemala City, soaking up the colour and life of the people, I sat down at a juice bar. Taking a refreshing mango drink, I heard, 'Uno Quetzal, uno Quetzal...' and looked into a little girl's imploring, coffee-dark eyes, her hand held passively open in front of me. Next to her was a deformed little boy, no older than eight years, in a little trolley.

I handed the girl some change, but still she stood there with a dignity beyond her years. 'Por favor, señora, por favor...' She seemed to imply, *I am here, you are there, a rich white woman. What price is your conscience?*

Yet there was no incrimination in her gaze. Her eyes never left mine. Then the broken, twisted body of her brother twitched and his enlarged head turned, prompting me to reach again for my purse. A faint hint of a smile lightened the little girl's face and she moved on. '*Uno Quetzal, uno Quetzal...*'

I finished my drink, and then a strange thing happened. Two young men started an argument across at another table and, as they did so, a third man in dark glasses came up behind me. From a corner of my eye I saw his hand as it reached for my rucksack containing the precious crystal skull. I grabbed the handle of the rucksack, yanking it away from him and pushing the table forward. Glasses of drinks flying, falling and breaking, caught the attention of the waiter. He yelled out something unintelligible to the fleeing thief.

Somewhat dazed, I heard a car pulling rapidly away from the corner of the street. Fortunately the skull was safe. I quickly made my way back to our cheap hotel, not wanting to be out late in a city that has long had a dangerous reputation, even before the drug trafficking reached the levels of today. Walking quickly, glancing sideways, rucksack safely on my back, I felt uneasy. I did not see the man in dark glasses following, one moment merging into the crowds, one moment walking quickly behind me.

Piedras Negras

Early the next day Mikhail and I set off for the ruins at Piedras Negras, a remote Maya sacred site in the Guatemala Petén rainforest, accessible only by a two-day-long horse trek and white-water rafting on the vast Río Usumascinta. For over half a century a mystery story has grown around its unrestored mounds of stone, which hide broken pyramids held in the grasping roots of giant trees.

It is an abandoned, unfathomable place. Hidden beneath the fallen temples of this city is said to be a 'Hall of Records' whose revelations could prove ancient contact between the Old and the New World. In the spring of 2006 I had tried to reach Piedras Negras from the Mexican side of the river but arduous wet conditions had made the tracks impassable, even by horseback.

Two years before that, in 2004, an expedition funded by A R E, an organization researching the work of Edgar Cayce, the American 'Sleeping Prophet' of the 1930s–40s, managed to reach the ruins with difficulty. During one of his deep trance states Cayce had indicated that an ancient city, probably Piedras Negras, was one of three locations of Atlantean 'Halls of Records', apparently placed there around 10,000 BCE.

Two people from the expedition spent a day at the National Museum of Anthropology in Guatemala City with a Guatemalan archaeologist, who had done extensive work at Piedras Negras. They reported, 'He was amazingly open and not only answered all our questions, but he gave us details of all the most recent digs at Piedras Negras, as well as revealing the ideas and hypotheses held by various archaeologists, who have an inordinate interest in Piedras Negras. In brief, archaeologists appear to believe that Piedras Negras conceals something very important and perhaps astonishing.'

Fortunately the damming of the River Usumacinta, adjacent to Piedras Negras, proposed in 2006, had not happened by 2011. If it had, four ancient cities and acres of virgin rainforest would now be under water, courtesy of Plano Pueblo de Panama.

A four-hour journey over rough tracks through the rainforest jungle took us to the wide, grey-green river. Everywhere dense forest provided an almost impassable wall of mystery. Brave indeed were the early European explorers and archaeologists who literally had to cut their way through it to get anywhere at all. However, we saw places where settlers were destroying ancient trees and burning the land, ready for fields of maize or new cattle ranches.

Such were the levels of denial prevailing at the time, that many ordinary people were trying to continue their lives along the lines of previous decades, hoping that business and ordinary life would revive, that this was just an ordinary downswing. But others, principally the farmers and others who listened to the spirit of the land, were aware that something else was going on, and that things were fundamentally changing – but in what direction, hardly anyone knew. Governments and social authorities were losing their grip, and barely able to do more than make it appear that they were doing something.

Reaching the river, Mikhail and I, together with my crystal skull, took a small boat downstream to Piedras Negras, paying an extortionate price to cover the smuggled fuel. This part of the journey took six hours. It left us little time to explore the ruins. We knew that we would have to camp and we had already planned to stay for at least two days, with the permission of our guide. He had travelled in the boat with us, glad to get any paid work at all.

We wanted to explore alone and, fortunately, our guide was happy to sit at the riverside with the boatman and enjoy the food provisions we had brought. So, late into the evening we walked through the ruins, still densely covered with the vegetative mat of time. Lianas hung from branches heavy with epiphytic plants, and strangler fig trees sought their victim saplings and grew headstrong up to the upper reaches of the forest canopy and sunlight. The site was now hardly maintained.

We walked quickly back to our planned rendezvous with our guide, for it was now almost dark and the forest had changed from what it was during daylight!

Tree roots crossing our path became snakes and huge leaves dropped on us, silently transformed into ethereal hands as they gently touched us. Then there were haunting night-time sounds – deep croaking from toads along the riverbank and eerie howling as male howler monkeys asserted themselves in their forest domain. We arrived at the river, breathless, hot and sticky, our journey lit by dancing fireflies. We hoped against hope that *los crocodillos* that the boatman had warned us about at night would not yet be seeking their supper!

We decided to leave our deeper, psychic investigation of the ancient city till the next day. Accordingly, rising early, we returned to the lush central plaza, where an unusual stone altar lay in two pieces. Apparently it had once stood on four stone heads, long since looted. It was in the shape of a large jaguar paw. Archaeologists say that when Chan Panak of El Cayo, a nearby Maya city, 'ascended the Paw Stone' in the presence of the Piedras Negras ruler, he would have been standing upon this very stone. Being an important ritual spot we took the crystal skull from my rucksack and placed it upon the Paw Stone.

Balaam Ek

Friends had often asked us what our crystal skull was called. Does it have a name? To which we replied, 'No, it is sufficient for us to know that it is a sacred object.' Over the years since the skull had been gifted to me in the *kiva*, many people had held it, looked at it with curiosity, in awe, or sat in meditation with it. Very often they would describe their experiences to us.

One person, Shandy, had said, 'I felt my higher chakras expanding with light. I have never felt so connected to the universe before. The skull beneath my hands was moving like liquid. It was extraordinary.'

Maria, who is extremely psychic, told us, 'I felt the skull moving in my hands. I felt a vortex and saw many things I could not explain, but one was a spiral galaxy and a huge amount of light.'

'I felt an incredible resonance and a shaking from the skull, going into my own eye sockets. It was telling me I could look at the skull of a person and tell how many times they have been reincarnated. The human skull is a map or a hologram of information, waiting to be discovered,' said Steve, looking visibly stirred by his experience.

I remembered Alfredo saying to us in Spanish that, when he held the skull, he went into a different time and space that was fast-moving and a mix of colours. He went on to add that it was a 'space-time wind'. Faces kept developing in the crystal and he said, 'I could have held it all my life.'

The previous night I had dreamt of being in a crystal cave. Sometimes the dream was not so pleasant, for real heads, severed from their bodies, kept appearing. It seemed threatening. But when I concentrated hard on the image of my crystal skull, mercifully it would appear and the bloody heads would disappear. When I awoke I wondered about the meaning of this dream that recurred time and again. It seemed a little ominous. Hoping it would not foretell anything disastrous, I put such an idea to the back of my mind.

Mikhail and I sat opposite each other, the crystal skull between us on the Paw Stone. We placed some forest flowers around it and each of us gave a little pinch of tobacco as an offering to *los aluxes*, the spirits of the place. Closing our eyes we asked, as always, what we could learn from the skull. Suddenly in front of me I saw the skull's eye sockets pulling me into a sparkling, endless cosmos. 'This is where I come from,' I heard.

Then, 'I have a name. It is *Balaam Ek*.' It somehow wasn't surprising to me that the skull should have a Mayan name, even though it came to me in the Anasazi lands. I immediately knew that *Balaam* meant jaguar and *Ek* is a star or planet, usually Venus.

Keeping very still and concentrating all my *nagual* power upon the skull, I replied 'Thank you. I am grateful for everything you have shown us, Balaam Ek. You really do shine like the Jaguar Star that you are. I pledge to protect you, with my *life* if necessary. I *will* take you to the End of Time.' And with that our meditation came to a close.

During the next two days we explored Piedras Negras and found a gigantic, dry *cenote* (an old water hole), with walls several hundred feet deep. We found the site's main buildings and pyramids around the apex of the mountain. We were looking for anything unusual that the archaeologists might have missed, that might give a clue to Piedras Negras possibly containing the Yucatec Hall of Records.

Quite what a Hall of Records would be, we couldn't imagine. Perhaps it could give us important clues in my mission to take the skull to the End of Time. We found tunnels and chambers appearing to go deep within the mountain, but they were so broken-down with time that we did not dare enter, even if they did contain some kind of hidden records from the past. This reminded us of the Maya elders, who had spoken of long tunnels beneath the Earth connecting one city to another.

Vision Quest

The caves were another matter. We came prepared with a strong rope that assisted our descent to around 50ft (15m) below the surface. One in particular seemed the perfect place to stay the night and go deeply into a vision quest with the skull. It is important to observe certain rules when undertaking a vision quest and, for this solo quest, I asked Mikhail to leave me in the cave and for him to swing in a hammock under a mosquito net in the trees outside.

Once he had left I began preparations ... safety, comfort, torch, drawing a medicine wheel circle in the soft dirt of the cave floor, followed by the personal ritual I customarily used for setting up a 'sacred space'. Above all, focused intention. Then the big questions: What should I do next with the skull? What was to be the destiny of the world as 2012 approached? I was convinced we were very close to the End of Time – we were teetering on the edge. It seemed so long ago that the skull's previous guardian, the old woman in the *kiva*, had spoken to me.

This was turning into a vision quest more powerful than any I had undertaken before. I was immediately surrounded by snarling jaguars that faded in and out of my field of vision. They were so close that I could feel their hot breath on the back of my neck. Quelling my fears I called out to them to be still and asked for an old friendly jaguar that had often protected me in my quests to step forward. Immediately I was swept quickly through the wild forest.

At one moment I seemed to be riding this jaguar, and at the next I was looking out through his eyes. Eyes, deep yellow eyes, turned into stars. Once again, fractal images enfolded me – pictures of resplendent Maya kings; people toiling in hot sun, struggling to lay massive stones on half-finished pyramids; the scorching sun kept blinding me and I repeatedly blinked my jaguar eyes. The forest was burning, the sacred corn dying. Gods of death were stalking, destruction was all around and people were screaming.

Then stillness, utter peace and a feeling that I was in the stars and that the crystal skull Balaam Ek was guiding me. Suddenly I saw more crystal skulls. They merged together and a mist arose above them, in which was held a shining golden figure with a most beautiful human form. Then the stars spun around me again and voices called from far away. Try as I might, I couldn't awaken from my vision.

Eventually, after a long night, during which I intermittently nodded off into some kind of sleep, I was jolted awake by the voices of the ancestors. The message they gave was clear. 'Your quest is almost over. You and Balaam Ek, Jaguar Star, must journey to the Heart of the World. There you will place the skull in the temples that radiate Light for humanity. But beware of unseen dangers. The time is not yet.'

My last task that morning at Piedras Negras was to offer a short prayer of thanks to the unseen *aluxes* and spirits, whom I had seen as tiny dancing lights in the forest. I would be leaving and meeting Mikhail, the guide and the boatman in 30 minutes. As I settled down, resting back against a huge sapote tree, I felt just a little uneasy, as if I was not alone. Probably a monkey or a jaguar, neither of which would hurt me, I thought. I felt protected by the great buttress roots of the tree, wrapping themselves around me.

I carried on, but a breaking branch in the distance disturbed me again. Something caught the light, like metal glinting in the sun, in the trees. I shuddered as I remembered my recurring dream about the severed heads and the long sharp machetes carried by forest workers. Tourists rarely came to this place and I knew there were no people living nearby. I started to feel anxious, picked up Balaam Ek, placing it carefully in the colourful Guatemalan fabric which padded out my rucksack, and made my way quickly to our meeting point.

Dangerous Encounters

Rushing to tell Mikhail of my fears, he urged me into the waiting boat. The boatman was alone. Where was our guide? Best not to wait for him. We asked the boatman to quickly untie and get away from the river bank, to where we would feel safer.

Over the years the crystal skull had caused a lot of envy, so I had revealed its existence to only a few trusted people. There were even rumours that government agents of more than one country had more than a passing interest in the properties of the skulls. We knew that FBI agents had been snooping around some of our ceremonies over the years, posing as charismatic leaders, photographers or film directors. They had chosen the wrong people to try to fool – most of us were keen students of human behaviour and some of us could read their telltale behaviour and negative auric emanations.

But still we were slightly fearful that there were many who would like to know the secrets of Time by possessing a crystal skull. Despite putting aside these fears, I felt a shiver pass down my spine as I recalled the incident in the juice bar in Guatemala City. Had the strange man in dark glasses even followed me here?

We pushed out into the river, the motor urging us forward against the flow. Suddenly a shot rang out. We were being fired upon! Crouching low in the boat, the boatman opened full throttle and headed for the centre of the river. More shots hit the water as we sped along. A small plane appeared from just over the forest canopy, turned and sped not more than 30ft (10m) above the river surface. Three bags were jettisoned and splashed into the water just as two speedboats left the Mexican shoreline.

For a moment we thought their interest was focused on the bags, but one of the boats swung round and came after us in hot pursuit. Shots again rang out, aimed in our direction, and a voice with an angry American drawl shouted at us to pull over to the far bank. There was no way we were going to stop. We heard another motor start up. Now we were being followed by two small boats.

Then, even more scarily, it dawned on us that we had stumbled across the dropping-off point for narcotic traffickers, smuggling drugs into USA, whom we'd previously heard about in a bar at La Frontera.

We knew that trading in ancient artefacts sometimes funded their drug trafficking. Perhaps they had seen me meditating with the precious crystal skull at Piedras Negras.

Great surges of tepid green water rushed past us as the macho pride of the boatman fed his adrenalin. We realized we'd be in deep trouble if caught in this remote area by traffickers, so it was a great relief to find we were increasing our distance from the pursuing boats – the boatman said we had a Kawasaki 400, while they had only smaller 250s. We had time to think. What did our pursuers want? Could it be the crystal skull? All the time we were drawing a bit further away.

The boatman, seeming a little pale even beneath his dark skin, looked questioningly at us. This kind of event didn't usually happen when he transported archaeologists to Piedras Negras. One hand held the steering, his other hand nervously fingering a gold crucifix. After going flat out for some three hours, we rounded a wide bend in the river. 'This where you get off, *amigos*,' he said, pulling into the bank, our craft hidden behind huge rocks jutting out into the water.

'But this is the wrong side of the river,' we said. 'This is the Mexican side.'

'I not take you back to Guatemala,' he gasped. Pointing to my rucksack, he said, 'You bring bad luck, you call up evil spirits with what you got in there.' With that he crossed himself and pushed us off the boat – into Mexico.

Far from being connected with anything evil, as the superstitious boatman had thought, crystal skulls are regarded by traditional priests and elders as a holy manifestation, even surviving through the changing times and Earth upheavals at each Maya creation. Yet the chase and the boatman's suspicions had ruffled me, and I was reminded of a teaching given by Mahatma Gandhi:

> Keep your thoughts positive, because your thoughts become your words.
>
> Keep your words positive, because your words become your behaviour.
>
> Keep your behaviour positive, because your behaviour becomes your habits.

Keep your habits positive, because your habits become
your values.

Keep your values positive because your values become
your destiny.

From *Life is Too Short*, Mary J Pryor, Pryor Group, 1999

The Voice of the Skulls

Still feeling rather shocked by this adventure we sat down on the
riverbank to decide what to do next. Of course I naturally turned to
Mikhail for ideas, and he acquiesced as I reached into my rucksack and
unwrapped the huge crystal. I was beginning to feel it was all part of
our present predicament. 'Up the river with no boat', as they say!

Balaam Ek needs to be held with one's free hand slightly off the
skull, within its auric emanation, in order to feel its full power. On one
occasion it told me, 'You have a head of flesh containing a skull and
circuits of silver light information. If you understand this, you will also
see that time is an illusion. What you call time is not real and, together,
we will begin to know this. Comprehend that there is an inner nature
to the Earth's energy about which you know little, but it is ready to
cooperate and to assist humans in their evolution. There is no time,
only the *now*, eternally in the heart of all that is.'

This time Balaam Ek again seemed to put words into my head,
saying, 'Humans play their games of politics, relationships and wars for
amusement, as a diversion from the essences of paradise. The birds and
animals do not count time or money. They, in contrast to humans,
work alongside Earth elementals to connect the luminous threads of
nature – like the Native Americans' Grandmother Spider. They hold our
planet Earth in a particular frequency to form a loving embrace of the
creative, generative forces of the cosmos. This embrace is a holding of
all in perfection and light in order for the "experiment" of humans in
the mind of the gods and goddesses to be fulfilled. Each and every living
creature in the vastness of the cosmos can look to Earth, Gaia, and be
blessed in their own spiritual evolution of perfection.'

When I related this to Mikhail, thinking about the practicalities of getting us out of our present situation in this remote part of Mexico, he said, 'But that's not going to find us a boat.'

We started walking away from the river. What else could we do? Finding small tracks through the tall grasses at the river's edge, we eventually came to a rough dirt road. Which way? We decided to head west, thinking that sooner or later we might get to the road on the Mexican side of the river. Eventually we arrived at a Maya village and asked for drinking water. With no chance of transport there, we walked on in the direction the villagers indicated.

Coming to a larger road, we stopped, exhausted. One or two trucks thundered by, loaded up with vegetables, but they didn't respond to our signals for a lift. We continued to sit, hoping for a kind passer-by or for a combi bus to take pity on us *gringos*. Day turned to dusk, fireflies darted between the trees and, in the distance, howler monkeys began a quarrel. Unearthly howls once again carried on the cooler air.

By now we didn't know what to do. We decided to get out Balaam Ek again in order to consult the Maya gods, for surely they would know. Just before nightfall we found some bright red forest flowers and made a little altar upon which to sit the crystal skull. We both began a shallow meditation. I was told, 'Trust, believe that all will be well.'

Two minutes later, the sound of tyres crunching along the stony road brought me back out of meditation. A car pulled to a halt beside us. Mikhail was already getting in. I rushed to pick up Balaam Ek. As I did so in the dimming light, and somewhat blinded by the car's headlights, something registered deep in my *nagual* self – it was a white car.

Now there was no going back. We were off at high speed, passing along murky passages of overhanging trees. The driver, wearing sunglasses despite the darkness, said nothing. Mikhail and I were bundled in the back seat, with Balaam Ek between us in my rucksack.

Fighting tiredness, with the jungle rushing past, the noise of the engine, and with fear rising and falling in my throat, my *nagual* self pushed my mind aside. Trying to stay awake, I daydreamt chaotic words, about the Time after Time, crystal skulls, sleeping, falling... Balaam Ek held in the paws of a jaguar... dark images quickening my *nagual*... be a warrior of Light... stars, lights, voices... and then, the car had stopped.

'Out,' ordered the driver. Only now did I get a good look at him, silhouetted in the moonlight. He was a young man, with a proud Maya face and the profile of an ancient king, steely, hard and handsome at the same time. The scary part was that we couldn't see his eyes or read his intentions. He pulled us over to a small thatched *palapa* house, menacingly holding a long, shiny, glinting machete.

'What are you doing to us?' I asked in Spanish.

His reply was short. Indicating three hammocks suspended in the small room, he just said, '*Tranquilo* (calm down). We sleep. Trust me.'

By the morning we needed explanations. The man produced his machete and proceeded to cut me a very welcome slice of papaya. Crouching down on his haunches and placing his sunglasses down on his knees, he looked directly into my eyes. 'Now you safe, I explain. For years they ask me to protect you, keep you safe. When you travel in these lands, I knew you had come. Cosmic Maya, we know all.'

I looked puzzled. He went on, 'You not know? I been following you always in my white car. Years ago, when you at café in Guatemala City, I protect the skull. At restaurant by river I chase your attacker. I know you take trek to Piedras Negras, but I cannot cross border to follow you myself. *¡Mierda!* (shit!). I think all is lost. Then, wow, I find you here! *Gracias a los dioses* (thanks to the gods). You not know I have mission to help take crystal skull to End of Time?'

Times of Change and Preparation

Our encounter with the gunmen and the river pursuit had really got us thinking. Drug trafficking is just one visible detail of the prophesied End Times. From all points of the compass we see evidence, both natural and human-made, that this is the Time of Change and the Time of Preparation. I was also prompted to think about what I myself needed to change in my own life. After struggling with this for a while, I remembered a quotation from a Buddhist *sutra* that I had written in my notebook, and dug it out.

The magnitude of the heart is measured by what can
   disturb you.

If it is small like a pond,

Even a small stone can create a big turbulence.

If it is like a lake, it needs a bigger stone to create
   a turbulence.

If it is vast, wide like an ocean,

Nothing can disturb that.

Even mountains can fall into the ocean

But the ocean remains as it is.

So often, while gazing into the starry depths of Balaam Ek, the skull, I
had questioned exactly what superconsciousness is. It seemed like an
ocean of possibilities that I couldn't quite pinpoint. Once I was 'told',
through my thoughts, 'Superconsciousness is the determination of full
awareness, of being fully *present*. It is the faculty by which one knows
one's own existence. In the context of superconsciousness, to know and
to exist imply deep levels of understanding about these two words.

'Normal consciousness may be described as being responsive to your
environment – this contrasts with being asleep or in a coma. The
term "level of consciousness" that you use denotes how consciousness
seems to vary during anaesthesia and during various states of mind such
as daydreaming, lucid dreaming, imagining and so on.

'Some of you say that consciousness may exist after death or before
birth. But that is inaccurate. It is through superconsciousness that we
understand that each of us always has a flame or divine light within.
With superconsciousness we know that there is existence in those
other realms of which your shamans speak, including after-death and
before-birth. Like the little facets of a crystal, we are always linked and
we are always part of the whole.

'You can hear me, Balaam Ek, the being within this crystal skull,
speaking in your head. I could tell you many mythic stories of humans

being blinded by the gods, who disempowered them and closed the doors between the dimensions. My message is important. If these memories have been dimmed in you, or if they never have been allowed to emerge, you can find them if you look with a consciousness of compassion and with unconditional love – firstly for yourself, then for all life that surrounds you.

'This opens you to the Light Within, which is your connection between soul and *Hunab K'u*, God, the Divine, Creation, or whatever names you feel comfortable with. It is awakening this special kind of consciousness that leads to superconsciousness.'

Each time I received a teaching from the skull, I thanked it. Each time I contemplated superconsciousness, I was given instantaneous flashes of inspiration for my artwork and flashes of realization about different patterns of beingness. One of these realizations concerned the recurring pattern that humanity receives from the past.

By then I was certain that we can choose to take ourselves back into the past in order to learn how to walk into the future. Conversely, Balaam Ek the crystal skull had given me another message.

'Wise beings from previous human civilizations have returned at this critical time to assist the spiritual evolution of humanity. There is a world stage. There is a galactic stage! You are the players.'

CHAPTER 12

The Blessing of the Crystal Skulls

Atlantiha

I n December 1998, Hunbatz Men of the Itzá Maya Tradition gave the following teaching to a large audience.

The Itzás of tradition can remember when we were in the continent of Atlantis, or *Atlantiha* in the Mayan language. For thousands and thousands of years we lived in these sacred lands. In those remote times our sacred religious symbols were in all the locations of the continent of Atlantiha and those that inhabited these lands could understand these symbols.

In the lands of the continent of Atlantiha, there existed many communities that understood the cosmic spiritual work. The old Itzás cohabited with this cosmic wisdom in the continent of Atlantiha.

All time begins and also finishes. The cycle indicated cosmically by the calendars suggested that the continent of Atlantiha would come to its end. When this began to happen, many communities emigrated to other places.

In this way great Atlantiha had arisen from the sea and in this way it returned to the sea. The magnetic pole of spiritual religious education had already fulfilled its cycle of educating humanity and, cosmically, the order had already been given that this great power would have to move to another location on Mother Earth.

Many teachers of Atlantiha emigrated to other lands and took spiritual and scientific knowledge with them to their new establishments. The Itzá Atlantihan community also had to emigrate to new lands. Before settling in these lands that we inhabit today, the Itzás travelled to many places. Among them are mentioned the sacred lands of today's indigenous Kogis.

These indigenous brothers settled in the high lands of Sierra Madre of Santa Marta. Also, what is today the Yucatán Peninsula, Mexico, and the lands of Central America, were under the waters of the sea. When these sacred lands arose from the waters, then the Itzás arrived. They already knew what would be the destiny of these new lands.

At that time, the Itzás ended up populating these sacred lands. They brought the sacred symbols of the inherited wisdom of Atlantiha to deposit here. In these sacred lands arose the high initiatory degree of *Ku-kul-kaan*, or *K'uuk'mexcan* in the Mayan language. In that time the Itzá educated initiates to understand the symbols of the snake and the eagle. When the initiates understood these symbols of consciousness, they understood the seven powers (seven chakras) of the human being. When they comprehended these powers of the body they were clever enough to understand the other two complementary powers, the high one of the cosmos and the one under the Earth.

The Itzá brought the knowledge of Atlantiha, but also, being in these new lands of *Tamaunchan*, they developed further spiritual knowledge together with the inhabitants who are today called the Maya. In this manner the Maya inherited the knowledge of the Atlantihas.

For many thousands of years this magnetic pole of spiritual education was in the power of the Maya. They, with what they learned from the Itzás, developed this cosmic wisdom even more. Then, with their sacred language they created the word *Hunab K'u*, so that, with this word, they would represent the great concept of the creation of the universe.

The words of Hunbatz Men gave me a great deal to think about. It was time to look into the depths of Balaam Ek's crystalline magic again, to ask the cosmic Maya to share their wisdom. Settling down, I went into a deep meditation. When I returned I wrote the following.

The Maya, like many great civilizations of the Americas, achieved a great wisdom – a *gnosis* – through the development of their seven powers (the seven chakras) and 'the other two complementary powers, the high one of the cosmos and the one under the Earth. As each successive civilization received gnosis, there came to be no necessity for a hierarchy of kings, queens or priests. The wisdom permeated through to everyone. Consequently there was no need for a hierarchical civilization, as we know it. The people just lived their lives in a simple but sacred way.

As Hunbatz Men said, the 'magnetic pole of spiritual education' changed. First there were Atlanteans, then Olmecs, then Teotihuacános, then Maya and, finally, Toltecs. The Aztecs too would have followed this pattern of development, but something arose in their culture at an early stage that caused it to run into excesses of sacrifice, and the Spanish Conquistadors finally halted any further development.

In South America, the Nazca people were replaced by the Moche. When their civilization fell, the Chimu carried the sacred wisdom until they passed it to the Inca. The Incas of Peru, like the Aztecs of central Mexico, were kept from reaching their ultimate evolution as a civilization, halted by the conquest of the Conquistador Pizzarro.

Each vanishing civilization left keys to their knowledge. They knew that, at some time in the future, others would come who would use these keys to open the door to higher knowledge, to *gnosis*, to the ocean of superconsciousness. I believe that this was the purpose of these great civilizations. People knew that their spirits were energy, and that it would not die. They knew their origins in the cosmos and, like the ancient Egyptians, chose to rise to power and then to set as a star in the sky.

They had hope, even a certainty that those coming after them would evolve so that, eventually, they would use the keys they left to bring forth an even more beautiful creation in the cosmos, a new kind of human being and a new consciousness.

Each and every one of you is a holder of those keys now, but will you open the door?

Exactly what the new consciousness would be was not precisely made known to me. I was left deep in thought. Whenever I received any revelations from the crystal skull, I always made a point of giving thanks and appreciation in the traditional way with an offering. I went outside and picked wild flowers and herbs, arranging them on my altar. I knew they would willingly give themselves to be offered in the presence of the sacred skull.

The Call of the Crystal Skulls – in the Year 2012

Late one night, after six months back in Europe, I received a mysterious phone call. It was now the year 2012, approaching the March equinox. The caller told me it was imperative I go to Chichicastenango in Guatemala. I had to go and wait to be contacted. In these dangerous and changing times it would be a big risk for me to go to that country again. But I felt I had to undertake this last part of my quest alone. Mikhail was to stay behind. I sat in a meditation with Balaam Ek, 'consulting' the Cosmic Maya, and then I became sure that I should go.

This, despite air travel being well-nigh impossible for the average person. Now only the richest person could travel by plane. Use of automobiles was restricted to those on 'official' business or to a few who could afford the exorbitant cost of a 'circulation permit'. Feeling somewhat overwhelmed by the task, I talked about it to a close friend, who said, 'I might be able to help. Give me till tomorrow.' The next day she rang to say, simply, 'You're going on Friday, and you'll be met at the airport by a contact of mine who will give you your ticket and permit.' *Wow.* It was one of those don't-ask-questions, just-do-it situations – all I could do was give thanks. I packed my bags immediately and, in two days, I was on the plane.

There is some kind of deep pain locked into the spirit of the land of *Guatemaya*. Her people were still being slaughtered. The original massacres began in 1523 when Conquistador Pedro de Alvarado (described by historians as a 'terrorist gangster' or a 'slave-hunter') arrived in Guatemala and discovered the remains of the great Maya civilization, at that time scattered in small city-states. His conquest was more than a matter of simply hanging influential indigenous leaders. Alvarado decided to exterminate the civilian population, a practice yet to be abandoned, given their recent history.

He directed eight major massacres, killing up to 3,000 indigenous people at once. Maya leaders were burnt alive as Catholic priests destroyed historical records going back thousands of years. Alvarado rewarded his soldiers with the right to enslave the survivors. Maya lands were stolen. People were herded into towns or forced to work on the Spanish estates in a system of debt peonage.

Today, the country that endured the Spanish invasion and the more recent horrors of the civil war of the 1990s was still struggling. Hurricanes and mudslides had wiped out whole communities. No tourists came here now that travel permits were difficult to come by.

Mother Earth was sighing. She turned and was restless. She was shaking more violently, like a dog ridding itself of fleas. There were signs of hope though. Some remarkable results had been achieved through globally organized meditations and positive projects driven by dedicated people who had a genuine wish to improve things. Perhaps Earth really did know about the huge amount of prayer, goodwill and hard work that had been offered to her.

It was just possible, just believable, that raising human consciousness was making a difference to the intensity of Earth changes in 2012. We stood on the 'edge of Time', vulnerable, questioning. We needed a planet to call our 'home' if we were to remain in physicality, and we certainly needed her if we were to continue with the great cosmic plan set out for humanity.

Large groups of people were cutting their way out of the binding cultural hypnosis of Western civilization and waking up to warnings about global warming and other issues and crises. They were now seeing clear physical evidence of rising sea levels threatening many lower-lying cities. Flooding in London was threatening to endanger parts of the 2012 Olympic Games, but focusing upon the goodwill that this event brought, everyone was determined that it should go ahead. In the Indian subcontinent a great surge of spirituality appeared to have turned the tide of cataclysmic seas of mud and water, brought about by floods, that had displaced millions of people.

The United Nations had at last managed to stop most of the wars and insurgencies in the new African states. Back in 2006 the charity Christian Aid had warned that global environmental changes could cause 180 million deaths in Africa – this was now looking like an accurate prognosis. Thousands of desperate sub-Saharan Africans were attempting to get into Europe by whatever route they could, storming the beaches at night in army-like raids.

Many countries hit by earthquakes had become poorer. Great efforts were made by the few still in a position to help to send humanitarian aid to the many who needed it. California had recently become the focus of attention for millions of people worldwide, who undertook days of global prayers and meditations to try to modify the terrifying rumble of 'the Big One' beneath Californians' feet. Despite this, secret controlling forces in USA continued to pursue a grand illusion in order to preserve their matrix of control.

Intrigue at high government levels was rife, with the virtual collapse of the dollar, the euro and now the Chinese yuan. Analysts agreed that world trade and money markets were standing on shaky ground. The pandemics we were warned about years ago had broken out sporadically, though their full effect was yet to be seen. When the truth about 9/11 finally emerged, the suicide rate in USA, Israel, UK and Japan escalated – these revelations undermined people's trust and belief in the institutions and media they had believed in for so long, bringing up far greater implications than most people had previously seen.

Great multifaith rallies were now held on a regular basis worldwide. Balaam Ek told me that their prayers had changed the course of human evolution.

'Without superconsciousness, without prayer and without unconditional love, the human race will not progress. You will be trapped in death scenarios. Diseases will wipe out most of the population. It is vital that all people raise their consciousness, for in this way you become energetically stronger and, like a tall tree, you can bend with the winds of change.'

Despite numerous difficulties I had managed, with the help of my friend's string-pulling, to get back to the Mayalands, where I needed to be as the Fourth Age ends.

I had heard Don Alejandro, Wandering Wolf, say at a private gathering in Spain in 2004, 'Everything has its time, everything has its end and there is a time for everything. Now we are still in the Fourth Creation. Its ending is going to be different to the ending of other suns, due to the contamination and warming of the planet. Our mountains have little vegetation. It will make it more difficult. So let's see how the Creator is going to take care of his children. Blessed be my children who listen to my messages, that are from our Creator. Blessed be you who are listening to these messages, as you are looking for the divine laws and for what we can do when that End Day approaches. These messages are not mine, they are from my ancestors.'

I went back to my old favourite place in Guatemala, the city of Antigua, still little changed despite the environmental disasters that had occurred elsewhere. Then on to Chichicastenango ('Chichi' for short) in the highlands, three hours west of Guatemala City. It was still the domain of thousands of Maya. On market days, Chichi's plaza was crowded with people dressed in an array of colour – like finely plumed birds they flouted purples, reds and blues, woven into traditional patterns on dresses, trousers, shawls and blouses. They were still the indigenous keepers of nature's wisdom.

I was waiting for someone to contact me by telephone and tell me more about my mission and why I needed to be in Chichi. Walking back to my lodgings I met an old shaman known to me from times past, during the peaceful years when I had been able to travel easily. He greeted me, sat me down on a flat tumbled-down wall, and began to speak.

'The Children of Time have kept to their mission, undertaken so long ago, to be present at the end of the age and to help its "birth pains". Like midwives, they have been preparing the Mother. Secretly, they have maintained their connection with her. Small groups of initiates have kept the light burning for her in these darkest times of history. They have continued to perform ceremonies to the Earth Mother, to offer prayers to love and honour her. And in return they have had food and sustenance.

'She has allowed them to grow their crops and trees, extract her life-blood oil and take her waters. She has let them cut her forests for their homes and sacrifice her fish and fowl to provide their food, because they only took what they needed for their sustenance. They are the indigenous of the Earth. They are the Children of Time, the Children of the Sun, the Children of Fire. They are still teaching these things to us, and to the White Brother and Sister, even as Earth says *Enough*. It is time for the prophecy to be fulfilled. It is time for the birth.'

As I wandered back after meeting the shaman, his words inspired me to sing to myself my favourite old Maya prayer:

May my heart be in the Heart of the Earth

May the Heart of the Earth be in my heart

May my heart be in the Heart of the Sky

May the Heart of the Sky be in my heart.

Chichicastenango

My mysterious unknown contact finally called and directed me to make my way secretly to the main church in Chichicastenango and to wait there until I was contacted again.

The market here extended right up to the steps of Saint Thomas's church. Using the crowds as cover I walked quickly past groups of men, the *cofradias*, brotherhoods of Maya priests and elders who still wore their traditional dress of hand-woven black jackets decorated with red wool fringes. Their hats were embroidered voluptuously with tropical flowers, trailing long, red woollen tassels down their backs. They carried old milk tins that smoked with the incense of copal tree resins, burning on hot charcoal. Each elder watched how straight his smoke rose, to see if he was sincere enough to communicate from his heart to the heart of the Maya sky.

Walking nervously to the side door of the church, I checked to see that no one was following me. I had Balaam Ek with me. It seemed more than just a weighty lump of quartz, since the responsibility of what I had been charged to do felt overwhelmingly heavy. It hadn't been easy to get here. All foreigners were now regarded as suspicious, especially when boarding the ramshackle old buses, remnants of the fleet of American school buses sold off to Guatemalan towns in the 1970s.

I had got off the bus in the outskirts of town, near the cemetery, so as not to draw attention to my mission. I hoped that not too many people would notice this light-skinned *gringo*. I darted through narrow cobbled alleyways and into a street which was being used as a market-place. It was searingly hot and crowded. Everyone was in a hurry, rushing from the shade of one shop to another in a rich mélange of sensations and sights.

The inevitable smell of *pollo asado*, roasting chicken, contrasted sharply with the fragrant perfumed lilies and tall red roses hugely bunched on the flower stalls. A table laden with spices and dried herbs and bearing labels in Mayan drew my attention. Next door was a plastics shop, heaped high with all manner of gaudy bowls and containers.

Then I almost fell over a man sitting on the pavement. I was forced to gaze at his withered hands, covered in scabs and sores, fingers twisted and missing. *This must be leprosy*, my mind registered. I looked down at what once had been feet and now were bleeding stumps. I tried to choke back emotion, but my tears flowed unheeded as I stood and stared. What was worse, the skin of his face and head was flaking off in great paper-dry pieces.

His eyes turned to me – eyes that seemed to have seen the tortured hells of Earth. Unfocused, he fumbled for the money tin between his feet. I turned, sobbing, and gave him some money. Couldn't this man be in a hospital? Day after day he must have been sitting on this hot pavement in the scorching sun, his face at the level of the bus exhaust pipes belching black smoke.

I remembered a shop I had just passed that sold water and went back to purchase some and calm my emotions. I carried on along the same street again, but was drawn by a perverse fascination to look at the beggar. He was shouting a tirade of abuse at passers-by, wildly and angrily waving what remained of his hands in the air, as the demons of fate possessed him and the old Maya gods of death looked down, waiting for him. In some strange way I felt his pain as my pain. I was angry that he hadn't even got basic healthcare and angry that the white-clad, pious nuns with their charity collection tins averted their gaze and stepped neatly around him. I gave him one of my bottles of water and carried on.

Church of the Skulls

Carefully I pushed the heavy old church door open. Inside a Catholic mass was being said at the altar. Down the centre aisle were rows of candles on the floor. Through the thick aromatic smoke of incense I could see Maya women kneeling in deep sorrowful prayer on palm mats. Piled up beside them were great bunches of flowers and herbs that they would leave behind as offerings when they go.

It was an atmospheric sight and, for tourists, it had once been wonderfully quaint and exotic. But most of them had had no idea that Chichicastenango had been the focus of Guatemala's civil war and killing fields. The hills around the town were littered with mass graves, which Guatemalan and Argentinian forensic doctors had begun to exhume some years before. Today, in 2012, there were reports of more graves throughout the country.

North from Chichi, the province of El Quiche stretches into the mountains where, again, soldiers ruled with terror and bodies appeared on roadsides showing horrible signs of torture and mutilation. Tourists no longer came here. I shuddered as I thought what my fate could be in this wild country. It seemed best if I stayed partly hidden to the side of the central nave, near to the door. I had been told I would be contacted here.

I slipped between the rows of women and fell silently to my knees on one of the palm mats. Drawing an old embroidered shawl over my backpack, containing Balam Ek, I waited and waited. Here in the church the day drew on, but in the dense smoky interior one would not have known it. I waited. One mass finished, another started and still I waited. I shifted into a kind of reverie, like a drug-induced haziness, and started to sway from side to side.

There was a sudden light touch upon my shoulder. 'Come. Now,' I was told. I followed a black-cloaked figure that disappeared into a side chapel which I had not noticed before. As I stepped through, a hand grabbed my arms and another hand held a damp cloth over my mouth and nose. Struggling to breathe, I kicked my legs out at my assailant, but then I knew nothing more.

I saw the face of the beggar in front of me, then it changed to a crystal skull. Spiralling through a wild jungle, I saw more faces, faces I knew. Crossing my vision there appeared a huge jaguar, which opened his mouth and swallowed up all the faces. He leapt across through the undergrowth, shining like a mythical astrological beast, and drew me through a spinning tunnel of light. How long I went through the tunnel I don't know, but then I heard voices and saw movements, and a hand lifted me up to a sitting position. '*Perdonenos* (forgive us), señora,' I heard, 'We must keep this place secret, even to you.'

Then hands unbound a cloth over my eyes and I blinked, trying to recognize my surroundings. Looking up I saw a kind face. Again, '*Perdonenos*, señora,' he says. 'Soon I tell you why we did this and what we must do. First, I must see if you really are the One We Have Been

Waiting For. I make astrological reading about you.'

I looked around and saw that I was in some kind of stone room. I shuddered a little, unaccustomed to the coldness. The man, seeing this, passed me my traditional shawl. It seemed as if we were somewhere deep in the earth, since the room had a kind of damp mustiness lingering within it. There was no light save for one electric bulb trailing a sinuous bare flex down one corner. An ancient studded wooden door, closed firmly shut, looked as if it would keep out Cortés himself – or me inside! It seemed I had no option but to wait while the man made some preparations in front of me.

'You, señora, please, call me Miguel,' he said. 'I just simple messenger.'

'What did you do to me?' I asked.

'Señora, it necessary. *Lo siento* (I regret), we give you just a *poco*, a leetil, leetil bit of drug. We must take you secretly from church without seengle sound, and without you know where you going. Soon you feel better. We talk to ancestors.'

Not really knowing what he meant, I watched him as he laid a red cloth down on the cold stones of the floor and placed tiny green and blue crystals upon it. On one side he piled up plant seeds, bright scarlet, known as *tzi'te* seeds. He wrapped the same red cloth around his head that had just bound my eyes and took hold of my hands across the impromptu magical altar.

'Please, tell me you name and date when you born, in Maya count,' he asked, seeming to look right past me into some vision of the future. He must be a fortune-teller of some kind. I recalled having read of the healers, the *Ah Q'ij* of the Kiché Maya, who are able to read the Threads of Time Future by studying the seeds and the patterns of four that they make, all in relationship to the sacred calendar count of days.

'Patricia. Ten *Ahau*,' I replied.

Adding more lumps of copal tree resin into a little tin, where it was smoking copiously, Miguel nodded. The aroma of the copal reminded me of all the traditional ceremonies I had taken part in over the years. I so hoped that now, in the year 2012, if it really was the Year Zero, the people would be able to carry on their traditions into a future golden age. The incense, and probably the drug that he had given me, caused me to feel quite sleepy. Miguel then told me to pick up some of the red seeds and, with this, he went into a kind of trance, repeating names of days in Mayan, groaning a little, then suddenly smiling.

'*Si, si,* ye-e-es…,' he said, 'It *is* you. Ancestors have spoken. You carry skull?'

Feeling confidence in this man now, I replied, 'It is here with me, as requested.'

'Then we must go. No much time. *Tenemos que marcharnos ahora* (we go now).' With that, he quickly cleared his altar, bundling everything up in a scrap of tattered cloth.

Enlightenment

Miguel opened the door. Creaking on its old hinges, it revealed a stone corridor and, at the end, a flight of steps going down. He motioned for me to follow. More and more I had the feeling that I must have been taken into a crypt under the church, or even under a pyramid. Passing me a lighted candle, Miguel said, 'Mind head. Our ancestors, very leetle people.' Stepping carefully, for in places the stone beneath my feet was slippery or broken away, we came at last to a stop.

The passage had widened and Miguel, holding his candle high, said, 'Look, ancestors!' He pointed to a huge face mask, one of many, cut into the stone itself. They still had traces of red cinnabar paint upon them, and other colours less visible. In each of the mask's eyes were the glyphic symbols for *Ahau*, the calendar day that refers to the solar deity.

'There is your day sign. Ancestors knew you would come.'

'Miguel,' I asked in Spanish, to be absolutely clear, '*¿Qué significa todo esto?* (what's all this about?).'

'Don't you know? Deedn't anyone tell you? You *el numero* tw… tw… twelve. *Doce. Duodécimo.* We waiting long, long time for you.'

'What do you mean, twelve, the twelfth?"

Miguel just beamed a huge smile at me, his gold-capped teeth glinting in the candlelight. '*Soy solo un mensajero* (I am only a messenger),' was all he would say.

It was then that I remembered. I mean, *really remembered*. Not just what I had learnt about the 12 crystal skulls having been kept in a secret location since around the time of the Spanish conquest, but I remembered what my heart had been telling me. Why had it taken me so long to realize it? Perhaps taking the crystal skull around to meditation groups, where lots of people used it for scrying or obtaining messages, had distracted me. Perhaps all that was a bit ingratiating to Balaam Ek. That wasn't the crystal skull's real destiny.

For the last few years, when it became more dangerous, even to walk on the streets, I had kept the skull carefully hidden when not in use, and moving it from place to place. My encounters with the thief at the café and the gunman on the River Usumacinta had taught me a lesson. I could count on protection from the cosmic Maya only when I was in their lands, not when I was Europe.

But now I was sure. This is what the old woman in the *kiva* had wanted me to do. She had asked me to take the crystal skull to the End of Time. Way back, when she gave me the skull, she knew that she wouldn't live through these last terrible years. Years when it seemed the world could end – such was the devastation across the lands.

By gifting it to someone younger, and to someone who would eventually realize its importance, she was securing a possibility for the world by getting me to take the crystal skull into the future. A future not for her, not even for her people. This, I realized, was a mission that could change all of humanity.

With Miguel leading the way, we continued along the subterranean passage, through twists and turns and passing side-passages through which a breath of warm, perfumed air occasionally rushed. Although sometimes we had to climb up steps, the passage appeared to be taking us down ever deeper. I wondered whether it was taking us to *Xibalba*, the Underworld itself. With my candle now burned down to a little stump, Miguel halted in front of another great door set into a typical Maya-shaped arch. Banging three times upon it with his fist, it swung open.

The Grail Mass in the Heart of the Earth

I rubbed my eyes. I thought I had stepped into a picture book about Maya history. We were in a huge, circular or possibly heart-shaped stone room that held the aura of an ancient temple. To one side of me, as I stood at the open door, there were women in traditional dress. To the other there were men in the costumes of the *cofradia*. They lined up in two rows and I walked between them, holding Balaam Ek in my hands.

In front of me, lit by candles, were Maya in ancient costumes adorned with jaguar skins, Hopi with feathered headdresses, Incas with gold pectorals of the face of the Sun God upon their chest. There was a tall, black-skinned man, a small Tibetan in orange robes and a number of indigenous elders, from which tribes I could not say. Each held a crystal skull! In all, I counted 12 skulls, including mine.

Slowly I walked in and joined them. Balaam Ek started to pulsate in my hands. At first everyone was silent, and then a low chanting began. Notes of songs long forgotten filled the temple. The sounds subdued then swelled in a crescendo. One lone female contralto voice sung a sweet, sweet song, one that I can only describe as a hymn to the Goddess.

The 12 crystal skull bearers began circling the chamber, presenting the skulls to the people present. It seemed to me as if the entire world was represented there, such was the diversity of faces in the onlookers. It seemed as if we were at the heart of the world, somehow representing the world and all its people.

Young and old alike dropped to their knees as the last skull passed and the bearers had formed a circle around a dais holding a large, glowing 13th skull. This skull had a most elongated head, deep-set eye sockets and a third eye carved in the centre on the frontal 'bones', bearing two wings. The 'mouth' of the skull was open, as if it was about to sing. Upon the top of the skull appeared a circle of light containing a cross – the symbol that assists astral travelling and the Maya symbol of the World Tree.

Each bearer, including myself, sat on palm mats, just like the women in the church. When they placed their crystal skulls simultaneously upon the dais, the chamber began to shudder physically with a deep Earth sigh, almost like an earthquake tremor. The chanting, which had not really ever stopped, reached new angelic notes, sending out waves of sound-induced light to swirl around the circular walls of the temple.

The earth sighed again, deep and low, but the voices ascended in pitch until, to my ears, they became like a high-frequency sonar that pierced the physical skulls of all present. Now I wasn't hearing sound with my ears – instead, each chakra in my body was vibrating coherently with everyone else's. Seeing clairvoyantly, I watched as my auric energy field merged first with the 13 crystal skulls, then with all the people's auras.

Looking now at the central skull, it began to change before my eyes, becoming chalice-like and golden. It was as if I could at once fill it with my unbounded love and it would fill me simultaneously with all the love of the Universe.

What do you most desire? I heard in my heart. There was only one possible answer.

'Peace on Earth. Let us walk the Beauty Path. Let us birth a new Creation of Light.'

The Crack Between the Worlds

The Mass of the Thirteen Skulls went on through several stages and eventually ended. Each person present received whatever he or she most desired for the world. I cannot recount what happened for others, but at one point I felt the expansion of light so great in my own skull that I lost consciousness.

I awoke to find myself being carried through the stone tunnels. Miguel placed me gently down. I was allowed to rest. Turning to him, I had so many questions still in my head. *Where have we been? Who were all those people?*

Instead of answering the questions I had, he told me, 'Here in Chichi, church and military authorities work together long time, try get rid of, they think, pagan beliefs. They even build Santo Tomás church on top our Maya temple. Like good Christian peepil, we go to mass. What *el Papa* (the Pope) don' know is, we always honour our ancestors' gods with incense, flowers, herbs. Our ways, they old, far more old than church ways. How can we stop believing? We refuse to be a... as... assimilated, I think you say in eengleesh.

'A temple, it is buried beneath church in Chichi, originally built for *Hun Ahpu*, one of the *beeg* gods in Maya universe. We don' forget that. Today, we have many Christian beliefs. But we know, all One in Spirit. So we, the Maya, in Chichi, we still worship how our ancestors did. There *ees nothing else* we can do.

'Because we may become *so* strong, the government, the aristocracy, they afraid of Guatemaya – nation run by Maya people. They kill us 'cos we never be conquered. *¡Vete al Diablo!* Go to hell! we say. Just look, we have determination, we keep our ways. We wear traditional clothing with pride. We speak our languages. There is invisible forms of resistance too.

'Villages harbour clandestine political and religious organizations. The timeless, secret training of Maya shaman-priests, it continue. Our resistance makes savage paranoia among *ladinos* (people of mixed Spanish and Indian blood) and Spanish-Mexican élite. They go *loco*, crazy about it. If we have power in government, our values grow *beeg* through country. All the land become a huge communal possession, not private property. That why they see us *beeg* threat.

'But come, it late. I see you safe back before dawn break.' So we continued walking through upward-inclining stone passages, for what seemed like an hour.

'*Silencio* (quiet now), señora.' Miguel cautioned me as we stopped beneath a great stone slab in the ceiling above.

Eyeing me up and down, he said, 'This most dangerous day, Seven *I'k*, but our calendar say, if we continue with caution, how could we not be safe in hands of gods?'

Miguel stood up on a rock and pushed a hidden plank that filled a hole, where a corner of the slab had broken away. He urged me upwards.

Emerging from a crack between the worlds, to my surprise I stood in the cool morning air – in the midst of a cemetery of brightly-coloured tombs, elaborately decorated. Miguel gesticulated and waved me toward a spot in the distance where the early morning bus would stop.

I hadn't even had time to say goodbye or thank Miguel for guiding me. I stood there, blinking, rather dazed. Suddenly a statement by Albert Einstein, the physicist, came into my mind:

> There are only two ways to live your life. One is as though nothing is a miracle; the other is as though everything is a miracle.

Love Letters to the Universe, Richard Kehl,
Darling & Co., 2005

CHAPTER 13

Song to *Homo Spiritus*

*There is no easy walk to freedom anywhere, and
many of us will have to pass through the valley of
the shadow of death again and again before we
reach the mountaintop of our desires.*

Nelson Mandela, South African statesman
(born 1918, Nobel Peace Prize 1993)

December Solstice 2012

I felt it best to stay more or less hidden, with a family I knew deep in
the Biosphere Reserve in Guatemala. It was no longer safe to travel
far and certainly I couldn't get back to Europe. I had had plenty of time
to reflect upon the significance of world events, as we slipped and
slithered on the Snake of Time towards the end of 2012.

As well as being a solstice, 21 December 2012 is of far greater significance because it is numbered with the critical date 13.0.0.0.0 in the
Maya Long Count of Time. We can envisage this portentous day as the
Snake of Time seeking release from its dark underground abode, seeing
a crack of light in his cave – a fulfilment of prophecy.

The Thirteen Baktun Long Count calendar date (13 x 144,000
days), has as its starting point the Gregorian date of 11 August 3114 BCE.
Its end is precisely calculated to coincide with December Solstice 2012
CE. Just imagine the astrologer-priests and day-keepers all those centuries
back, sitting together, studying the motion of sun, moon, planets and
stars. Using knowledge and records already ancient and handed down

to them, they constructed calendar dates way beyond their physical life cycle or that of future generations of their own families.

Imagine for a moment trying to predict something that will take place in 7137 CE. Chances are, most people would shrug their shoulders and say 'Well, I shan't be around then anyway' – end of story!' But these astrologer-priests and day-keepers chose to do what they did in the knowledge that, one day in the distant future, their records would be read and understood. And that date is *now*!

With amazing awareness of the precession of the equinoxes, these wise men also knew of a cosmic event that could occur only once every 25,625 years (5 x 5,125 years), known to the ancient Greeks as the Platonic Year, the precession cycle. We met this in Chapter 9, when quoting John Major Jenkins, who mentioned that Izapa had been like an astronomical observatory calibrating the alignment of the December solstice sun with the Dark Rift in the Milky Way.

In our Milky Way galaxy lies the Dark Rift, Great Cleft or, as the Maya call it, the Road to the Underworld or the Black Road. It is a relatively small, dark gap, mostly devoid of stars, toward the centre of the galaxy in the constellation of Sagittarius. The Sun will conjunct and enter the area of the sky marked by the Black Road exactly on the December Solstice 2012. Precession would make it pass over or under the Black Road at other stages of the cycle.

According to Maya mythology we humans are born on Earth through the Dark Rift, the cosmic birth canal leading to the womb or the centre of our galaxy, around which our galaxy revolves. This reflects the pronouncements of today's shamans and day-keepers who know that we are rapidly approaching the End Time of this the Fourth Creation, with the Earth preparing for a rebirth.

What everyone wants to know is, *what will happen?* Some Native Americans say that a Sun Dog Rainbow will be visible. A Sun Dog is a full rainbow circle around the sun, displaying bright white lights at the four compass directions. It is a rare but natural phenomenon. It will be visible to those who will understand the reasons for the falling away of old forms of living, and for the release of cultural hypnosis. They prophesy that it will be a sign that their ancestors have returned in white bodies with red hearts, to teach the old ways. The Sun Dog

Rainbow will be a good strong omen, indicating that it is time to share 'medicine' with all who come to learn.

I remembered when, years ago, Don Alejandro said that we must anticipate 72 hours of darkness as we approach Year Zero. We will experience either great heat or great cold. He told us that we must not be afraid. We must be sure to remain in meditation, even as the Earth changes occur.

I thought also of Sri Aurobindo who, in *The Human Cycle* (Dutton, 1953) wrote: 'The coming of a spiritual age must be preceded by the appearance of an increasing number of individuals who are no longer satisfied with the normal intellectual, vital and physical existence of man, but perceive that a greater evolution is the real goal of humanity and attempt to effect it in themselves, to lead others to it, and to make it the recognized goal of the human race. In proportion, as they succeed, and to the degree to which they carry this evolution, the yet unrealised potentiality which they represent will become an actual possibility of the future.'

Cosmic Snakes and Ladders

As the year 2012 progressed I felt an increasing urgency to be near the sea at Tulum, in eastern Yucatán. Memories of Atlantis have always been very strong for me there and, in the present unstable times, it was a kind of comfort to be near to where, according to Don Alejandro, Atlantean survivors had built their first city. I respected his 'ancient word', *ojer tzij*, translatable as 'prior word', meaning an extended discourse that carries the authority of a long tradition, rather than mere hearsay.

Esoteric information about Tulum tells that its 'birthing temples' celebrated the rebirth of the Atlanteans as the Maya people. The goddess *Ixchel*, keeper of wisdom's memory and goddess of childbirth and rainbows, protected them. They even carved images of descending 'gods' – upside-down, being birthed – into their new world consciousness or age.

I met an extraordinary traveller on the beach near Tulum. In these times there were many people without homes, and it was common to camp out on the sands with many others. The old wooden beach *cabañas* (cabins), despite falling into disrepair, were now desirable residences for families. I had stretched my hammock between two palm trees and found that I had a very interesting neighbour. Tall and bronzed, of an age I could not guess, his deep blue eyes implied an inner spiritual knowing, perhaps enlightenment.

He explained to me that the 'shift', or the Earth Awakening, would most likely be caused by a rapid magnetic pole reversal. This is a different event, but not entirely separate from the culmination of the calendar cycle. Hunbatz Men had mentioned that the Earth Mother once gave an order to change the magnetic pole. Scientists measuring the magnetic field confirm it has dropped 38 per cent in 2,000 years, at an average of 1.9 per cent per year. However, over the last 100 years it has dropped by an average of 6 per cent per year. If the field drops to zero, the Earth's polarity will reverse.

Ken Carey, in *Starseed: the Third Millennium* (Harper, San Francisco, 1991) had written, 'At the moment of quantum awakening, change will occur rapidly, rippling across the terrestrial surface like a wave. Everything in the Earth's gravitational field will be affected in some way. There will be a time of massive change, of change on a scale that has no historical precedent, though it does have antecedents in the prehistoric events of this and of distant worlds.'

My hammock neighbour told me, 'Once before, in the hidden history of the world, humans did experience a shift in consciousness. Simultaneously, the Earth's magnetic field reversed, the position of the poles shifted and caused a great movement of land masses. It moved humanity from consciousness into subconsciousness.'

'Yes,' I said, 'This was the time that the Maya recount in their myths, when humanity was "blinded".'

He responded by saying, 'However, the shift in consciousness we expect to come soon is not a shift into subconsciousness, but into super-consciousness.'

Swinging gently in my hammock, I was lulled to sleep by the sounds of the waves and of little groups of people sitting chatting around driftwood fires. I reflected dreamily how, currently, most people do not remember even a little about other worlds or their previous incarnations. It is really unusual for anyone to fully remember.

However, children are now being born in preparation for the new times, who can carry the memory of their previous incarnations and who can fully recollect their *nagual* self. These children, whose dormant DNA will be awoken to full realization of their destiny, will become the new guardians and leaders. They will know that, once again, the Earth is to be respected and cultivated as a beautiful garden.

Breaking this reverie for a moment, my thoughts began to be drawn to my present predicament. Here I was, without Mikhail, on a beach in a land far from my own, carrying a crystal skull to the End of Time, and wondering exactly why things had worked out like this. This led to further questions. How will we know that the changes are actually occurring? How I wished Mikhail was here to talk over these questions with me!

Balaam Ek had shown me that, as the Earth magnetics lessen, those who are spiritually awake and ready to fulfil their purpose will place themselves in the optimum position and location to fall into a kind of deep 'slumber', similar to meditation or trance. Within the 'slumber' will be a profound sensation of No Time. Other, less aware, people will continue to struggle against the Earth changes, hanging on to the bitter end, slithering uncontrollably down the Serpent of Time in a cosmic play of 'snakes and ladders'.

At some point those who have been 'slumbering' will awaken into another dimension, having climbed the 'ladder' of consciousness into a spiritually superconscious state outside and beyond time itself. Although everyone's biocircuitry is able to undertake this raising of consciousness, fear, greed and detachment from the wisdom of Earth Mother Gaia will block the impulse for many to enter into it.

One night, whilst holding Balaam Ek and watching the stars reflecting light on the ocean, I was able to see, with my own eyes, a generative Ray of Creation streaming from the stars in Orion, linking into a celestial web of light. It was as if every star and every part of the universe was singing together, connected through golden threads. Throughout this experience I felt the presence of a mystical guardian, clothed in purple, standing just behind me, urging me to look deeply and listen.

When I was asking questions of Balaam Ek, after seeing the Ray of

Creation in the night sky, I was told, 'Your modern mystics and prophets should understand that this light prepares Earth for a "birth" which will occur through the Dark Rift of the Milky Way. This is because, when the Earth is in this precessional alignment with the Milky Way, a much more spiritually evolved cosmic energy radiation will be received over the whole planet. Just one result of this will be that children of the new time will intuitively understand how to utilize this energy and quickly be able to reach a superconscious state, transiting at will into the fifth and sixth dimensions.'

This information from Balaam Ek rather seemed to confirm my much earlier feelings (*see* Portals in Chapter 8). It did appear as if something really *big* was about to happen. But still the information coming through Balaam Ek was mystical and somewhat ambiguous. However, being only human, it was a scary realization to face on my own, without Mikhail. On the beach it felt as if we were already on the edge of Time.

It was such a strange situation to be in. We were a small isolated group, thrown together by the hand of fate. We lived as best we could from day to day. Food was scarce. I was beginning to know real hunger. Sometimes here on the edge, Time broke into little crystalline shards. Occasionally bigger pieces, much bigger pictures, complicated possible futures, were presented to me, but always still broken, not yet complete.

Enigmas

I continued to discuss further deep matters with my friendly hammock-neighbour, as we walked along the shoreline. I didn't want to scare him or explain how I knew time – or was it me? – was cracking up. Instead I fell back on my research, things I felt safe with, and said, 'Astrophysicists have mentioned that a source of a particular quality of ultraviolet light from the Orion Nebula has influenced our DNA on Earth. Do you think, this ultraviolet light will increase dramatically at Year Zero, when our sun is in a prime position within the Dark Rift to "lens" increasingly powerful energies from outside our solar system?'

My questions poured out. 'Will the resultant energies be key frequencies that our superconsciousness will recognize?'

He stopped, gazing far out to sea, beyond the fine white strip of breakers on the reef. Seeming to avoid my questions, his response was, 'You know, we can allow the message of the crystal skulls to form a bridge into our own skulls. We can integrate dimensions that we are as yet unable to understand.'

'What dimensions do you mean? The same dimensions that shamans travel into?'

Again he was a little evasive. In reply he said, 'Dimensions one and two resonate with the Earth frequency, that has already begun to increase. Dimension three is linear space and time. Dimension four follows – this is the dimension that feeds upon human emotions. Next come dimensions five and six, that resonate with "creation frequencies" integrated within, and by, the crystal skulls.

'Then there are dimensions seven to nine, that humans can barely comprehend at the present time. You know, the skulls themselves are carriers of many types of light-encoded stellar energies, the kind of things your quantum physicists have been calling "entanglement" theories. For these reasons the skulls are precious messengers, beyond time, able to "sing" their songs of the spheres.'

I thanked my newfound, wise but mysterious friend and walked back alone to write in my diary. On a couple of occasions I had surprised him while he was meditating with two strangely marked flat stones in his hands that appeared to fit together. Upon being disturbed he quickly hid them away. As I splashed back through the wavelets on the silvery sand, I wondered why he would on no account give me his name. 'You would never believe me if I told you,' was all he had said.

Revelations

Slowly I walked back enjoying the comic spectacle of a pelicans' fly-past, a regular occurrence as they patrolled the inshore waters searching for fish. I went past many people fishing on the shore too – *they are not as successful as the pelicans*, I mused. Because there is nothing else to do here except keep up a constant search for food, just about everyone engages in fishing.

Piles of large empty *caracols*, a kind of shellfish once regarded as a delicacy, are piled up on the beach, having provided some good meals. Sometimes this onetime holiday paradise feels very bleak on a mainly fish diet, but it could be worse. I could be trapped in a city where there is little more than rats and dogs to eat until the relief trucks arrive – if, that is, there are any.

I chose a secluded sandy spot in which to rest for a while. There, partly hidden by dry grasses, I came across a huge upturned turtle almost a metre long. This presented a dilemma. This amazing creature was right here in front of me – should I right it? Someone must have deliberately turned it wrong side up to leave it to die. Knowing it was a valuable food for all the people on the shore, what should I do? I was hungry too. But years before I had joined campaigns to protect these self-same turtle-nesting beaches. So I would be hypocritical to leave this lumbering creature to slowly die of sunstroke and exhaustion.

My decision made, I quickly discovered that there was no way I alone could move the turtle. Looking along the shore I spotted my friendly neighbour returning. I knew I could trust him to help me save it. The poor creature must have been there for days already. We heaved and pushed and turned her over. It was almost certainly a female who had come up the beach to nest and then had been caught. She was so heavy that we could only move her a few metres at a time and then rest.

The turtle seemed almost dead but nevertheless we carried her to the water, splashing a little onto her crusty, leathery head and closed eyes. Within about ten minutes she began to revive – her life force was returning and her eyes opened. If you have ever looked into a turtle's eyes you would know eternity!

It brought tears to my own eyes and I sobbed as she began slowly making her way into deeper water. But my tears were those of intense happiness as she made a final effort and began swimming, now out of view, towards the gap in the reef.

Together my neighbour and I jumped around in joy, splashing each other excitedly. We ran off into deeper water to swim. By the time we got back to our camp the setting sun was beginning to send magenta and orange shafts of light across the pink western sky.

Far out to sea, ominously shaped storm clouds were gathering – we could be in for a wet night. We had picked up a few small edible shellfish on our way and, when we returned, we proceeded to boil them up for our meal over a little driftwood fire.

When I had finished eating I settled down in my hammock and began inspirationally writing a stream of notes.

'In Year Zero, the new Maya Creation begins. The "spheres", including our solar system, will be ideally placed, as happens once every 25,625 years, when the sun crosses the Dark Rift of the Milky Way at the December solstice. Astrophysicists predict that the polarity of the sun will reverse. Increased atmospheric destruction of the "crystalline shield" around Mother Earth will allow more ultraviolet radiation to affect us. The Earth's magnetic field is expected to continue to decrease, providing fertile ground for human psychic experiences and dream states.'

I began spontaneously sketching little pictures of Egyptian Pharaohs and Olmecs with elongated heads. Then I made further notes.

'In Classical Maya times, royal babies had their skulls bound and reshaped so that, as they matured, their heads became elongated, perhaps mimicking a desirable royal or extraterrestrial cranium. Or were the elongated heads of people long ago shaped that way because they once used higher chakras and senses of perception? Will we use our higher chakras in the future, when our superconsciousness is "switched on"?'

I wrote in bold letters, 'Superconsciousness will be primed by increased ultraviolet light penetrating the atmosphere of our planet.'

This caused me to stop. *Hang on a minute...* I realized with a jolt that, in the past, we have been adequately shielded from ultraviolet radiation by the Earth's atmosphere. Now there are huge holes in the ozone layer. Ultraviolet radiation has a frequency vibration at the fastest end of the visible light spectrum.

Feverishly, I wrote, 'As far as I understand it, medical research has found that the pineal gland in the centre of our skull is affected by light coming in through our eyes. This gland in turn is linked subtly to the Third Eye chakra. It excretes melatonin (a neurohormone) and converts serotonin (a neurotransmitter) into a number of potent hallucinogens, similar to LSD and the Amazonian vine *Ayahuasca*. Melatonin is necessary for dreaming and psychic states.

'The pineal gland reacts in an extremely complex way, making it likely that our biochemical composition could be changed in proportion to our exposure to a higher vibrational quality of light.

'From the ultraviolet vibration upwards, frequencies become increasingly hazardous for humans in our present form. Apart from much-feared skin cancers, what else can we expect to occur with increased ultraviolet light? Will its higher frequencies activate hitherto dormant parts of our DNA, at or around now, the beginning of the Year Zero?'

I placed a large question mark on the page. Alongside it I wrote in capital letters: HUMAN GENOME PROJECT – recent research findings of extraterrestrial factors in DNA.

'If an activation at a deep level of DNA occurs, those raising their spiritual awareness to a state of superconsciousness could also find themselves more able to deal with the increasingly difficult and challenging physical life. They would know how to overcome the obstacles.'

I was excited by this realization and wanted more people to know, to have hope for a better future. On the beach I felt thwarted. There was no means of electronic or telephone communication. Yet somehow I knew that all was working out according to a vast blueprint that people accessed when giving prophecies or making scientific discoveries. I sighed, reflecting on what I had written. I looked at the sparkling light on the sea, thinking about the turtle, wondering if she had made it safely out past the reef. I thought also about Mikhail, back in Europe, and wondered what was happening for him at this moment. I was really missing him.

Back to my notes, whilst I still had a little light left. My one remaining pen was barely able to keep up with my thoughts. Once again I held the crystal skull Balaam Ek, in order to connect with its wisdom and receive answers to my questions. It spoke.

'Those of you who allow yourselves to change will feel the effect of huge amounts of energy being released upon the Earth. This will further assist your shift into superconsciousness, your reunion with Creation. It is your "return to the stars". It will involve a dimensional shift to a different frequency, for the Earth and her peoples.

'Some of you will find it easy to shift as you enter into "slumber"

– actually it is a spiritual awakening! It may be perceived as infinity, an eternity, or a flash of concentrated radiance revealing contiguous lifetimes.

'In these moments all people will realize their interconnection with one another upon the WorldWideWeb of Life and Light. Each of you will know why you have incarnated on Earth. You will have the choice of returning to physical form or remaining as highly evolved, multidimensional beings.'

It was almost dark now. The crystal skull was pulsating and glowing with a golden light. 'There is a great Cosmic Plan. Those that return will be called the Children of Time, the Children of Fire, and they will have a new title upon the family tree of humankind. No longer outdated *homo sapiens*, the currently existing species of human. A new humanity will be born.'

Putting down the crystal skull, I took a rest to reflect on this. At last, what the skull had wanted to communicate was becoming clearer to me. What it was saying was mind-blowing! Then I continued with some notes of my own, inspired by what Balaam Ek had 'said'.

'In the hearts of many people lies a sense of the spiritual dimension within life. It has been calling to human consciousness for a much greater time span than any religion. Throughout the ages, we have heard prophetic words, trying to awaken us to our greater potential. Avatars and teachers have watered and picked fruits of the spiritual World Tree, giving them freely to us to digest.

'This spiritual food leads to the quickening of the Greater Plan. It is difficult to comprehend it while we are in our physical bodies, especially when we are challenged by life experiences, the polarization of darkness and light and the depths as well as the heights of God-beingness. But there is to be no completion of this Greater Plan unless the darkness is grasped as intrinsic to the experience we gain as we create the God Being that we are.'

I wrote in bold letters, '*Evolution from homo sapiens to a spiritual human is birthed through the transformation of the dark shadows in our minds, as part of our reaching out for superconsciousness.*'

I continued to write, 'Now we are at a special point in this Greater Plan. We are due to enter the Maya Fifth Creation, as the indigenous prophecies state. It is the end of gestation, bringing an urge to birth. People desire a world without wars. They seek to grow toward a state of happiness, of superconsciousness, of unconditional love.

'In these End Times, the Time of Preparation, we are in a time of the birthing of the spiritual, beyond the power of mind. If sufficient collective power manifests through each of us – 144,000 are prophetically mentioned – and if we are conscious enough to understand this Greater Plan, discard old ways and transform our shadow selves, we can avoid much of the destruction. Otherwise, destruction will be necessary to erase the "unwanted", in order for the Earth to evolve into a new being.'

It was now too dark to write more. I placed my worn-out ballpoint pen down in a safe place, hidden beneath a piece of driftwood on the sand – pens have become valuable! I closed my diary and thought about Balaam Ek. Pulling a tattered old Mexican blanket over myself, I enjoyed the gentle swinging sensation of my hammock in the light breeze that kissed the shoreline and the myriad of stars in the night sky.

I heard the crystal skull speak again in my head.

'The Great Remembering is coming. The Children of Time, of the Time after Time in the Maya Fifth Creation, will carry full consciousness of their eternal self. They will be called... *homo spiritus*.'

Birth Night

December Solstice was fast approaching. There had been unconfirmed reports of more troubles in Asia and the United States. There really was no way to get news. Those of us on the beach just lived from day to day as best we could, isolated in a world of our own.

Despite this, high excitement was building up amongst people around me. We created a little beach altar from dry, white coral and shells, preparing for an all-night vigil that many of us were intending to undertake in the 20 nights leading up to the solstice.

That night, at the vigil, I heard great rumblings in the belly of the Earth herself – earthquakes, perhaps. I renewed my prayers to Earth Mother, to allay increasing anxiety about the times ahead. Here on the beach we were vulnerable. As the days passed, the rains were sometimes torrential. Hurricanes were passing nearby with increasing regularity. It wasn't easy. On these occasions I would huddle with others in the old ceremonial buildings, or find sanctuary in hidden caves nearby. The limestone rocks were riddled with them, if you knew where to look for their entrances.

Then came a night when it seemed that the Earth could no longer sustain her balance. The wind grew wilder. In the caves we drew closer to one another. A tremendous hurricane which had by now built up outside was flattening everything in its path. Roofs of small buildings were ripped from their walls, and palm trees had their leafy tops completely broken off. Any precious boats that had not been secured broke free from their moorings and smashed to pieces on the reef.

It felt as if this was to be The Night. But the night went on, and on. There was no dawn, and the sky was cloud-covered. We never did see the Dark Rift of the Milky Way above the dawn horizon, as promised. The darkness continued. We used up what little food and water we had in the cave, then it was all gone. Our dwindling supplies had caused some tensions between us, but now they were shared out and gone, acceptance came. And still the darkness did not lift. We felt Earth Mother moaning in pain, as if all the earthquakes were now concentrated in just one place.

It was not possible to venture outside. We waited, in darkness, sleeping little, hoping the hurricane would move on and hoping that the seas, whose intensity we could hear, would subside. Years before, I had said that I wanted to be at Nah Chan when the Earth changes came. Now, here I was, not so far away, at Tulum.

Where, you might be wondering, was Balaam Ek, my crystal skull? When I had first arrived at Tulum I had explored some of the deeper passages of the caves. I had found a little rocky niche behind a pillar made of conjoined stalagmite and stalactite, where the skull would be completely unseen and safe.

Suddenly there was a great roaring of the Earth beneath our feet. It moved, it cracked and, in the darkness, panic gripped the people in the cave.

Gradually the Earth settled, but still it was dark outside. Then another tremor, this one more intense. Some people began a great wailing, praying in concert with the howling wind. I was scared too.

With a rush of concentrated intent, some people fought one another to get deeper into a small passage leading deeper down – perhaps there, enfolded in the suffocating blanket of deep Earth darkness, was a hidden place of sanctuary.

Fearful of such panic, I too wanted to get away, but first to retrieve Balaam Ek. In complete darkness I felt my way further into the cave, groping the walls, keeping my head low so that I would not hit protruding rock. Stumbling and grovelling, I made my way deeper into the cave system to the place where I had hidden Balaam Ek. If I was about to die, I would best be with the crystal skull.

Again the Earth trembled. I thought longingly of Mikhail and got ready to say goodbye. Now we really were on the edge of Time itself – it couldn't get any worse than this. I was close to Balaam Ek, I thought. I tripped and lost my balance on some loose ground, fell backwards and hit my head. Then nothing.

I slipped in and out of consciousness, with half-formed thoughts and dreams circulating inside me. I recalled prophecy after prophecy. Each went through my head, coming alive with characters from the past. Here an Inca chief, there a Maya day-keeper taking solar alignments from a pyramid; a Hopi clan sitting together in a tipi listening to stories of their origins in the stars, Don Alejandro telling a vast crowd of people all about Year Zero and the Children of the Sun, Hunbatz Men initiating me into Maya cosmovision with a crystal skull pulsing in his hands, the shining face of the old woman who gave me Balaam Ek, the mass of the 13 crystal skulls at Chichicastenango...

It all seemed so long ago. So long. Picture after picture. Fractal, broken shards of Time, images of people and more people. Those I had loved. All I had learnt, all their wise words began to merge into one sweet song. It rose and fell as the waves crashed upon the beach above me. One moment conscious, one moment slumbering. I knew the End of Time had come. This was *it*.

The Earth trembled more, the ocean roared and the wind set up a high-pitched whistling musical note through the tunnels of the cave system. Waters began flooding into the tunnels. I started to awake.

Surely this was the Earth giving birth, I told myself.

I felt a great surge of energy pass through me. All my fears were gone. A momentous radiance filled my head – light moving in all directions. From somewhere far away a sound, a low soulful note – a sacred OM – vibrated through my skull, rearranging light into ever-changing patterns. Scintillating seeds of light moved in and out of my consciousness.

In the darkness, in the utter pitch-black darkness of Earth Mother's soft belly, I heaved myself up and moved around on the rocks where I was lying. My hand touched something. Amazingly, I felt the smooth rounded surface of the crystal skull, there at my side.

In my dazed excitement at finding Balaam Ek, I kissed the cold crystal. Curling up around it, I dropped off. I slept and slept. And I dreamed, on and on.

I dreamt a birth.

The birth of *Homo Spiritus*.

1 *above* Dzibalchaltún, Mexico. At the Spring Equinox the sun rises through the doorway of the Temple of the Seven Dolls, the only known Maya temple to have windows and an observatory tower in place of the more usual roof-comb.

2 *below* Temple of the Sun, Nah Chan (Palenque), Mexico

3 *above left* A modern serpent head showing the cosmic G symbol of our spiral galaxy. Made by a Maya woodcarver in Chichén Itzá, Mexico.

4 *left* Don Alejandro (left) at the fifth annual Gathering of Indigenous Elders and Priests of the Americas, Mayapan, Mexico, 2003

5 *below* Sunset at Frontera de Corazal on the River Usumascinta, the border between Mexico and Guatemala

6 *right* Small amethyst crystal skull, used in a ceremony of 13 skulls in 2006 (courtesy of its keeper, Star Johnsen-Moser, USA)

7 *below* Ebmnagine, a life-size quartz crystal skull used in ceremony by the author in Spain (courtesy of its keeper, Elmera)

8 *above* Group of small figures with strangely elongated heads, found in a tomb at the Olmec city of La Venta, Mexico

9 *left* Hunbatz Men, Itzá Maya Tradition day-keeper

10 *below left* Part of a doorway, this large frieze at Ek' Balam, Mexico, depicts life-size winged Balaams with elongated heads who journeyed from the Pleiades to bring civilization to the lands of the Maya

11 *below right* The Maya Sun God 'Kinich Ahau', from Campeche city, now in the National Museum of Anthropology, Mexico City

12 *right* Perhaps the best-recognized Olmec symbols are these colossal heads, representing either kings or ballgame players. To date 17 have been unearthed, some weighing up to 40 tons.

13 *right* The cave at Tulum on the Caribbean coast of Mexico, from which Maya elders say Atlanteans emerged after the destruction of their lands

14 *below right* Equinoxal serpent pattern of life-force energy descending from the solar god at the Great Pyramid of Ku-kuul-kaan, Chichén Itzá, Mexico

15 *above* **Huayna Picchu (Quechua: 'Young Peak') stands majestically over Machu Picchu, Peru**

16 *above* The Temple of the Sun God, Apu Inti, at Machu Picchu was inhabited by high priests and the Virgins of the Sun (chosen women)

17 *below left* The legendary lost city of the Incas was built on the summit of Machu Picchu ('Old Peak')

18 *below right* Inca ruins at Machu Picchu, where many mysteries still remain hidden underground

19 *above* **Xamuk'u, a life-size quartz crystal skull used in ceremony by its keeper, Star Johnsen-Moser, USA, and the author, in Yucatán, Mexico**

APPENDIX 1

Prophecies

Hunbatz Men, Itzá Maya Tradition

This is an extract from *ETs and Mayas – Educators of Humankind*, a sacred study text, privately circulated by Hunbatz Men, Itzá Maya Tradition.

We are just beings in this universe. We have a universal essence and our spirit is the essence of many Suns and Moons. When we watch the sky at night, we can admire the greatness of the celestial vault and we feel attracted to hundreds of celestial bodies. Usually we feel we can reach even the most distant and brightest star.

Hundreds of years ago, some ancient peoples like the Mayas built thousands of temples and large squares, as well as planetary observatories, so that the people could watch the sky any time of the day and night. The purpose of this was to let each Maya observer remember and identify from which of those celestial bodies he had inherited his genetic essence.

In the old times the Maya priests of Ek' Balám and other ceremonial centres used to teach their people how to look for their essence in the stars through certain rituals. They also taught people how to awaken their genetic memory through magic rites so that they could use this memory to remember which of those bright points in the universe they had embodied on this sacred planet called Earth.

When the Maya priests of Chichén Itzá and other ceremonial Maya centres, known as *Hau K'inoob* and

Ek' Baalamoob, did their rituals and meditations, it was with the purpose of finding the origin of their essence in the universe. In their roles as educators, these priests had the duty to teach their people the relationship between them and cosmic law.

We human beings are the cosmic seed. Therefore, there are other cosmic seeds in other sites of the universe – either in our same solar system or in other galaxies. It would be absurd to think that we are the only beings who inhabit the universe because our creator *Hunab K'u* made the universe, this great dimension of millions of celestial bodies floating in a never-ending cycle, to be inhabited by an indefinite number of beings.

Hundreds of years ago, the priest class was able to communicate with any kind of life. In those times the Maya owned the real power of human beings and, by using that power, Maya initiates were able to communicate with the *Muxub*, a Mayan name given to the extraterrestrial ones, to those beings who came from very distant planets and stars.

Nowadays, the cultural development reached by the Maya amazes many scientists and just 10 per cent of the whole Maya culture has been understood so far. This is due to the fact that current patterns of mental development of human beings are very limited. This and the Western education we receive make our physical and mental faculties vanish day after day.

In ancient times, when we still owned cosmic knowledge and applied it in our everyday lives, our cosmic faculties worked perfectly. It was the time when we were able to communicate with the *Muxub*, or extraterrestrials. It was the time of the cosmic harmony between *Muxub* and human beings, and this is the reason why we learned from each other during so many centuries we spent together.

It is important for us to try to understand why the Egyptians', as well as the Incas' and Maya people's knowledge of the cosmos, was so vast. Evidence of this knowledge can be found in their temples, codices and pyramids, and shows that these peoples had a close relationship with the *Muxub*. We can say that it was the time of the light of wisdom, when human beings lived happily watching the celestial vault and learning the mysteries of the universe.

All these facts make us conclude that, thousands of years ago, the wisdom of extraterrestrials and the Maya got spread to all the corners of our planet Earth. Therefore, the *Muxub* and Maya were considered to be Educators of Humankind. Today, we must retake this knowledge from extraterrestrials and the Maya since they are the only ones who can show us the right pathway of cosmic wisdom. This wisdom is the only one thing that will be able to save the humankind from their destruction.

To conclude, I am here attaching some other Maya manuscripts that were written on different dates. Ancient Maya had a real communication with the *Muxub* – extraterrestrials. This fact was recorded in Maya history, as shown in the following books.

Prophetic Book: *Chilam Balam of Chumayel*

The centre of the land will be shaken the day when the true cosmic lords, Ah Bentan and Ah Paymil, come.

Maya cosmic culture was created in order to respect all the manifestations of life on Mother Earth and also for every being that lives outside our planet. I believe that when this culture was formed, cosmic consciousness played an important role. In that time, many beings gathered together in order to set up the cultural basis of respect that would be at the service of human beings and other beings that live outside this third dimension, such as the Ah Bentan and Ah Paymil.

Verse 778:

We shall return to our home, to rest in our community, because our time here has come to an end and it is time to depart. Because our all-mighty Lord is coming.

The Comet, furrowing the sky with great power and glory, marking the end of our times. We have come here only as pilgrim visitors. Our mission has already been completed. Our days are over! Do not forget us or think we will not return! Keep us always in your memory and think of us continuously.

Sacred Book: *Popul Vuh*

The prophetic and scientific book, the *Popul Vuh*, has already warned us. The Comet has already marked the end of our times. This was said to us by the *Popul Vuh* in this way: those who came before the comet warned us that they had only come as pilgrim visitors. Halley's Comet was seen in the sky in 1986. On 21 March 1996, the great cosmic messenger named Hayakutake was sent to us, bringing life in its great tail of several thousand kilometres longer than any other comet. On 21 March 1997 we were sent another messenger named Hale-Bopp, the light of its head surpassing that of the Sirius star. The two last comets were seen in the sky on 21 March in their respective years, and were perfectly visible in Maya ceremonial centres. In 1998 the comet Tempel-Tuttle was also seen. On these occasions, people of the Maya tradition were very glad to see the great sign of our all-powerful Lord the Comet again.

Maya of tradition know our Maya culture very well and are very proud of the culture our ancestors developed in this sacred American continent. Maya culture says that each comet marks the end of a cycle. At the same time, we know that with Maya culture we will be able to understand the law of cosmic changes. For this reason, Maya culture was developed for all living beings that inhabit any corner of the universe.

It is prophesied that in the second *K'altun* Nine *Ahau* in the series of years *Chichan*, *Men*, *Oc*, and *Ahau*, the incarnated teachers with cosmic consciousness will come back to the ancient ceremonial centres, such as Chichén Itzá, Dzibanche, Altun Ha, Xunan Tunich, Tikal. These teachers will bring with them tempests and whirlpools of change already announced by the Eight Great Suns that govern us.

Book of Songs: *Dzitbalché*

To you, human being,

I come to tell you

That here in this region, here in the plains,

Here in the land of our ancient giant men

And also of the hunchbacks,

When no man like the ones

We can currently see,

Had settled down in these lands,

X Ah Cha Paat, the one

Who had seven outstanding heads,

Had already wandered here

Since immemorial times.

The sacred book of *Dzitbalché*, written in 1742, tells us about the memories of the ancient Maya. It is important to understand these words: 'Giant Men who had seven outstanding heads and with the name of *X Ah Cha Paat* already wandered here since immemorial times'. Passages such as this one are frequently quoted in the Maya tradition. I understand that some brothers and sisters will find it difficult to accept realities such as this. I want to tell those sceptical people that we Maya of tradition already knew of this information and accepted it. We knew that we were not the only inhabitants on this planet, and we will not be the only ones that will live here on our Mother Earth.

Great Priest Ah K'in of Cabalchen Mani

> Good is the power of the deity *K'u* who comes to enliven us. Do not be afraid, creatures of the world. Oh, Father! You are *Hunab K'u*, the unique cosmic deity, the Creator, our creator. Good is your cosmic power! Oh, Father! Keeper of our universal soul. The one who accepts us and also accepts all the other beings of the universe. The one who brings the sky behind him when he comes! When you come again, it will be the time of the beginning of the humankind under the sign of the Two Suns!

'*Hunab K'u*, Keeper of our universal soul. The one who accepts us and also accepts all the other beings of the universe. The one who brings the sky behind him when he comes!' This was written by Maya priest *Ah K'in*, of Maní town, in 1562.

This phrase quoted above was difficult to understand for many researchers. This is why even today not many people understand Maya culture. Fortunately, we are beginning to experience a great opening of cosmic understanding of the light of knowledge in this new age. The new teachers of this new age will now be able to understand everything *Ah K'in* of Cabalchen Mani said.

Reproduced with kind permission of Hunbatz Men, Itzá Maya Tradition.

The Seven Fires Prophecy of the Anishnabe People and the Process of Reconciliation

'At a time when the Anishnabe People were all living in peace and harmony along the shores of the Great Salt Ocean (Atlantic), there came among them seven prophets.'

So begins the reading of the Seven Fires Prophecy as woven on a Wampum Belt, sacred to the Anishnabe people throughout Turtle Island.

Some years ago, in Mexico, I was honoured to meet Chief William Commanda, who at 87 was the spiritual elder of the Algonquin Nation and holder of this belt until his death. In a moving Ceremony of the Seventh Fire he told us the history of the belt, which is believed to have come into existence around 1400 CE, and about the Seven Fires Prophecy.

The Anishnabe are a family of indigenous peoples who, historically, lived along the eastern coast of North America. Anishnabe is translated as 'good person' or, connecting with starry origins, 'one who came down from the sky'. Somewhere between 1000 and 1400 CE a great migration of the Anishnabe took place. In this migration 10,000 large canoes filled with people headed inland, following what is now called the St Lawrence River toward the Great Lakes.

Today, original Anishnabe people are known by many names, including Cree, Pequot, Wampanoag, Abenaki, Algonquin, Mikimaq,

Shawnee, Innu and Chippewa. They are probably the largest of all the indigenous nations living on the North American continent along the East Coast of USA and Canada, as well as the shores of the Great Lakes, the Rocky Mountains and even as far south as Mexico.

What could have been so important to make the people move away from a place where they had lived for many hundreds of years, leave their homes and travel many thousands of miles to new and unfamiliar lands at a time when, according to Anishnabe traditions, they were living in peace and harmony? The answer lies in their knowledge of the Seven Fires Prophecy and its implications, not only for the Anishnabe people living 1,000 years ago, but also for everyone today.

The Seven Fires Prophecy speaks not only to Anishnabe but also to all people. It is a warning and, at the same time, a promise of better things to come if all of us living on Turtle Island can learn to put aside our cultural hypnosis and come together as one people, for our collective healing and the healing of Mother Earth.

Anishnabe tradition says that the first three prophets who came amongst their people brought a prophetic warning that came to fruition. They told them to be aware that a race of people, referred to as the 'light-skinned race' would be coming to their lands. They advised the Anishnabe that, in the interest of the safety of their people and their nation, it would be wise if they divided into two groups. One would leave and go deep into the interior of the continent and wait until the intentions of the light-skinned race were made known. The other would wait and greet the newcomers as brothers and sisters.

These prophets also told the Anishnabe where they would travel and how they would be guided to their ultimate destination. They told of a sacred 'Megis Shell' that would appear and lead the way to a series of islands where their journey would end. The final destination would be a place where the 'food would grow on water'. That place was the Great Lakes region where *pagwadjanomin* or wild rice grows on water. For the group of people who were to stay and greet the light-skinned race, the fourth, fifth and sixth prophets gave the following warnings and prophecies:

If they come with the face of brotherhood, you will
become one people. Their knowledge of the material
world and your spiritual wisdom will be joined together
to create a mighty spiritual nation and you will be
joined by two other races, (we believe) Asian and
African, to create the mightiest nation of all.

If they come bearing nothing in their hands, you
must still be cautious for they may be smiling, but in
reality they may be wearing the face of death. Do not
accept them readily but wait and see. You will know
them by their actions.

If they are wearing the face of death, then a great
calamity will befall the people of this land. Great
suffering and pain will be visited upon your people.
The very cup of life will almost be overturned.

You will know which face the light-skinned race is
wearing when the fish are dying and the water is unfit
to drink.

The sixth prophet warned that the natural people of Turtle Island
would be attacked by a light-skinned race and that a great period of
despair would ensue. He foretold of a darkness which would
overshadow the land, and of suffering, which would be inflicted on the
Anishnabe people, as well as on all indigenous peoples.

Then the seventh and final prophet came to the Anishnabe. He was
different from the others and had a strange light in his eyes. He came
with a message, not only for the Anishnabe people, but directly for the
light-skinned race.

At the time of the Seventh Fire, a new people will
emerge. They will retrace the footsteps of their ancestors
and will try to find those things which have been lost
along the way. They will approach the elders in search
of guidance. It will not be an easy task but, if they are of
good heart and purely intentioned, they can prevail.
Some elders will be sleeping and will have nothing to

say. Others will say nothing out of fear.

The new generation must be fearless in their quest.

The light-skinned race will be at a crossroads. If they continue down the road of materialism, it will be their destruction, and for all humanity as well. But if the light-skinned race chooses to join with the natural people of this land on the spiritual path, then they will again have the chance to create a nation, the greatest spiritual nation ever to have existed. Two other races will join these two races. Together, they will light the Eighth and Final Fire, an eternal fire of peace, harmony, brotherhood and sisterhood.

APPENDIX 3

Prophecies of the Americas

A list of the prophecies from the people of the Americas:

Anishnabe: Seven Fires Prophecy of Chief William Commanda. *See* Appendix 2

Aztec: Aztec Sun Stone Calendar. *See* Chapter 8

Cherokee: Calendar Prophecy. *See* Chapter 12
Thirteen Crystal Skulls – Harley Swiftdeer. *See* Chapters 6 & 12
Disaster – Thomas Thunder Eagle. *See* Chapter 10

Hopi: The Two Water Serpents. *See* Chapter 5
Nine Prophetic Signs. *See* Chapter 6
Prophecy Rock. *See* Chapter 6
Two Hearts. *See* Chapter 6
Pahana the Great White Brother. *See* Chapters 6 & 10
Great Purification. *See* Chapter 10
144,000 Enlightened Beings. *See* Chapter 7
The Fifth World of Illumination. *See* Chapter 9

Inca: Willaru Huayta Prophecy. *See* Chapter 9
Q'ero Priests' Prophecy and Festival of Snow Star or *Qoyllur Riti. See* Chapter 9
Golden Sun Disc of Coricancha, Peru. *See* Chapter 9
Alberto Villoldo, psychologist and anthropologist reports on Quechua shamans. *See* Chapter 9
Pachakuti, period of upheaval after which Homo Luminous, a new human species will emerge. *See* Chapter 8

Willaru Huayta – Eagle of North and Condor of South
Prophecy. *See* Chapter 9

Kogi: Earth Prophecies from the Mamas (shamans), and Alan
Ereira documentary 1990. *See* Chapter 4

Maya: 2012 Calendar Prophecies. *See* Chapters, 1, 5, 8, & 9
Mural of the Four Suns at Toniná, Mexico.
See Chapter 10
Prophetic Book: *Chilam Balám* of Chumayel.
See Appendix 1
Sacred Book: *Popol Vuh*. *See* Appendix 1
ETs and Mayas: Hunbatz Men. *See* Appendix 1.
Book of Songs: *Dzitbalché*. *See* Appendix 1
Great Priest: *Ah K'in* of Cabalchen Mani. *See* Appendix 1
The Thirteen Crystal Skulls. *See* Chapters 6, 9 & 12
Alignment of the Pleiades Stars. *See* Chapter 6
Return of Quetzalcoatl/*Ku-kuul-kan*. *See* Chapter 2
Prophecy of the Nine Hells. *See* Introduction &
Chapter 2
Kechi Maya, Guatemala. Don Isidro. Messengers from
Xibalbay. *See* Chapter 5
Return to Natural Time – José Argüelles, *Valum Votan*.
See Chapter 5
The Heart of Heaven. *See* Chapter 8
The End of the Fourth Sun – Don Alejandro.
See Chapter 12

Mexican: The Pyramid of the Sun, Teotihuacán. *See* Chapters
6 & 9

Native American (general prophecies):
Sun Dog Rainbow. *See* Chapter 13
Rainbow Warriors. *See* Chapter 3

Navajo (Dineh):
Mother Earth in Pain. *See* Chapter 7

Salish: Speech of Chief Seattle. *See* Chapter 3

Sioux: Black Elk, Oglala Sioux. *See* Chapters 6 & 7
Chief Crazy Horse, Oglala Sioux. *See* Chapter 5
Birth of White Buffalo Calves, Lakota Sioux. *See*
  Chapter 6
White Buffalo Calf Woman, Lakota Sioux. *See* Chapter 6

Zuni: Cloud Swallower. *See* Chapter 6

APPENDIX 4

Maya Timekeeping and Archaeological Periods

The Maya developed around 20 different calendars. However the three which are most relevant and used today are as follows.

The *Haab* – a 365-day solar year, comprising 18 months of 20 days each, along with an additional 5-day period to total 365 days. These last 5 days were considered to be particularly unlucky.

The *Tzolk'in* – a sacred calendar of 260 days created by the Olmecs and developed by the Maya. It has been called the Ritual Almanac and is regarded as the oldest and most widely used calendar in Mesoamerica. (The Aztec name is *tonalpohualli*.) It consists of repeating interlocking cycles of 13 days and 20 names of the sun. Subsequently the early Maya adopted two different time-keeping systems, the Short Count and the Long Count. The Short Count derives from combining the *Tzolk'in* cycle with the solar year and the Venus cycle of 584 days. In this way, 'short' periods of 13, 52 and 104 years are generated. The best way to imagine these cycles is as intermeshing gears.

The Long Count – throughout Maya history dates were fixed by this calendar that began on 11 August 3114 BCE. It is based upon cycles of days as follows:

1 kin =	1 day	
20 kins =	1 uinal =	20 days
18 uinals =	1 tun =	360 days
20 tuns =	1 katun =	7,200 days
20 katuns =	1 baktun =	144,000 days

13 baktuns = 1 Great Cycle (5,200 Tuns) = 1,872,000 days

Long Count dates begin with the baktun place value and are separated by dots. For example: 6.19.19.0.0 equals 6 baktuns, 19 katuns, 19 tuns, 0 uinals and 0 days. Each baktun has 144,000 days, each katun has 7,200 days, and so on. If we add up all the values we find that 6.19.19.0.0 indicates that a total of 1,007,640 days have elapsed since the Zero Date of 0.0.0.0.0.

The much-discussed Thirteen Baktun cycle is completed 1,872,000 days (13 baktuns) after 0.0.0.0.0. (hence it is written 13.0.0.0.0). This period of time is the 'Great Cycle' of the Long Count and equals 5,125.36 of our Gregorian years. This is the period of our present Fourth Maya Creation that is set to end on 21 December 2012 when this Thirteen Baktun count is completed.

The complete 21 December 2012 date combines 13.0.0.0.0. (Long Count date) with Four *Ahau* (*Tzolk'in* date) and 3 *Kankin* (*Haab* date). Additional time units:

20 baktuns	= 1 pictun	= 2,880,000 days
20 pictuns	= 1 calabtun	= 57,600,000 days
20 calabtuns	= 1 kinchiltun	= 1,152,000,000 days
20 kinchiltuns	= 1 alautun	= 23,040,000,000 days

Archaeological Periods in the Mayalands

14000 BCE	Clovis culture
7500 – 1500 BCE	Archaic (proto-Maya) period

1500 BCE – 250 CE Pre-Classic period

1500 – 1000 BCE	Early preclassic. (Olmec)
1000 – 300 BCE	Middle Pre-Classic (Olmec and cities of Nakbé and Tikal)
300 BCE – 250 CE	Late Pre-Classic (Edzná, El Mirador, Calakmul)

250 – 925 CE	**Classic period**
	Divided into Early, Late and Terminal Classic. The 'Golden Age' of the Maya. During this period all cities in the main Maya region reached their peak of civilization and then declined.
925 – 1500 CE	**Post-Classic period**
925 – 1200 CE	Early Post-Classic (Chichén Itzá occupied by Toltecs)
1200 – 1500 CE	Late Post-Classic (Itzá invade. Coba and Tulum thrive. New capital established at Mayapán. Tayasal established. Kiché state dominates.)
1519 CE	Cortés lands in Mexico
1521 CE	Aztec capital of Tenochtitlán falls to Spanish
1521 CE	Alvarado arrives in Guatemala

APPENDIX 5

Crystal Skulls

At the present time a small number of genuine ancient clear quartz crystal skulls have been revealed to humanity. Maya wisdom teachers have not said exactly how many crystal skulls are in their possession. Some crystal skulls are old, others are contemporary. The most well-known crystal skulls 'discovered' in the last four or five centuries in the Americas are in private hands or museums and are listed below.

1. Perhaps the most famous and beautiful is the 'Anna Mitchell-Hedges skull', sometimes called the Burney skull, which for many years was kept in Canada with Anna, the daughter of Maya explorer Mitchell-Hedges, waiting to be returned to the Maya people. I have already mentioned the story of this skull. It has a moveable jawbone carved from the same piece of quartz as the skull. When subjected to tests at Hewlett-Packard's laboratories in California it was found to have been made from an extremely pure type of quartz and inexplicably cut against the axis of the crystal. They could only assume that it had been carved by hand, perhaps over many hundreds of years.

2. The only known crystal skull that comes close to resembling the Mitchell-Hedges skull in quality is one named the Rose Quartz Crystal Skull, which apparently came from the border between Honduras and Guatemala. It is slightly larger than the Mitchell-Hedges, and it too has a movable jawbone.

3. The British Museum has a crystal skull of brilliant sparkling quartz, now in the Department of Ethnology, London, but rarely on view to the public. It has been there since 1898 and, in the mid-1990s, was subjected, along with other skulls, to a number

of tests to determine authenticity, but whose results were inexplicably kept secret. (*See The Mystery of the Crystal Skulls* by Chris Morton and Ceri Louise Thomas, Thorsons, 1997.)

4. The skull called Max (or the Texas skull) in the collection of Jo-Ann and Carl Parks, USA. Larger than the Mitchell-Hedges skull, it is said to have come from Guatemala but was once in the possession of a Tibetan monk. 'The monks honoured the crystal reverently. They would chant and talk Tibetan to it. It was used by the monks to direct energy into the bodies of the people who came to be healed. They would tap in to the energy of the skull and run it through the meridians of the patient's body to assist their healings.' (Interview by Debbie Smoker with Jo-Ann Parks, Houston, July 1995. www.v-j-enterprises.com.)

5. The skull called Sha Na Ra formerly in the keeping of Nick Nocerino (deceased), in the USA, who used it for a method of obtaining information from it called 'scrying' or, more simply put, crystal gazing using his activated Third Eye chakra. When scrying, Nick said that he was shown that Earth has changed its geography four times and UFOs removed people each time, bringing them back after the Earth stabilized again. He believed every crystal skull had a UFO/ET connection, and that maybe they act as a portal to them and to all life force in the universe

6. The Paris skull in the Trocadero Museum. This is smaller than the Mitchell-Hedges skull and also made from clear quartz.

7. The Smithsonian Institute skull, given to that institution by an anonymous donor. It is larger than life-size, cloudy crystal and completely hollow, enabling one to look right through its eye sockets deep into its empty interior. This particular skull carries a dubious reputation – that it has a curse upon it.

8. The Mayan Crystal Skull was discovered in Guatemala in the early 1900s, and the Amethyst Skull was found in Mexico around the same time.

A number of other skulls are in private collections, including those called *Xamuk'u*, Magnificent Star, *Chuen* – a smoky quartz monkey-looking skull – Grandmother Rainbow, Madre, *E hay u*, Maha Samatman, Harley Swiftdeer's skulls and DaEl Walker's quartz skull called Rainbow.

Yoke Van Dieten, living in USA, has a collection of skulls. One of them, ET, is a smoky quartz skull found in the early 20th century in Central America. It was given its nickname because its pointed cranium and exaggerated overbite make it look like the skull of an alien being. Yoke tours with her skulls to share the healing powers she believes they possess.

Life-Sustaining Systems of Exchange and Reciprocity

Arising from the Declaration of La Paz, made at the Continental Encounter of Indigenous Pueblos and Nations of Abya Yala (the Americas), held at La Paz, Bolivia, on 12 October 2006, the Council of the Indigenous Nations of Abya Yala has identified seven 'Global Currencies' of the Indigenous Peoples.

Each is a life-sustaining system of exchange and reciprocity. The third Intercontinental Council meeting of the Indigenous Nations held in 2007 is to translate their objectives into actions to be presented at a national and state level.

This is a timely reminder. The Intercontinental Council is identifying vital resources, a visionary model that could be adopted worldwide. Once again the indigenous of the Americas are showing us that their power base, crucial to their survival and ultimately to ours, is rooted in our deep relationship with the natural world.

The seven 'Global Currencies' of the Indigenous Peoples are:

The Breath of Life –
  the air, winds and atmosphere

The Water of Life – the waters, clouds, waterways,
  rivers, streams and oceans

The Giver of Life – the sacred species: Buffalo, Deer,
  Salmon and Eagle

The Sustainers of Life – Corn, Beans, Squash
  (agriculture)

The Foundation of Life – the land and territory,
  Mother Earth

The Sharers of Life – Community and Nations

The Seed of Life – Spirit and Light

For further information, see www.tonatierra.com.

BIBLIOGRAPHY

Argüelles, José, *The Mayan Factor*, Bear & Co., 1987

Beckingham, Adrian, *Stories that Crafted the Earth*, Gothic Image, Glastonbury, 2005

Brown, Joseph Epes, *The Sacred Pipe*, Univ. of Oklahoma Press, 1953

Carey, Ken, *Starseed: the Third Millennium*, HarperCollins, 1991

Coe, Michael D, *The Maya*, Thames & Hudson, 1966

Dalai Lama, His Holiness, Tenzin Gyatso, *Freedom in Exile*, Abacus, 1990

Diaz-Bolio, José, *The Geometry of the Maya and their Rattlesnake Art*, Area Maya, 1987

Eisler, Riane, *The Chalice and the Blade*, Harper & Row, 1987

Eltringham, Peter, Fisher & Stewart, *The Maya World*, Rough Guides, 1999

Gillette, Douglas, *The Shaman's Secret*, Bantam, 1997

Goetz, Delia & S Morley, *Popol Vuh*, Univ. of Oklahoma Press, 1950

Hunbatz Men, *Secrets of Mayan Science/Religion*, Bear & Co, 1990

Jenkins, John Major, *Maya Cosmogenesis 2012*, Bear & Co, 1988

Johnson, Kenneth, *Jaguar Wisdom*, Llewellyn Worldwide, 1997

Landa, Fray Diego de, *An Account of the Things of Yucatan (1566)*, tr. 2000, Monclem

Mercier, Alloa Patricia, *Maya Shamans – Travellers in Time*, Vega, 2002

Mercier, Patricia, *Chakras*, Godsfield Press, 1999

Meyer, Karl E, *Teotihuacán*, Readers Digest, 1973

Morton, Chris & Ceri Louise Thomas, *The Mystery of the Crystal Skulls*, Thorsons, 1997

Roney-Dougal, Serena, *Where Science and Magic Meet*, Chrysalis, 1997

Schele, Linda and David Freidel, *A Forest of Kings*, W Morrow, 1990

Schele, Linda, Freidel and Parker, *Maya Cosmos*, Quill, 1992

Stray, Geoff, *Beyond 2012*, Vital Signs, 2005

Tedlock, Denis, *Popol Vuh*, Touchstone, 1985

Timms, Moira, *Beyond Prophecies and Predictions*, Ballantine, 1994

Tomkins, Peter, *Mysteries of the Mexican Pyramids*, Harper & Row, 1976

Websites

Indigenous Wisdom
www.shiftingages.com
Major film production of Don Alejandro Cirilo Perez Oxlaj (Wandering
  Wolf), Guatemala

www.tonatierra.org
Indigenous Peoples' Peace Initiative

www.healingtheland.com
Restoring the voice of the indigenous people

www.narconews.com
Action and news of the Zapatistas in support of indigenous life

www.nativeweb.org
Resources of indigenous cultures around the world

www.wovoca.com/site.htm
Authentic website of the native people

www.taironatrust.org
Tairona Heritage Trust. Historical and cultural, the Kogi indigenous
  people in Columbia.

www.un.org/depts/dhl/indigenous/
United Nations site in support of indigenous nations

www.hopi.nsn.us
Official website of the Hopi Nation

Maya/Inca/Eco Tours
www.ponyexpress.net/starseed
Hunbatz Men, Itzá Maya and Star Johnsen-Moser

www.planeta.com/ecotravel/mexico
Eco-tourism

www.manataka.org/page260
Willaru Huayta, Inca/Quechua messenger, Peru

Practical help
www.puebloapueblo.org
Rebuilding Hospital Atitlan, Guatemala, post-hurricane

www.survival-international.org
Helping indigenous people determine their future and protect their
land

www.ixcanaan.org/project
Project Ix Canaan, Guatemala, rainforest guardians

www.mayaecho.com
Environmental and Maya projects

www.amnesty.org
Amnesty International

Calendars Maya/Time
www.alignment2012.com
John Major Jenkins' website, Cosmogenesis 2012

www.dr-rock.biz
Convert Gregorian dates to both traditional Maya and Dreamspell
dates

www.diagnosis2012.co.uk
Comprehensive database of Geoff Stray's prophecy work

Archaeology

www.mayaexploration.org
Non-profit research and education centre

Eco/Planet Earth

www.un.org/cyberschoolbus/indigenous
Especially educational for young people

www.ghrc-usa.org
Guatemalan human rights abuses

www.gomaya.com/glyph
Ancient News, Future History

www.myfootprint.org
Personal audit of your impact on the environment

www.lacaravana.org
Sensible education in environmental preservation and the values we
inherit from the indigenous cultures of the American continent

www.tortuga.com
Planet Art Network. A global hub for Earth regeneration of humanity
on Mother Earth.

www.sacredsites.com
Worldwide reference to places of peace and power

INDEX

Abya Yala 44, 60, 79, 177
Africa 204
Agent Green 68–9
agriculture 37, 44–5, 92, 93–4, 133
Ah K'in of Cabalchen Mani 238
Ahau 14, 16, 81, 211
Ahau Kines 14
Altar Q, Copán 19
Aluna 60
aluxes 80, 87, 125–6, 151, 189, 191
Amatitlán 30
Amethyst Skull 165
Amnesty International 35
Anasazi people 19, 92–5
Anishnabe Seven Fires prophecy 239–42, 243
Anna Mitchell–Hedges Skull 109, 121–2, 249
Antigua 30, 205
Apu Ausangate 146–8
archaeoastronomy 29
archaeology, archaeologists 17, 20–1, 29, 42, 43, 58, 61, 74–5, 88, 121–2, 153, 159, 160, 186–7, 188
Argüelles, José 76–7, 78, 79
Arizona 19, 72, 92, 98–9, 100, 178
Asian tsunami 29
'assemblage point' 7, 11, 115
astrology 28, 152–3, 157, 159
astronomy 28, 77–8, 143–4, 145, 152–4, 155, 156, 157
Atlantis (*Atlantiha*) 17, 134, 164, 167, 186, 199–202, 219
atomic weapons 102, 104
avocado (*ahaucatl*) 37
Aztecs xx, 25, 38, 39, 49, 110, 112, 114, 134, 135, 140, 201
  Sun Stone Calendar 137, 140, 243

Balaam Ek (author's crystal skull) 109, 116–17, 132, 134, 139, 141, 148, 152, 156, 158, 170, 171, 187, 188, 207, 211, 229, 230, 231
  author receives 97
  author's fears for 192
  author's protection of 125, 126, 167, 181–2, 189
  divination of 22, 62
  End of Time mission 97, 149, 182, 184, 189, 212
  at Grail Mass 213–14
  illumination 107, 119, 120–1, 137
  images within 143, 144, 161–2, 174
  and interdimensional travel 172–4
  meditation with 107, 123–4, 150, 172–3, 143–4, 188–9, 195, 201, 203
  messages and teachings 110, 124–5, 137, 144, 175, 176, 194, 197–8, 205, 221–2, 226–7, 228
  reveals name 189
  theft attempt 185–6
  Teotihuacán ceremony 112
  vision quest with 190–1
Barrios, Carlos 127–8
being in the Now 34–5, 51
Beings of Light 48, 83–4, 120, 149 *see also* ethereal beings; Shining Ones
Belize xix, 3, 38, 121, 163
Beyond 2012 (Stray) 138, 140
Big Dipper 145, 155
'bioluminescence' 113
Black Elk, Nicholas 96, 102, 108
Black Elk Speaks (Neihardt) 108
Blackgoat, Roberta 128–9
Bonampak 116–21, 125–6
Book of Revelation 76
Bravo, Don Pedro 7, 8, 142
Buddhist *sutra* 196–7
Buffalo Bill 108
Bush, George 78–9, 160

Cablicot 86
Caddy, Eileen 77
Cakchiquel Maya 79
Calakmul 173
California 204
Camalzotz 86
Canada 44, 49, 91
Caracol observatory 153
Carlos I 38
Carmen (anthropologist) 64–9
Cassiopeia 167
Catholicism 22, 208
Catholics 107, 203
Cayce, Edgar 186
Central America (Mesoamerica) xvii, 3, 8, 15, 17, 18, 25, 39, 56, 62–3, 72, 79, 140, 200
Ceres 59

Chaak (Chac) 45, 58
Chaan Muan 119
Chaco Canyon 19, 92–7
chakras 7, 58, 114, 139, 188, 200, 201, 214, 225
Chan Panak 188
Chavez, President 79
Cherokee people 49, 60
Cherokee prophecies 243
  calendar prophecy 211
  disaster 179–80
  thirteen crystal skulls 109, 111, 213–14
Chiapas 73, 168, 171
Chíchén Itzá 43, 45, 78–9, 153, 156
  spring equinox ceremonies 151, 160–2
Chichicastenango 202, 205–16
Chilam Balam of Chumayel 235–6
Chile 44
Chimu people 201–2
Christian Aid 204
Christianity 39, 40, 120, 135, 148, 176, 214–15
Christians 9, 64
CIA 79
climate change 9, 82–3
Cloud People (*Chachapoya*) 134, 135–6, 150
Coatzalcoalcos River 17
Cocos Plate 30
Coe, M D 17
Colombia 63, 65, 68
Columbus 91
Cortés, Hérnando xx, 24–5, 38–9, 109
Cosmic Maya 17, 174, 196, 201, 203, 212
cosmic universities 59, 61, 75, 84, 88
Crab Nebula (M42) 157
Crazy Horse 85
crystal skull prophecies xvii, 109–12, 162–5
crystal skulls 48, 98, 128, 160, 167, 193, 249–51
  Cherokee legacy 180
  encoded messages (*lembal*) 109, 113–14, 121–5, 122, 164, 166–7, 223
  52 skulls legend 164, 167
  Grail Mass 213–14
  meditation with 110, 113, 124–5, 172–3, 164, 188–9
  'singing' 109, 110, 122, 163
  13 skulls legend 110, 163, 164
  Teotihuacán ceremony 112–15
  see also Balaam Ek; Ebmnagine
crystals 119, 123, 165–7
Cusco 133, 134–5, 139, 146

Dalai Lama 129
Day after Tomorrow, The (film) 48
De Alvarado, Pedro 203
De Ursua, Martín 39
Declaration of La Paz 44
Demeter 59
Dineh *see* Navajo people
'disaster inertia' 47–8
divination 21–2
DNA 123, 157, 163, 221, 222, 226
Dogon people 156
Dresden Codex 27, 85–6
duality 12–14, 50, 51, 53, 58, 87
Dzibalchaltún 29
Dzitbalché 237–8

Earth/Earth Mother xvii, 5, 20, 21, 29, 30, 32, 35, 164, 177, 194, 228
  'Crystal Veil' 28, 225
  'impregnation' 45, 144
  indigenous peoples' concerns about 10, 41, 68, 82–3, 91, 99–100, 128–9
  indigenous peoples' reverence for 33, 44, 49–50, 55–6, 57, 63, 128, 206
  kiva represents 93
  link with crystal skulls 163–4, 167
  magnetic pole reversal 137, 179, 220, 225
  Milky way alignment 143, 222
  omens and portents 29, 144
  orbital changes 88
  pain and suffering 55–7, 71, 128, 174
  return to beauty 46–7, 160, 176, 221
  2012 changes 27, 137, 175, 179–80, 203–4, 220, 228–31
Earth Monster 171–2
Ebmnagine (crystal skull) 163, 165, 166–7
Egyptians, ancient 120, 156, 165, 202
Einstein, Alert 216
Ek'Balaam 120–1, 123, 156
El Quiche 209
El Salvador xix, 3, 37
Elder of the Twisted Hairs Society 179–80
Eliade, M 87
Elizabeth (fire priestess) 4
Elmera (crystal skull keeper) 163, 164–5, 166–7
End Day, Apocalypses (TV programme) 149–50
End of Time 183, 190, 230–1
  author's mission 97, 149, 182, 184, 189, 212
  cosmology 145
End Times 41, 88, 159, 196

change and preparation 41, 196–8
End Times prophecies xx, 23, 28–9, 81–5,
140
challenge of 175–6
countering destruction xxi, 10, 47–8,
52–3, 83, 87, 128–31, 159, 228
and the destiny of the world 127–8
doom and gloom 9, 23, 51–2
positive aspects xx, 13, 48, 86–7, 130,
138–9, 145
'entanglement' 223
environmental change and damage 26,
41, 67–8, 68–9, 71, 128, 204
environmental movement 69, 130, 175
ethereal beings xviii, 172–3, 174 see also
Beings of Light; Shining Ones
Evehema, Dan 82–3
extraterrestrials (ETs) 83–4, 113, 115,
120, 153, 156–8, 163, 165, 226

Father Sun see sun
FBI 35, 192
feminine 56, 59–60, 65, 87
Fifth Age (Hopi) 104, 158
Fifth Creation (Maya) 25, 28, 33, 41,
159, 171, 227–8
harmony and love 86, 87
'seating years' 27, 82
Fifth Era (Aztec) 140
fire ceremonies 3–6, 11–12, 28, 31–3, 93,
152
First Father 157
First (Great) Mother 59–60, 66, 74, 144,
145, 155
Flores see Tayasal
Four Balaams 81, 120, 121, 123, 156
Four Corners 99, 128–9
Fourth Age (Hopi) 93, 100, 158
Fourth Creation (Maya) 140
commencement (3114 BE) 9, 33, 42,
74, 111, 154
end (2012) 26, 27, 34, 40, 43, 63, 81,
112, 130, 153–4, 171, 205, 218
Four Winds, The (Villoldo and Jendresen)
138
Franklin, Benjamin 65
From the Heart of the World
(documentary) 64
Frontera de Corazal 127

Galactic Centre 143, 145, 155
Gandhi, Mahatma 193–4
Gathering of Indigenous Priests and
Elders of the Americas xviii, 49, 62–3,
70–2
Glastonbury Tor 71

global warming 175, 204
globalization 159
gnosis 201–2
golden age 48, 82, 138, 139, 145, 147, 149
Golden Sun Disc 134, 135–6, 136–7, 140
Great Mother see First Mother
Great Spirit 7, 10, 16, 20, 46, 48, 62, 65,
73, 78, 79, 101, 131, 139, 177, 178
Gregorian calendar 5, 63, 76, 79, 217
Guatemala xix, 3–8, 9, 11–12, 18, 21, 28,
30–5, 36, 44, 85, 116, 127, 165, 182,
183–93, 202–17
civil war 5, 203, 208–9
Guatemala City 3, 30, 79, 183–4, 185–6,
192, 196, 205

Hall of Records 186, 190
hallucinogens 142
'Harmonic Convergence' 25
Hau K'in 58
Haudenosaunee League (Iroquois) 60, 64–5
Healey, Giles 117–18
Heart of Heaven 144–5
Heart of the World 191, 213–16
Hero Twins 80, 145, 154–5
hierophanies 87
Himalayan skulls 165
Homo Spiritus 228, 231
Honduras xix, 3, 19, 37
Hopi Clan Rocks 105–6
Hopi people 49, 64, 65, 68, 70, 72, 92–3,
128, 157–8, 213
Hopi prophecies 73, 98–103, 127, 175,
243
Fifth World of Illumination 158
Great Purification 178
Nine Prophetic Signs 103–5
144,000 enlightened beings xxi, 129–30
Pahana the Great White Brother 105–8,
177–8
two heart people 101
two water serpents 82–3
Hopi Prophecy Rock 100–1
horses 38–9
Huayta, Willaru 133–4, 149
Human Cycle, The (Aurobindo) 219
human evolution 130, 138–9, 194, 227–8
Hunab K'u (Hunahpu) xxi, 14, 21, 61, 62,
131, 145, 157, 198, 201
Hurrukaan 45

Inca Pachacuti 139
Inca people 49, 132–6, 146, 202, 213
Inca prophecies 13, 136–9, 243–4
Eagle of the North and Condor of the

South 149
emergence of new humans 137–9
Golden Sun Disc 137
Qoyllur Riti 138, 147
Willaru Huayta 133–4, 149
indigenous peoples xvii, xx–xxi
  agriculture 37, 44–5, 92, 93–4, 133
  democracy 64–5
  Gathering of Priests and Elders xviii,
    49, 62–3, 70–2
  'Global Currencies' 252–3
  massacres of 64, 91, 169, 203
  preservation of 178
  reverence for the Earth 33, 49–50,
    55–6, 63, 65, 128, 206
  rights xix, 44, 64, 71–2, 168–9, 171
  share prophecies 27, 56–7, 105, 159
  spiritual custodians 104–5
  superconsciousness 16
  and unity 13
  warnings xviii, 26, 67–8, 70–1, 91, 176
  wisdom 68–9
interdimensional portals 6, 123, 141–5
interdimensional travel xviii–xix, 6–7,
  172–4
Isidro, Don 85–7
Itzá Maya xviii, 36–9, 43, 44, 156, 157,
  199–201, 233–5
Itzamná 164
Ixchel 31, 45, 59, 219
Iximché 79
Izamal 164
Izapa 143, 154–5, 218

jaguars 18–19, 55, 56, 58, 81, 187, 190–1,
  209
Jenkins, John Major 143, 145, 154–5,
  218
Jews 9, 176
Johnsen-Moser, Star 113–14

Kekchi Maya 85
Ker 59–60
Kiché Maya 4, 33, 79, 80, 98, 157, 210
k'in 24, 78
Kin 14
kivas 92–3, 94, 100
  crystal skull gift 94–7
Kogi (Elder Brothers) xxi, 63–8, 70, 200
Kogi prophecies 244
  Allen Giraud documentary 64
  message from Mama priests 67–8
Koré 59
Ku-kuul-kaan see Quetzalcoatl
Kuna people 44

La Luna 68–9
La Venta 18
Lacandón Forest 116, 125
Lacandón people 73, 117, 172
Lambson, Titus 106
Laura, Insurgente 169
laws of time 76–80
lembal 109, 164
Lhuillier, Alberto Ruz 74–5
Light 84, 85, 113, 123, 124–5
'light messages' 52
Loo, Frank 165
Lords of Time 41, 80
Lost Kingdoms of the Maya (Stuart and
  Stuart) 19
Lyra 158

Maasaw 99, 100
maize (milpas) 37
Mandela, Nelson 34
Marcos, Subcomandante 50, 168
masculine 56, 57, 58, 87
Matrix 50, 56, 77, 79, 80
Maya arches 61
Maya astrology 152–3, 159
Maya astronomy 58, 143–4, 152–4, 155
Maya calendars 5, 28, 40, 42–3, 111, 134,
  159, 175, 246–7
  agricultural 37
  Haab 140, 246
  Long Count xviii, 9, 23–4, 26, 40, 43,
    112, 140, 153–4, 175, 217–18, 246–7
  Thirteen Baktun Cycle 63, 154, 247
  Tzolk'in (*Cholq'ij*) 24, 55, 63, 77–8, 79,
    140, 170, 246
Maya cities xviii, xix, 12, 36–7, 42, 128
  astronomical alignments 3, 12, 29, 45,
    87
  Bush's visits 78–9
  decline 42
  implanted vibrations 123
  underground tunnels 170, 190
Maya Cosmogenesis (Jenkins) 154
Maya cosmology 5, 111, 170–1
Maya cosmovision ('sacred science') 9, 15,
  16, 23, 58, 67, 152–3
Maya creation mythology 98, 145, 154–5,
  157
Maya Heart of Heaven prayer 144–5, 206
Maya National Council of Elders, *Xincas*
  and *Garifunas* 28
Maya New Year 12
Maya people/s xvii, xix, 3, 14, 49, 70,
  36–41, 106, 183

Atlantis origins 199–201, 219
Classic Period xix, 22, 36, 42, 117, 152, 160, 225, 248
and Conquistadors xx, 24–5, 36, 38–40, 203
and crystal skulls 109, 110, 121–2, 166
disappearance 19, 40, 42–3
and ETs 120, 156, 141, 164, 233–5
forced Christianization 22, 39, 40, 214–15
gnosis 201
harmony with the land 44–5
modern oppression 25–6
original Anasazi 92
resistance 215
respect for others 128
rights activists 168–9
in 2012 206, 207–8, 213
UFO sightings 173
Zapista rebellion 168–9
Maya prophecies xvii, 13, 62–3, 73, 75, 233–8, 244
alignment of the Pleiades 111–12
Book of Songs 237–8
end of the Fourth Sun 205
ETs and Mayas 233–5
Heart of Heaven 144
Great Priest Ah K'in 238
Mural of the Four Suns 170–1
Nine Hells 25
One Reed xx, 24–5
Prophetic Book 235–6
return of Quetzalcoatl 24
return to natural time 76–7
Sacred Book 236–7
2012 xviii, 8, 9–12, 26–30, 81–2, 86–7, 98, 127–8, 143–5, 154–5, 217–18
Xibalbay messengers 85–6
Maya Vision Serpents 12, 40, 42
Mayalands 3, 5, 16, 21, 24, 29, 128, 164, 170, 184, 205
archaeological periods 247–8
map xxii
Mayan Crystal Skull 165, 251
Mayan Factor, The (Argüelles)
Mazatlán 50
medicine men 6–7, 108
Medicine Wheel 31, 97, 190
meditation 15, 16, 43, 67, 71, 96, 107, 110, 113, 141, 150, 164, 201
with Balaam Ek 107, 123–4, 150, 172–3, 143–4, 188–9, 195, 201, 203
with crystal skulls 110, 113, 124–5, 172–3, 164, 188–9
with crystals 123

melatonin 225
Men, Hunbatz xviii, 43, 58, 59, 61–2, 63, 75, 130–1, 141–2, 152–3, 156, 161, 199–201,220, 230, 233–5
Mendez, Alonso 87
Mérida 62, 73, 156
Mesoamerica see Central America
Mesopotamia 176
Mexico xix, xx, 3, 8, 17–23, 29, 37, 38, 44, 49, 55–63, 64, 73–5, 79, 109, 110–15, 116–21, 125–7, 136, 143, 145, 151, 154, 156–67, 168–74, 181–2, 193, 194–6, 200, 219–31
Pyramid of the Sun prophecy 244
Mexico City 140, 156
Miguel (messenger) 210–16
Mikhail (author's husband) xviii, xx, 4, 10, 23, 49, 117, 126–7, 156–60, 162, 168, 170, 171–4, 176, 181, 183–4, 186–9, 191, 192, 194–5, 203, 221, 226, 230
Milky Way 143, 145, 150
Dark Rift 143–4, 155, 218, 222, 225, 229
mining 99, 128–9
Mitchell, Edgar 34
Mixco Viejo 3–7, 8, 11–12, 29, 45
Moche people 201
Montezuma II 135
Moon/Sister Moon 37, 153, 175, 217
lunar alignments 29, 45, 135
lunar cycles 77–8
lunar mysteries 59
Mother Earth see Earth
Mu 134
Mural of the Four Suns 170–1
Museum of Anthropology, Lima 136
music of the spheres 164, 167
Muslims 9, 176

nagual 19, 73, 146, 182, 189, 195, 221
Nah Chan (Palenque) 59, 73–5, 84–5, 87, 141, 159, 229
National Museum of Anthropology, Guatemala City 186
National Museum of Anthropology, Mexico City 118
Native American prophecies 244–5
Rainbow Warriors 45–8,
Sun Dog Rainbow 218–19
Native Americans 7, 11, 35, 53, 60, 64–5, 83, 90–4, 103, 176–7, 194
natural time 76–7
Navajo (Dineh) people 49, 109
Mother Earth in pain 128–9, 244
Nazca people 201
New Economics Foundation 13

Nicaragua 37
9/11 205
Nine Hells prophecy 25
North America 45, 49, 56, 62–3, 72, 74, 91
Nostradamus 8

Oaxaca 110
Ocosingo 168
Olmecs 17–20, 163, 201
One Reed prophecy xx, 24–5
Orion 21, 22, 33–4, 75, 96, 157, 167, 221, 222
ovnis see UFOs

Pahana (Great White Brother) 104, 105–8
Pakal Votan 74, 80, 81, 84
   tomb 75, 76–7, 78, 80, 84, 159
Papal Bulls xix, 64
Paytiti 135, 138–9
Peltier, Leonard ('Wind Chases the Sun') 35
Peru 132–3, 134, 135, 137, 138, 141, 146, 150, 202
Petén Itzá Lake 37, 39
Piedras Negras 186–8, 189–93
pineal gland 110, 225–6
Pizzarro 202
Plains Indians 10, 90–4, 105
Plano Pueblo de Panama 187
Pleiades 24, 93, 111–12, 120, 152, 153, 158, 162, 164, 167
Pokoman Maya 3
pollution 55, 99, 180
Pope, the 28, 214
Popel Vuh 9, 33, 80, 85, 86, 98, 236–7
prophecy/ies xxii, 8, 23, 152
   of the Americas 243–5
   and extraterrestrial intelligence 156–60
   and the feminine impulse 60
   Guatemalan elders xxii
   inner essence 20
   origins of xviii–xix, 85–8
   see also crystal skull prophecies; End Times prophecies *and* specific peoples
Pueblo Bonito 92

Q'enko (zig–zag) rock 136
Q'ero 137, 139, 141, 148
quartz 48, 112, 122, 165–6
Quechua people 133, 146
Quetzalcoatl (*Ku-kuul-kaan*) 24, 44, 111, 160, 161, 171, 200

Rafael 30–3
Rainbow Warriors 45–8, 49
Reyna, Sonne 91
Rights of Indigenous Peoples 64, 71–2
Roberts, Chuck 102
Rosemarie (fire priestess) 4
Ruiz, Samuel 168

Sacred Hoop 60, 83, 96, 97, 108
Sacred Pipe, The (Brown) 108
Sacred Valley 133, 134
Sacsayhuaman 139–40
Salish speech of Chief Seattle 49, 244
San Bartolo 43
San Cristóbal de las Casas 168, 182
San Lorenzo 17–18
San Vincente Pacaya 31
Santa Domingo church 134–5
Santa Elena 41, 51
science and technology 55, 66, 68, 77–8
Seattle, Chief 49
Secatera, Leon 163–4
Seneca people 109
Serpent of Light 160, 161–2
Serpent of Time 20–3, 21, 171, 217
Seven Fires prophecy 239–42
shamanic flight 171
shamanic techniques 11, 141
shamanic training 146, 182
shamanism 40, 85
shamans xviii, xxii, 5–6, 7–8, 16, 20–1, 23–4, 28, 29, 47, 62, 81, 109, 110, 112, 115, 138, 139, 152, 159, 166, 206, 216
Shapiro, Joshua 164–5
Shining Ones 134, 138, 147, 148
silica/silicon 122, 163, 165
Sioux creation stories 100–1
Sioux people xxi, 49
Sioux prophecies 245
   birth of white buffalo calves 96
   Black Elk 96, 108
   Crazy Horse 84–5
   White Buffalo Calf Woman 96–7
Sirius 156, 166, 167
Sister Moon *see* moon
Sitting Bull 85
Snow Star (*Qoyllur Riti*) festival 137–8, 146–9
Sonora Desert 7
soul retrieval 7
South America 56, 62–3, 79, 147, 201–2
Spanish Conquistadors xx, 21, 24–5, 26, 36, 38–40, 43, 65, 109, 135, 160, 201, 203

Spirit of the Land 42, 43–5, 49–50
St Vincente Pacaya 35
stars 57, 93, 143, 152–4, 167, 173, 218
  return to 119–20, 124, 226
Starseed (Carey) 20
'starseeds' 157–8
stelae 12, 123
Stories that Crafted the Earth
  (Beckingham) 91
Sun/Father Sun 4, 13, 37, 62, 74, 144,
  150, 153, 161, 162, 164, 175
  'little pieces' (*k'in*) 14, 24, 78
  magnetic pole–reversal 82, 225
  solar alignments 3, 12, 29, 45, 87
  solar priests 14, 58
  2012 galactic alignment 143, 155, 218,
  225
Sun Dog Rainbow 218–19
superconsciousness 15–16, 18, 19, 23, 35,
  52, 53, 85, 87, 110, 118, 124–5, 130,
  159, 164, 183, 197–8, 205, 220, 221,
  222, 225, 226
Swiftdeer Reagen, Harley 163

Tairona civilization 65
Tayasal (Flores) 36–41, 44
Teotihuacán 109, 110–12, 112–15, 163
Teotihuacános 110–11, 201
Tewa 92
'third vector' 13–14, 51
Threads of Time 5, 8, 10, 11, 19, 20, 23,
  24, 27, 28, 40, 42, 46, 47, 70, 80, 81,
  82, 83, 85, 110, 113, 119, 130, 144,
  164, 166, 183
  Time Future xxii, 5, 10, 42, 48, 131,
  210
  Time Past 27, 42, 92
Thunder Eagle, Thomas 179–80
Titicaca lake 135
Toltecs 160, 201
Tonantzin 22
Tonatiuh 140
Toniná 42, 168–74
truth 14
Tulum 59, 219–229
Turtle Island xvii, xx, 11, 79, 113
2012 43, 63, 80
  allegory 183, 202–31
  Aztec prophecy 140
  December 21 (December solstice) xviii,
  xxi, 9, 26, 27, 34, 81, 112, 127, 143,
  154,
  155, 217–19, 228–31, 247
  Hopi prophecy 158
  Inca prophecy 137–8, 148

Maya prophecy xviii, 8, 9–12, 26–30,
  81–2, 98, 127–8, 143–5, 154–5, 217–18
  return to natural time 76–7
'two heart' people 101
Tzotzil Maya 168

UFOs (*ovnis*) 102, 113, 114–15, 162–3, 173
ultraviolet radiation 157, 222, 225–6
Underworld (*Xibalba*) 19, 80, 86, 137, 212
United Nations (UN) 28, 64, 71, 204
United States (USA) 10, 90, 91, 132, 165,
  192, 228
  founding 64–5
  indigenous land rights 44
Usamascinta River 127, 186, 187
Uxmal 20, 48, 57–62, 79, 128, 153

Venezuela 79
Venus 58, 153, 189
vibrational energy 115, 123, 125, 142
Virgin of Guadaloupe 22
vision quest 190–1
Vision Serpents 12, 40, 42
Volcán de Pacaya 30–4

Wandering Wolf (Don Alejandro Cirilo
  Perez Oxlaj) 3–5, 7, 12–13, 28–9, 62–3,
  174, 205, 219, 230
Web of Life xix, xxi, 10, 28, 37, 49, 53,
  115
White Buffalo Legend 96–7
women 56, 59–60, 61, 65, 66–7, 119, 169
world shakings 96, 101–2
World Tree 25, 39, 213, 227
  'Earth Fruit' 8
World War I 101, 102
World War II 101, 102, 130
WorldWideWeb of Light (and Life) xxi,
  11, 16, 27, 28, 34, 50, 83, 85, 97, 115,
  183, 227

Xibalba 80, 86, 166, 212

Yax Pac 19
Yaxchilan 126–7
Yucatán Peninsula xviii, 37, 43, 45, 57,
  79, 151, 156, 160, 219, 200
Yucatec Maya 58, 190

Zapista Army of National Liberation
  (AZLN) 50, 168–9, 171
Zotz (Bat of Death) 50
Zuni people 92
  Cloud Swallower prophecy 95, 245